Jack Denslow

THE ERNST & YOUNG GUIDE TO TOTAL COST MANAGEMENT

Michael R. Ostrenga
Terrence R. Ozan
Robert D. McIlhattan
Marcus D. Harwood

JOHN WILEY & SONS
New York • Chichester • Brisbane • Toronto • Singapore

Library of Congress Cataloging-in-Publication Data

Ostrenga, Michael.

The Ernst & Young guide to total cost management / by Michael Ostrenga with Terrence R. Ozan, Marcus D. Harwood, Robert D. McIlhattan.

p. cm. — (The Ernst and Young business guide series)

Includes bibliographical references.

ISBN 0-471-55877-X (cloth)

1. Cost control. 2. Cost accounting. I. Title. II. Series.

HD47.3.088 1992

658.15'5--dc20 91-45066

CIP

Printed in the United States of America

10 9 8 7 6 5 4 3 2 1

PREFACE

Few problems threaten American business today more insidiously than uncontrolled costs. Even companies known for excellence in both their products and services can lose money because they fail to use significant opportunities to improve their costs—particularly, overhead costs. Companies often adopt strategic imperatives such as total quality, close-to-the-customer, and time-based management, yet fail to develop the proper information structure to include meaningful cost information that could help them achieve these strategic goals.

This situation is unfortunate for many reasons. One of the most important is that more sophisticated, adaptable, and powerful cost management methods not only exist, but they are readily available to any firm willing to try them. These new methods are collectively called *Total Cost Management* (TCM).

This text is an introduction to TCM and its potential for helping you better understand the underlying dynamics of cost thereby facilitating better decision making concerning products and services, work flows, capital investments, as well as the day-to-day monitoring of your business. *The Ernst &*

Young Guide to Total Cost Management is not a step-by-step how-to guide to implementing TCM in your company. It is, however, a thorough examination of the cost-management methodology which will most likely make a difference to your corporate profitability.

The Ernst & Young Guide to Total Cost Management is composed of three parts. Part One is an executive overview. Discussing TCM in the most general terms, this first part of the book provides a chance to understand the issues without tackling them in full detail. Executives can either start with this overview and then proceed to read the more detailed sections if they wish, or they can delegate those sections to their managers as needed.

In Part Two, we examine the full range of techniques that make up Total Cost Management. TCM has three fundamental components: *business process analysis, activity-based costing,* and *continuous improvement.* We discuss these components in detail with an emphasis on how each builds on the previous. These discussions provide an in-depth view of TCM, how it works, and how it can strengthen your company's competitive advantage.

Finally, Part Three explores how to implement TCM in your business.

Total Cost Management is not a panacea for all the ills and challenges facing American business today. It is, however, a remarkably powerful set of techniques for identifying and controlling cost; techniques that U.S. companies can no longer afford to ignore.

ACKNOWLEDGEMENTS

Like all complex endeavors, the process of writing *The Ernst & Young Guide to Total Cost Management* has benefitted from the ideas, insights, and experience of many people. Although the following acknowledgements cannot recognize every individual who has made a contribution, we want to at least thank all those who have helped us in significant ways.

First and foremost, we want to thank the clients with whom we have worked on total cost management engagements over the years. It was through that collective work that our ideas about the integrative power of the TCM techniques took shape.

We owe an immense word of thanks to June Tyler, who molded the original draft into a manuscript. June provided the project management for the editing and reviews, and she spent countless hours ensuring the material reflected our Performance Improvement methodologies and application experience. In addition, we wish to thank Edward Myers, whose stylistic edit of the manuscript helped us bring the work to a broader audience.

We also owe deep gratitude to our colleagues. We would like to thank Mort Meyerson and Mike Salvador for their energetic work in getting this project started. Likewise, we would like to thank Richard Sasanow for his feedback on the initial chapters and for his efforts to bring the overall project to completion. We also greatly appreciate Greg Stratis's review of the final manuscript.

CONTENTS

PART ONE

EXECUTIVE OVERVIEW

Total Cost Management and Corporate Strategy

INTRODUCTION TO THE EXECUTIVE OVERVIEW

Few corporate executives are unaware of how quickly competitive pressures have intensified in recent years. The strategies for attaining market share (among them product and service innovations, emphases on quality and speed to the market, and considerations of cost) are more numerous and more complex than ever. Yet, many companies continue to launch new strategic initiatives without analyzing or understanding the likely profitability of these moves. Other companies are satisfied with the status quo and fail to recognize competitive opportunities. Small wonder that many of these companies end up disappointed in the results.

This text is a direct response to this situation. By describing the approaches in management accounting that have been developed over the past five years, this book provides executives with the analytical base they need to manage their companies' profitability more successfully.

New methods have been designed and field-tested for measuring, reporting, and managing profitability. Ernst & Young calls its approach to these new methods *Total Cost Management* (TCM). What follows is an overview of the Ernst & Young approach, an executive summary intended to help you understand TCM and to decide if it suits your company's purposes for analyzing profitability and controlling costs. This overview has three chapters:

Ch. 1. *The Business Environment Has Changed: Cost Information Must Change with It*—How the changing opportunities and imperatives of the business world have rendered traditional accounting systems inadequate. TCM offers the right alternative.

Ch. 2. *TCM in a Nutshell*—How TCM provides integrated cost information concepts that help you analyze business processes, improve your analytical basis for planning, and improve performance throughout your company.

Ch. 3. *The Role of TCM in Sustaining Competitive Advantage*—How TCM can help support key business processes no matter what your strategic approach.

Let's now turn to the first issue: How cost information must change to keep pace with changes throughout the overall business environment.

CHAPTER 1

The Business Environment Has Changed: Cost Information Must Change With It

Economic realities have made it necessary for most companies to operate with a "lean and mean" philosophy. In one industry after another, markets have become global with worldwide competitors offering high-quality, low-cost goods and services. In the service sectors, customers' demands for speed and accuracy prompt many firms to try dismantling long-standing bureaucracies. Industries previously operating under regulatory rules which allowed them to pass all costs on to the customer, now face a changed regulatory environment. Streamlining and restructuring have become common goals in all industries.

At the same time that pressures to streamline have intensified, businesses are experiencing demands to offer new services and new product features as well. Companies have worked hard to understand their customers' needs; that understanding has in turn sparked the marketers' and product designers' imaginations and enthusiasms. Those companies that are effective at rapidly bringing innovative new products and services to the market have gained a huge competitive edge in today's business world. Similarly, companies that are ineffective at quick responses are extremely vulnerable if a variety war breaks out in their industry. In fact, improving the process of introducing new products and services has become a strategic objective in company after company.

Yet, the proliferation of products and services can add to the complexity of getting work done throughout an organization: in engineering, in operations, in support functions, in customer services, in human resources. This complexity is one of the chief causes of rising costs everywhere.

Above and beyond the demands from customers and competitors, businesses have an additional complexity derived from their own mergers and acquisitions. Certain business combinations often result in duplicate product lines and redundant bureaucracies. Until a firm can resolve redundancies, the costs associated with organizational complexity are often high. The "lean and mean" reality remains an elusive goal.

Finally, one other factor continues to change the business environment: automation. Much of the work previously performed by a direct labor force is now done by machines. More and more employees are now engaged in indirect or support functions. Similarly, more and more of the administrative functions are transacted with assistance from computerized information systems. All these instances help to explain why the ratio of indirect costs to direct costs keeps rising steadily.

Facing all these new challenges, executives have begun to question how well their old cost techniques provide them with the information needed to make management decisions. These old techniques were developed at a time when the business environment differed dramatically from what companies face today. Some of the old techniques stressed the following points:

- Minimizing direct labor costs was considered the key to high productivity.
- Indirect costs were low compared to direct labor costs.
- Companies had a largely domestic view of their markets, their suppliers, and their competitors.
- Mass production, not product/service variety, was the dominant strategy.
- High product or service quality was seen as a way to charge higher prices rather than as a condition for being in the market.
- Services played a much smaller role in defining strategy.

THE ROLE COST INFORMATION PLAYS TODAY

In almost all companies, accounting departments periodically (weekly, monthly, quarterly, and so on) produce a set of management reports. These reports usually appear as income statements individualized for department heads and summarized for higher-level management. Typically, such reports show budgeted amounts, actual amounts, and the difference between the two for the current period and the year-to-date.

Companies using a standard cost system generate reports that show the standard cost of goods produced or services performed along with any variances incurred. In each of these cases, the reporting basis is the predefined cost; the budget in the first case, the standards in the second.

The major purpose of periodic management reports should be to allow managers a means of monitoring progress toward their goals and for directing their energies to situations needing attention. Yet, these reports achieve their purpose only if they organize and calculate costs in such a way as to reflect the true dynamics of the business. This is achieved only if the timing of the report is synchronized with changes in underlying activity. Unfortunately, these reports have several significant shortcomings.

Shortcoming #1: An Account Focus Rather Than A Management Focus

Costs are collected into accounts that translate directly into specific lines on financial reports. For each transaction, the department incurring the cost is noted as well as the account. Missing from this data collection mechanism, however, is the link between the cost incurred and the activity that required the cost. As more and more companies adopt a philosophy that managing the business processes is the key to managing the entire business, the link between activities and costs becomes crucial in making management accounting relevant to today's managers. Most current financial systems do not provide this link. The key to understanding the cost dynamics in an organization is documenting:

1. the relationship between activities and their causes; and
2. the relationship between activities and costs.

Shortcoming #2: Product/Service Planning Decisions

Firms use cost information to make decisions about which products and services to offer and how to price them. In the ideal situation, cost information is complete and all parties (marketing, engineering, production, customer service, and so forth) have a high level of confidence in the cost numbers. When these two conditions can be met, the cost information can be used appropriately as the basis for deciding questions about product and service lines, and for setting improvement targets.

When these two conditions are not met (a common occurrence in many companies), product line planning decisions more often reflect the relative power of the different functional areas (marketing, production, customer service, etc.) rather than a deliberate profit planning process. Because today's cost information does not model the cost dynamics well, the cost information that companies obtain about products is likely to be seriously in error. And the cost information they have about services, customers, and business processes is likely not to exist at all.

Shortcoming #3: A Questionable Role in the Capital Justification Process

As companies compete on the basis of quality, time, flexibility, innovation, and responsiveness, some of their major decisions in building the competitive infrastructure involve acquiring capital assets. Building the operations facilities, automating certain processes, and building in additional capacity to add flexibility at key points in a process are all decisions that have a major impact on the firm's ability to compete. They are all decisions subject to the *capital justification process.*

The formal techniques in use today for evaluating capital acquisition proposals rely heavily on calculating the internal rate of return of cost savings—particularly, savings in direct labor. Yet, most of the benefits of new capital acquisitions are in areas other than labor savings. Most of the benefits are in quality, time, flexibility, innovation, and responsiveness. But today's cost information provides little insight into the likely relationship between the investment and these benefits or between these benefits and overall profitability.

Some companies are now making strategic investments by relaxing their reliance on the capital justification *hurdle rates* and dealing with benefits on an intuitive basis. Other companies are continuing their reliance on the hurdle rates and continuing to force requestors to quantify all benefits. Both of these kinds of companies are all too often experiencing the pain of such inadequate techniques when faced with a lack of support in important decision making.

Shortcoming #4: An Incomplete Picture of Performance

Even though the purpose of today's management accounting information is to help managers improve the efficiency and effectiveness of their operations, this information sometimes has exactly the opposite effect. Because cost dynamics are often not well modeled, the performance information provided by today's management accounting systems is, at best, incomplete. Typically, it provides a very unbalanced picture of performance which can lead managers to miss important opportunities for improvement. In fact, it can lead managers to actions that actually obstruct the organization from achieving higher-level goals. This is particularly true when reward systems are closely tied to these unbalanced performance measures.

THE ROLE COST INFORMATION COULD PLAY IN MANAGING YOUR BUSINESS

Cost information concepts do have their shortcomings, but a well-planned, effective method for cost management can present a complete picture for managing your business. Recognizing the shortcomings and emphasizing a deliberate profit plan can translate into successful cost management. Some of the possible solutions are easily explained through examples of three recent success stories.

Speeding Service to the Customer

The executive committee of a large life insurance company made a strategic commitment to reduce the required time for responding to customer requests. They wanted to make sure, however, that the methods used to plan and implement these time reductions did not result in higher costs or in any deterioration of their service quality. They implemented Total Cost Management techniques in order to simultaneously analyze the time, quality, and cost of their services.

The scope of the project included nine business processes involving just over 300 people. They looked at such processes as new policy applications, loan applications, policy surrenders, premium receipts, and customer inquiries. Within each process, the project team documented each activity necessary for completing the work and calculated an average cost for each activity in the process. The team then classified each activity according to how valuable it was in the policyholder's eyes. Activities that policyholders did not value were investigated further and the team categorized each one to reflect why that activity was performed. The team then analyzed the categories to identify the greatest opportunities for improving the time, quality, and cost of the processes.

The team then grouped recommendations into three implementation phases:

1. short-term "hits";
2. system changes; and
3. people/organization changes.

Typical of the suggestions on the short-term "hits" list was the recommendation to change the format of premium notices so that they could be processed with scanning equipment rather than manually input. The company had excess capacity on scanning equipment it already owned. So the only investment required to implement this change was a redesign of the standard form and some programming to automate the scanning.

The system in use for processing universal life policies had been in place for only a few years, but it seemed to be the source of many problems identified by the team. Further investigation revealed that the system had been poorly implemented, with many important features not included at all. The recommended system changes were largely a re-implementation of the system already used in-house.

The people or employee changes centered on training (both system training and cross-functional training). The layout of desks and employees was also physically reorganized to facilitate multi-functional work teams.

In addition to achieving their cycle-time reduction goals, the added cost savings from implementing these recommended actions were estimated to be 30 to 35 percent of the insurance company's expense base for these processes.

Improving Quality Within a Planning Organization

In another company—a high-technology services corporation—the development of business plans and budgets were viewed as independent events. The director of the product planning division worked with an analyst to estimate the headcount and travel expenses required to support commitments within the business plan.

Due to the nature of the work performed, this division had by far the largest unreimbursed travel expenses in the company; in fact, it was the second highest expense category—only salaries were higher. Travel expenses were maintained in the general ledger by category: airfare, hotel, ground transportation, and the like. But these categories alone provided no help to the director in trying to plan or control these expenses. The director needed to know cost by activity, not by travel expense category. Activities requiring travel included:

1. investigations of companies being considered as business partners or as acquisition candidates;
2. detailed walk-throughs of designs for the integration of the services of different divisions of the company; and
3. regular meetings of customer advisory committees.

The director then had his managers prepare their travel budgets on an activity basis. During the next year, they maintained a sub-ledger noting the nature of the activity for all travel expenses. The sub-ledger required no new system development—only the implementation of a previously unused feature in the general ledger system. The history collected in the travel sub-ledger dramatically improved the division's ability to plan and control these costs.

An additional part of the analysis was to identify and study the causes of poor-quality travel. (*Poor-quality travel* was defined as the expenditure of time and travel monies on a trip that turned out to be a waste of time.) Typical causes of poor-quality travel included:

1. a lack of clear objectives;
2. premature technical reviews; and
3. key personnel missing from meetings.

New procedures, including a pre-trip checklist, minimized the incidents of poor-quality travel from predictable causes. As a result of these changes, the division was able to model the cost dynamics of its own work so that the reliability of its commitments were greatly improved, as were its budget estimates.

Getting Close to Profitable Customers

In a third sample organization, getting "closer to the customer" became a major corporate objective. Before developing plans to achieve this objective, the management team wanted a better understanding of which combinations of services and customers represented its most profitable business. It also wanted to understand better the costs of the processes used in interacting with its customers.

To gain this understanding, the team conducted an analysis using Total Cost Management techniques to determine the factors that most influenced its costs and profitability. The scope of the analysis included almost all the processes of the business.

Upon completion of this analysis, the management team had the information needed to target the most profitable segments of its market for developing business alliances and for providing more personalized services. It also identified certain of its services that were both costly and ineffective. By redesigning these services, the company was able to turn a significant number of just marginally profitable customer segments into profitable ones.

The company attributed this analysis with giving focus to its "close to the customer" strategy and giving directions to its continuous improvement efforts.

Reading these stories, you may be saying, "I see ways that my company could benefit from the information possibilities you've just described. But it sounds so *new*. My people would have to break too much new ground—both conceptually and practically." This is a common response reflecting a valid concern. However, the reality of the situation is reassuring.

YOU DON'T HAVE TO REINVENT THIS WHEEL

A debate about whether these concepts are new or not has been under way ever since the concepts were first proposed. Some writers and speakers, in fact, have shown that material from the 1920s (and even earlier) proposed many of the ideas that have regained popularity during the past five years. The accounting historians have added a valuable perspective to the interchange. The truth is that some of the ideas have been around for a long time; others are new. But even the ideas that have been in academic treatises for a century were never implemented on any wide scale. They are new in application, even if not new in theory.

Management Accounting is a New Science

The real breakthrough in improving management accounting came when Computer-Aided Manufacturing—International formed the *Cost Management System* (CMS) program of collaborative research.

Computer-Aided Manufacturing—International (CAM-I) is a non-profit organization whose mission is to facilitate collaborative research among manufacturers. In 1985, CAM-I initiated CMS as a general business project with the intent of using the techniques and structure of collaborative research to create a positive forum for developing improvements to cost management systems. Since its creation, the project has had over 70 companies sponsoring and participating in the development of new methods, tools, and techniques. The project has also had the participation of the leading management accounting researchers from both academia and from the Department of Defense.

The CAM-I CMS project exemplifies another phenomenon as well—one occurring throughout the century. Many cost accounting concepts and changes orginated in the manufacturing industry, but the concepts now have been extended and adapted for other industries. This phenomenon happened previously in standard costing and flexible budgeting. With the cost management techniques now being developed and implemented, the extension to the non-manufacturing industries is more pronounced than ever. The reason is obvious: The troublesome issues in today's industries are *overhead* and *administrative services*. There is little controversy concerning the techniques to account for direct materials and direct labor. The main focus of attention is on overhead, namely, operations overhead, plus selling, general, and administrative expenses. The techniques being developed are equally applicable to all industries because the business issues being addressed are the same throughout.

An Implementation Strategy that Forces Benefits

The second reason why you don't need to reinvent the cost information wheel is that not only do companies *not* have to develop the underlying accounting theory themselves, they do not have to start from scratch in developing an effective implementation strategy. The new techniques have been implemented in enough companies that patterns are beginning to emerge from the success stories. In fact, the objective is never to change an accounting practice; the objective is to achieve an operational improvement.

One company developed the following statement in describing its cost management project to its executive management team:

> There are many new ideas and techniques in the world of management accounting. We stay current with all those ideas. But our objective is not to implement new accounting ideas. Our objective is to increase the value to our customers of all work performed in our com-

pany. We adopt only the techniques that help us make progress toward that objective, and we tailor the ones we do adopt to fit our unique strategic direction and personality.

The most effective strategy could be described as a learning strategy: "Try it, learn from it, then decide your next move." Key elements of this strategy include:

- Starting small.
- Testing the value of a concept by using it to address a real business problem.
- Using a prototype approach.
- Using a prototype initially to improve organizational integration rather than system integration, even though the new techniques have a potentially tremendous systems integration potential.
- Doing the project as an analytical project, not as a project to replace your current accounting systems.

One executive calls this the *wing-walker strategy*. Wing-walking stunt artists who perform at air shows have a fundamental safety rule: Never let go of one strut until you have a firm grasp of another.

Your company's approach eventually may evolve to the point that you are ready to make significant changes in your systems. But if redesigning your systems (or software implementation) is your starting point, two unfortunate events are likely to occur:

- the project becomes so massive that it loses its momentum before showing results or realizing a benefit; and
- you get the system requirements wrong.

Moreover, you will miss a fabulous opportunity to learn more about the processes of your company than you ever dreamed possible.

Real learning takes place when you see the business results of the initial projects. Only then can you tailor the requirements to maximize benefits to your organization. You will know what to emphasize and what to de-emphasize. You will know what works and what doesn't work in presenting the information to your company's management. You will know what level of detail is most effective in your data collection and in your presentation of results. You will know the process and people needs as well as the system needs. You will know if a technique produces information that proves unhelpful in addressing your business issues. On the other hand, if an extremely large and expensive system is required before your people have the opportunity to take advantage of learning, you may have to live with sub-optimal results for a very long time.

These initial projects are critical in helping you discover your system requirements. Moreover, they are not just techniques for learning the practical applicability of new concepts; they can be a source of funding for a longer-term improvement effort. Since each project is designed to solve a real business problem, the benefits achieved in each can be used to pay for the follow-on project. Time and again we have seen the results of these analyses give management teams new insights into the cost dynamics of their businesses and point the way to important opportunities for improving their performance.

CHAPTER 2

Total Cost Management in a Nutshell

Since the time of its early development, the TCM concept has been refined and enriched as managers have applied it in numerous companies. But in order to understand TCM's potential, we must first position it within the context of the currently used cost systems.

There are four levels of cost systems:

1. infant systems;
2. traditional systems;
3. integrated information systems; and
4. Total Cost Management systems.

In *infant systems*, controls are poor, providing management with essentially no usable information. Such systems are currently found primarily in new organizations or companies that are undergoing extreme growth but have not yet acquired the resources to formalize their control systems.

Traditional systems have better controls, but the cost systems are independent of the operational systems. The only circumstances under which these traditional systems are appropriate in today's environment are in companies with:

1. very few product or process changes;
2. few products being manufactured or few services being offered; and
3. a highly labor-intensive process that produces goods and/or services.

In *integrated information systems*, the controls are excellent and the systems are fully integrated with the operational systems. But the emphasis in these systems is not well matched to the operational technology or to the organizational environment. Although the current environment may be machine-driven and material- and overhead-intensive, even the best of the integrated systems are labor-driven providing little guidance in overhead control.

Finally, *Total Cost Management systems*, as developed by Ernst & Young, are a comprehensive management philosophy for proactively managing total company resources (material, capital, and human resources) and the activities that consume those resources. Total Cost Management is an ongoing process of planning and improving the tactical and operational aspects of a business while providing the necessary foundation to support the strategic direction of that business.

The chief characteristics of Total Cost Management systems are that they:

- Focus on cost prevention as opposed to cost reporting.
- Provide a direct link between operating performances and strategic objectives.
- Focus on measurements of product or service profitability and cash flows in addition to cost flows and cost accumulation.

- Include selling, general, and administrative costs in the decision support function of cost systems.
- Equalize the importance of using technology for profit improvement as well as cost reduction.
- Allocate overhead on a cause-and-effect basis.
- Become a way of doing business, not just an accounting function.

As should be evident, Total Cost Management systems are more comprehensive, flexible, and proactive than the alternatives. What makes Total Cost Management so adaptive and powerful? The answer lies partly in the nature of TCM's three key principles. These are *business process analysis, activity-based costing*, and *continuous improvement.*

BUSINESS PROCESS ANALYSIS

The TCM approach is based on the belief that in-depth understanding and continuous improvement of business processes are the driving forces behind effective management of costs. Since a business is an aggregate of interrelated processes, executives need to develop a process orientation in their management philosophy.

Corporations tend to view their firms as a group of departments. This is a consequence of the old division-of-labor paradigm—a paradigm that has influenced how companies traditionally have been organized. For example, the organization chart of a manufacturer may show product engineering, manufacturing engineering, and production departments. An insurance company may have underwriting, rating, actuarial, and claims processing departments. Such organization charts suggest that each department is made up of a collection of tasks that can be measured and managed in isolation. This phenomenon creates departmental walls and ignores the work flow of the business.

Individually, each of these departments does contribute to the creation of a product or service. However, many activities cross departmental lines to produce the product or service. This series of activities is called the *process*.

For example, consider a typical process in a property and casualty insurance company's structure.

PROCESS: Issue a Commercial Lines Automobile Policy

1. Agent: Completes policy application
2. Underwriting: Evaluates risk and assigns rating factor
3. Rating: Codes policy, calculates premium, and produces the policy
4. Quality assurance: Checks policy for completeness and accuracy
5. Mailroom: Mails policy
6. Agent: Reviews policy, signs it, and mails or delivers it to policyholder.

Viewing the organization as a collection of processes rather than as a hierarchy of departments is the single most important conceptual requirement for improving your management accounting. This is important for two reasons:

1. It is the foundation for accomplishing business process improvement programs or cost-reduction programs; and
2. It is the foundation for initiating activity-based costing programs and continuous improvement programs.

Business Process Analysis is the Foundation for Business Process Improvement

On the surface, this process orientation may look like a conceptually easy way to view the organization. In practice, however, it is not the way people think and behave in organizations. Managers acquire authority and power around the reporting hierarchy. People build their careers by building their functional department roles—increasing the headcount, budget, and span of responsibility they control. Yet, the work itself flows across departments. Only when you view the work in its entirety can you identify the leverage points for streamlining the work. Exhibit 2-1 illustrates the difference between these two views. Each of the processes in the exhibit requires participation from multiple functional areas. No one department has complete responsibility for any process.

If you view the work only on a department-by-department basis, your efforts to streamline the work may result merely in a shifting of problems downstream, or in creating additional problems, complexity, or rework in other parts of the company. This happens because people and systems elsewhere in the organization have policies, procedures, and resources based on assumptions about the work done outside their own areas. The overall enterprise is most effectively improved by making improvements to the business processes rather than through individual initiatives (no matter how well intended) within individual departments.

Only two kinds of improvements are possible in an individual department: those that affect other departments; and those that don't. If you limit yourself to making improvements only to work that has no effect on other areas, you may be limiting yourself to less significant opportunities. If, on the other hand, you initiate improvements to work that does affect other areas (without the other areas being involved in designing and executing the improvements), then the improvement will be at best less effective than it could have been. Even if the

Processes	Departments					
	Sales	Marketing	Order Management	Engineering	Purchasing	Accounting
Proposals/Quotations	X	X				X
Customer Negotiation	X	X		X		
Order Entry	X	X	X			X
Order Engineering		X		X		
Procurement				X	X	X

EXHIBIT 2-1. Processes vs. Departments

output from your own department is improved, the pattern of the flow of work into downstream departments is likely to be affected.

Yet, every corporate improvement process needs something to give it focus. That focus-giving element needs to be so substantive and so logical that it can serve the organization through a wide variety of improvement efforts. Otherwise, the improvement process becomes little more than this year's fad. A suggestion to "improve everything, everywhere" doesn't exactly give insight to the people trying to identify improvement opportunities, nor does it suggest a logical way to go about the improvement effort.

By making business processes the object of long-term, continuous improvement efforts, you can determine key characteristics of each process. These characteristics can be derived from the answers to such questions as these:

- What work flow is required to complete the process? How does the work move from one activity/person to the next?
- Where are the bottlenecks?
- At what points in the process is the quality of the output unpredictable?
- Are there steps performed in the process that are irrelevant to the customers' requirements?
- How much time does it take to complete the process?
- How much money does it cost to perform the process?
- What causes the need for activities within the process?

Once the attributes are known, you can target a process for improvement. The criteria for selecting targets for improvement may vary depending on the business *objectives*. In some situations, the objective may be to reduce cost. In other situations, the objective may be to improve quality or to reduce cycle time. These objectives are not, of course, mutually exclusive. Reducing cost, improving quality, and reducing cycle time are all accomplished by the same analytical approaches to processes. But the selection of the process or sub-process with the greatest improvement opportunity may differ depending on the objective dominating the improvement effort.

Business Process Analysis is the Foundational Step for the Other TCM Components

Even if the primary objective in a company's management accounting improvement program is more accurate product cost or customer costs, a business process analysis may still be the first step in accomplishing that objective. It is also the organizing technique for improving performance measurement systems and decision support functions within the organization.

Managing Costs by Managing the Activities that Consume Them

Finally, it's worth noting that a process view of the organization facilitates an important new theme in management accounting: managers cannot manage costs directly. Rather, they manage the activities that consume the costs. Only by changing the activities that make up a business process or by taking action to reduce the demand for those activities can the manager have an effective and sustainable impact on costs.

ACTIVITY-BASED COSTING

The second component of TCM is *activity-based costing*. Even though the business process analysis is the cornerstone concept for improving management accounting, activity-based costing (more commonly known as ABC) has become the catch phrase to describe the new techniques in management accounting. In this book, we use the term "activity-based costing" to describe the specific techniques for costing business processes and for costing "objects." The objects may be products, services, product lines, service lines, customers, customer segments, or channels of distribution.

Activity-based costing (ABC) is a technique for accumulating cost for a given cost object that represents the total and true economic resources required or consumed by the object.

Organizations that sell goods or services already cost their products for inventory valuation or regulatory purposes. But many people who must rely on these costs for internal decision-making consider them both incomplete and distorted. They are incomplete because they include only the costs to acquire or produce the end products. They may not include any of the costs to warehouse, advertise, distribute, or sell the product or service. They are distorted because each product typically includes an assignment of overhead that was allocated on some arbitrary basis such as direct labor, sales dollars, machine hours, material cost, units of production, or some other volume measure.

Four questions can help you evaluate whether significant distortion is likely to exist in your cost calculations of product/service costs:

- Do you have products/services that are intuitively easier or harder to design and/or produce?
- Do you have both high- and low-volume products/services that are produced in or serviced from the same facilities?
- Do you have an overhead allocation base that is volume-oriented (labor, machine hours, units of production)?
- Do you have a significant amount of overhead (production and selling, general, and administration) cost relative to the total cost of the business?

Similar questions could be posed for other "objects."

- Do you have a combination of high- and low-volume customers?

- Are some customers easier or more difficult to serve?
- Do some customers purchase a higher concentration of high-margin products than do other customers?
- Do some customers require higher standards of quality or precision than others?
- Do some customers require additional services?

If you answered "yes" to many of these questions, you may be relying on distorted costs to make decisions.

What Difference Does Distortion Make?

The consequences of distorted costs depend on the decisions you make based on the cost calculations. Those decisions can be divided into two categories—those whose prime effect is *external* (within the marketplace) and those whose prime effect is *internal* (within your company).

External Focus An important category of cost-based decisions involve marketing issues: what products/services to offer and what prices to charge for them. If your product/ service is a commodity item for which the market sets the price, your cost-based decision may be so fundamental as whether you should be in the market for that particular item at all. Other related decisions focus on which opportunities to pursue:

- Which contracts to bid on and at what price.
- Which customers to pursue.
- Which products to carry in the product line.
- Which products to promote.
- Which services to offer.
- Which services to charge for, and which simply to bundle with the product or with a general service package.

- How to encourage (that is, to compensate) the sales force to work toward maximum margins rather than maximum revenues.

The most extreme but most graphic case of unfortunate results from product cost distortion can be termed a "death spiral." Consider this example:

> A manufacturer has a factory that produces both high- and low-volume products. This factory has a high level of support from overhead functions, and most of that support is not volume-based. (For example, production volume is not a factor in determining how long it takes a production planner to plan and release a manufacturing order. That process is much more dependent on the complexity of the product than on the volume to be produced.) Overhead is assigned to all these products using a plant-wide overhead rate applied according to the direct labor content of the product. As a result of this overhead assignment, the high-volume products are systematically overcosted and the low-volume products are systematically undercosted. The calculated cost is used as the basis for determining what to bid in contracts for new orders.
>
> Over time, fewer and fewer orders are received for the high-volume products and more and more orders are received for the low-volume products. Even though the volume of output of the plant diminishes, the overhead required to support the plant does not diminish proportionately. So the large pool of overhead is now spread across fewer products, thereby increasing their calculated costs. More contracts are lost, leading to even higher overhead cost to spread across even fewer products.

This story strikes a chord with many manufacturing executives. The story is particularly disturbing when an executive believes that competitors are developing improved costing techniques. As long as all players in a market had relatively equal costing systems (even if the systems were poor) no individual player was at a significant advantage or disadvantage on the playing field. However, once even one of the competitors in a market has improved cost systems, the rest of the players can be at a serious disadvantage if systematic distortion is present in their own cost calculations.

Yet, calculating more accurate product costs or object costs is not the only solution required for keeping your business cost-competitive.

Internal Focus For external focus, the relevant question is "What does the object actually cost?" Once you have confidence that you know what the object costs, what do you do if you don't like the number? Are you limited to the options of raising the price you charge for it, dropping the project, or living with a product euphemistically known as a loss-leader? Not at all. In addition to knowing what a product/service/customer costs, you clearly also want to know *why the cost is what it is* and—if you don't like it—*what can you do about it?* The power to address these two internal questions comes from the deliberate coupling of business process analysis and activity-based costing.

An Overview of the Technique

Let's first consider the ABC technique, then see how this important coupling can be achieved. (See Exhibit 2-2.) The logic of activity-based costing is simple. Companies expend resources to fund activities. They perform activities to benefit products, services, or other cost objects. The goal in activity-based costing is to mirror this causality among resources, activities, and cost objects in assigning overhead costs. For exam-

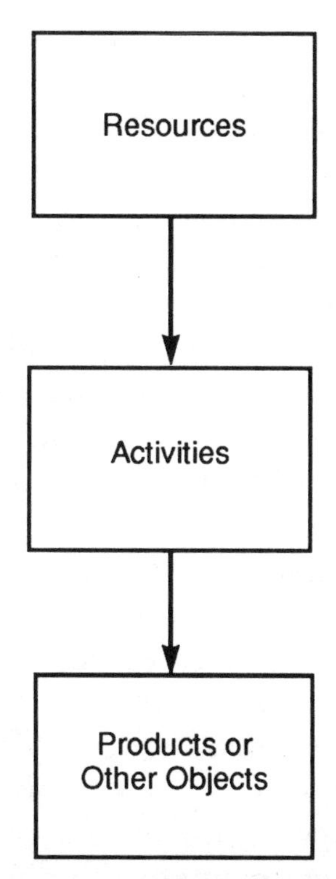

EXHIBIT 2-2. Logical Model for ABC

ple, salaries, facility costs, and computer costs may be spent to support production planning activities. Production planning activities are performed to support individual products. In this example, the cost of each product should reflect the cost of the production planning activity required to support it.

At first glance, this ABC process may appear to require extremely elaborate data collection systems. This is not necessarily the case. Companies may want to assign overhead costs to objects more accurately, but they are also looking for ways to simplify rather than complicate the work their people do. To continue this same example, ABC would not require that the staff members in production planning begin keeping track of how much time they spend supporting each individual product. Rather, ABC would make use of data that already exist as a natural consequence of the work.

Production planning decisions are analyzed and then communicated throughout the organization by using a computerized planning and control system (in this case, an MRP-II system). ABC could get the data it needed for its calculations by scanning the MRP-II files and determining how many production planning transactions were processed for each product. In fact, the very existence of rich databases is precisely what makes the actual implementation of ABC systems feasible. (A sidenote: in its infancy—before someone coined the ABC acronym—what people now call "activity-based costing" was called "transaction-based costing.") (See Exhibit 2-3.)

The cost data contained in a company's general ledger is reorganized into *activity cost pools* and then the amounts in the activity cost pools are assigned to products/services or other cost objects based on some causal factor. (In Part II of this book, we will show details from a variety of ABC implementations that address many of the practical issues in completing an ABC analysis of costs.) Once the object costing is completed, the costs are compared to selling prices or revenues to analyze profitability by product, service, customer, and so on.

CONTINUOUS IMPROVEMENT

The third component of TCM is *continuous improvement*. The most constant theme in business today is the need for leadership, attitudes, and support structures that foster continuous improvement in the performance of the enterprise. And the targets for continuous improvement cover all dimensions of an organization:

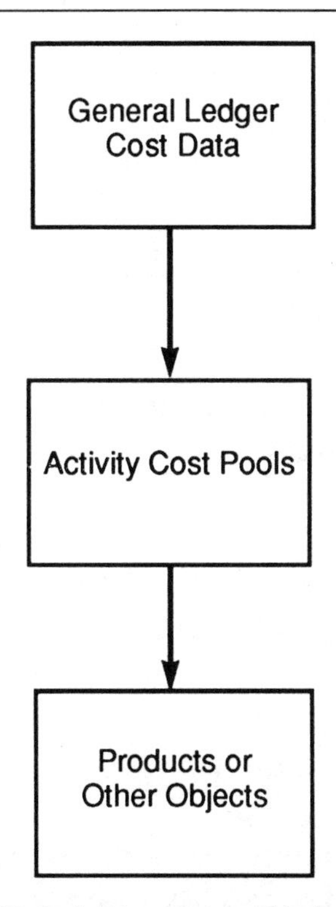

EXHIBIT 2-3. Implementation Model for ABC

- The quality of the products and services.
- The responsiveness to customers.
- The quality of the worklife.
- The time required to get new products or services to market.
- The ability to pinpoint customer needs and requirements.
- The financial health and wellbeing of the business.
- The ability to leverage assets (i.e., the ability to do more with less).

TCM plays two important roles in helping an organization get (and stay) on a path of continuous improvement:

1. TCM provides a means for measuring performance; and
2. TCM provides information to support key tactical and strategic decisions.

Improvement implies change. It implies that you know what your performance was yesterday and that you will know when you have bettered that performance. Improvement requires that the performance be measured. Without that measurement, you are only guessing whether improvement has actually occurred. Unless the measures cover all important dimensions of performance, what looks like an improvement may actually be only a performance exchange—trading better performance on one dimension for poorer performance on another.

Performance measures do not substitute for communicative leadership, but they can assist the leadership in communicating the performance objectives.

Measuring Performance

There is, however, a difference between measuring something and making it an objective. As Duncan McDougall points out, "We can measure to track progress toward an objective, but also must measure to maintain constraints." (Duncan C. McDougall, "The Principal of Slack Ropes or Managing on Purpose," in *Operating Management Review*, Spring, 1987.) One approach is to measure all important dimensions of performance, but to seek improvement in only one area at a time. That way, no backsliding is permitted on any performance dimension, while improvement is sought on strategic objectives.

In many companies, the current performance measurement system is actually an impediment to achieve continuous improvement. Often, the internal financial system is the most formal and most public performance measurement system the company has at its disposal. When that is the case, achieving favorable financial results can become the prime motivator of behavior. While achieving financial success is a primary objective of any business, a narrowed focus can create problems if not properly balanced.

The problem is threefold:

- A focus on short-term financial results can dilute the effort to achieve longer-term strategic objectives.
- In a misguided effort to achieve favorable financial results, managers may produce excess output (e.g., inventory) in order to absorb fixed overhead or earn standard labor hours. Such actions are directly contrary to strategic objectives of increasing throughput, decreasing cycle time, and eliminating waste in a business.
- Financial results are sometimes calculated as variances from budgets or variances from standards, and, typically, the budgets or standards are "frozen" for a year. The attitude of continuous improvement, however, never sees the goal as frozen. To the contrary, under continuous improvement, achieving one goal implies "raising the bar" and setting a new goal.

What is Needed to Make Measurement Systems Mirror Goals and Objectives?

There are three types of changes needed in most performance measurement systems. The first is *an alignment with the critical success factors of the business*. Critical success factors are those attributes that a company must possess, or actions that it must perform especially well, in order to survive and thrive. It is crucial that a business's performance measurement system reflect its critical success factors.

A quick exercise can set the tone for whether there is a serious gap between the measurements used to run the business and the factors critical to its success. Take a sheet of paper. Along the left-hand margin, list from top to bottom the performance elements currently measured. Along the top, list from left to right the critical success factors. For each performance measure, check the critical success factor that it supports. If you are like most people who do this exercise, you will invariably find critical success factors that are not adequately supported by measures. In addition, there are almost always existing measures that do not support any of the success factors of the business.

The second type of change needed in performance measurement systems is *a structure that provides balance and integration between financial and non-financial measures*. Most businesses have plenty of financial measures. However, these measures alone are not enough. Operational or non-financial measures are needed to manage the business at the process level where cost is incurred and where cost must be controlled. People at the lower end of the organization often do not understand or cannot relate to these financial measures.

There must be a balance in two important areas with regard to performance measures. A balance must exist between financial and non-financial measures. Within non-financial measures, a balance between measures of efficiency, effectiveness, productivity, utilization, speed, and quality must exist.

All too often, we measure *efficiency* (which is a measure of how well we are doing) without measuring the *effectiveness* (which measures whether we are doing the right things). Consequently, we may be doing very well at the wrong things and are none the wiser. *Productivity* (the measure of output for a given set of inputs), *utilization* (the uses of resources), *speed,* and *quality* round out the non-financial measures needed to provide comprehensiveness and relevance to the measurement system.

The functional balance also needs to be improved in many organizations' performance measurement practices. Typically, companies do not equitably measure the entire value chain. For example, they may over-measure operations and then under-measure marketing effectiveness—or fail to measure marketing at all.

The third type of change needed in performance measurement systems is *a format reflecting the spirit of continuous improvement.* For the performance measures to help foster the goals of continuous improvement, the measures need to be calculated and displayed so that they show a progress over time. It is not sufficient to show only the performance of the current period. Each measure needs to be reported in the context of a *trend.* The reader needs to be able to see whether current performance is better than, worse than, or the same as the performance in prior periods.

There is great value in seeing significant progress being achieved over time as constant efforts to improve performance actually show results. But reporting performance in trends is still not sufficient to move an organization toward world-class performance. A company can fall into the trap of comparing itself only against itself. In addition to seeing its own performance over time, a company must also compare itself against the performance of other organizations. This approach to measurement is known as *competitive benchmarking, best practices comparison,* or *best-in-class comparison.*

Improved Decision Making

In addition to performance measures, continuous improvement requires good decision support. The decision support relevant to operational issues should build upon the process orientation of cost behavior and the activity-based costing information. This allows the company to employ activity-based information in many different areas of the business such as evaluating capital investments, life-cycle costing, and target costing. (We will explore these topics at greater length in Chapters 12 and 13.)

Evaluating Capital Investments One of the most critical decisions that executives make in terms of competitive positioning is the investment in facilities, equipment, and technology. The company's future financial health is closely tied to the investment decisions.

How do you justify investments today? Not long ago, most companies made these decisions by determining the amount of direct labor savings, then multiplied that savings by an overhead factor to determine the total savings. Today, most companies recognize that overhead—whether in production or administration—is not driven by labor. Rather, it is driven by variety, complexity, and activities.

Direct identification of costs that change as a result of the investment is always the best method for evaluating new investments. But this approach has limitations because the effect of change on the process cannot always be measured in hard dollars.

Two organizations (CAM-I and the U.S. Department of Commerce) have developed, field-tested, and introduced new investment justification models. These models center on using both hard and soft data. For instance, quality improvement, reduced cycle time, improved service, better flexibility, and the like were all known to improve the competitive position. All of these factors are used in the evaluation models in addition to any directly traceable cost savings.

Life-Cycle Costing Product life cycles are becoming shorter and shorter. This has certain implications for business.

Clearly, "time to market" is of competitive importance. In addition, the up-front costs of development, design, prototyping, process validation, quality engineering, marketing, promotions, and so on occur long before the first dollar of revenue is generated.

The integrated principles of TCM can provide valuable insights into the management of product life cycles by providing:

- The foundation for costing the stages of the life cycle.
- A mechanism for understanding the cost trade-offs between life-cycle stages.
- An understanding of the total cost of the product over the life cycle.
- An understanding of "when and if" the total investment in new product development has been recouped.
- A basis for simulating process changes during the life cycle.
- A methodology for improving serviceability, quality, and flexibility as the life cycle evolves.

The techniques for *life-cycle costing* provide information to decision makers (particularly design engineers and product/service managers) to help them evaluate the potential long-term impacts of their short-term decisions. These techniques shift the cost control emphasis from the activities in which costs are incurred to the activities in which costs are determined.

Target Costing A technique closely related to life-cycle costing is *target costing*. Target costing is most frequently associated with Japanese cost methods. By means of this cost management technique, the "allowable" cost for a product is calculated according to market share and profit margin considerations. In effect, the product/service cost is specified as one of the requirements that must be met by the product/service development team. Strategic-level improvements to the business processes are sometimes needed for the organization to achieve the target cost.

This discussion concludes our overview of TCM's three key principles. Chapter 3 now sketches how you can apply TCM to your own business.

CHAPTER 3

The Role of TCM in Sustaining A Competitive Advantage

The three most prevalent emphases in business strategy today are *customer focus, total quality management,* and *time-based competition.* These three strategies are not mutually exclusive. A company must perform well in all three dimensions to be a major player in its industry. In many cases, actions taken to improve performance in one dimension will also improve performance in the others. But given an acceptable level of performance in all three dimensions, a company may choose to earn its competitive advantage by then excelling in one or more of these areas. TCM can play an important role in supporting any and all of these business strategies.

CUSTOMER FOCUS

Not too long ago, one of the most popular phrases found in corporate objective statements was "satisfying customer needs." That language has recently changed in many companies to reflect a new level of aspiration for interaction with customers. A typical new phrase within such companies is the objective to "excite and delight" the customer.

This change in language reflects a heightened appreciation of the advantage you can gain by knowing your customer's business so well that you recognize needs that the customer doesn't even know he has. It means, too, that satisfying customer needs is a necessary but insufficient condition for becoming and staying a leader in your industry. It means that the key to leadership is based on understanding the business processes, tactical and strategic directions, and personalities of your customers so well that you can effectively use your imagination to develop new ways to please them. It means an element of surprise.

On the surface, this is an invigorating and enticing approach. Ultimately, however, the desire to "excite and delight" the customer must be translated into new products, new features for old products and services, and a wide array of new services. Some of the changes may be small or subtle, while others may be much more substantive. For instance, you may alter your packaging to accommodate a particular way in which a customer uses the product or service. You may alter your method of invoicing to simplify the customer's processing of your bill. You may alter the procedures that your employees follow in communicating with the customer. Given the fast-paced environments of most of today's industries, there is a high probability that you will be developing a whole new generation of products and services.

You may dramatically increase the frequency of your communication with the customer. You may also increase the range of people within your organization who interact with the customers. Instead of interactions occurring primarily through sales representatives and customer service representatives, you may now actively encourage customer interaction with technicians, engineers, and operations personnel. In effect, all employees engage in some activities for servicing the customer and all employees also become an extension of market research. Traditional market research itself takes on increased importance.

The approach is indeed exciting. It is also one that poses a major challenge to traditional management accounting. With an increased variety of products and services (and with much of this variety individualized to particular customers), the job becomes more difficult. At the same time, it becomes more important to know how much specific products and services actually cost and to know which products, services, and customers offer real profit potential.

Without that analytical base, pricing policies may not translate delighted customers into a satisfying bottom line. On the contrary, it may be easy for your sales reps to "give away" the new features and services if you don't know what they cost.

There are many ways in which TCM supports this *customer focus strategy*. Three of the most important are:

1. *Business process analysis* utilizes your market research conclusions to make sure that all work performed in your organization is work that your customers value. This keeps the costs of those processes at a minimum while optimizing value.
2. *Activity-based costing* provides the cost information you need to decide which products and services to offer and how to price them. ABC also delineates the true cost of servicing your customer base.
3. *Performance measurement* keeps the corporate attention focused on accomplishing the goals most critical to the profitable success of your business.

TOTAL QUALITY MANAGEMENT

The second strategic emphasis is *total quality management* (TQM) which has become the dominant strategy in North

American industry for the past decade. Beginning with the automotive industry and eventually permeating almost all manufacturing and service sectors, companies have implemented programs to improve product/service quality since the late 1970s and early 1980s.

A process view is fundamental to these programs:

Suppliers→Inputs→Process→Product/
Service→Customers

Inputs are processed to create a product or service. Only those characteristics of the product or service that customers value can be used to specify the quality attributes of that product or service. *Quality* is then defined as conformance to specifications. To produce perfect products/services, you must know the specifications and then concentrate on the quality of the inputs and on the reliability of the process.

The most important common link between TQM and TCM is this process view. In fact, defining the business processes is fundamental to any performance improvement effort.*

There are actually two different scenarios for the relationship between TQM and TCM:

1. Where the quality program has taken root in the organization, is viewed as successful by senior management, and in fact influences the day-to-day actions of all personnel.
2. Where the quality program was never initiated or (more commonly) never took root in the organization.

---

* For an elaboration on the extent to which process improvement techniques are practiced in the United States, Japan, Canada, and Germany, see *The International Quality Study: Top Line Findings* (American Quality Foundation and Ernst & Young) 1991.

Let's examine each of these scenarios.

When TQM Already Permeates the Organization

In organizations with strong, mature quality programs, people usually already think with a process view. People view their work in terms of its participation in a business process. Tools and techniques are in place to monitor and control process variability. Activities not valued by customers have been declared waste, and much of this waste has been eliminated. Independent inspection activities have been largely eliminated; responsibility for quality now rests with the person who converts inputs to outputs. Process improvement teams are formed to solve business problems.

Many of the today's companies with the strongest quality programs are companies that previously lost market share, profits, or both because of poor quality in their products and services. Even though their quality programs have been promoted throughout the organization, the greatest improvements have occurred in the processes that directly make products for or deliver services to external customers. The greatest opportunities for improvement of processes and for further elimination of waste in these companies lie in the administrative areas of the business.

Once again, there are many important possible ways that TCM can support companies with mature quality strategies. Three of the most common are discussed here.

First, when attention turns to the administrative areas of the business, certain "products" are likely to be deemed unacceptable in value to their customers. One such example is the managerial accounting reports. Many business processes use accounting data as input for such decisions as:

- Product/service line composition;
- Product/service pricing;

- Product/service abandonment;
- Excecutive compensation; and
- Make/buy decisions.

Once managers see these decisions as made within the context of a business process, they can challenge the inputs to that process as well as the process itself. TCM provides techniques (particularly, activity-based costing and decision support tools) to change the specifications of the accounting inputs to these important business processes. Moreover, in implementing activity-based costing and decision support techniques, you can often complete the first steps of the analysis very quickly. This speed is possible because companies with mature quality programs often have already defined the activities comprising their business processes.

Second, once the initial quality problem is solved, the challenge is to make "continuous improvement" a reality. TCM's performance measurement techniques assure that complacency or backsliding do not unknowingly creep into the organization's performance.

Third, when managers truly view all work performed in the organization in terms of activities within business processes, the financial planning, budgeting, and control systems of the organization will naturally evolve to reflect that view. TCM's activity-based budgeting and control is the technique that structures the financial information around the business processes.

When TQM Has Not Taken Root within the Business

The second scenario occurs when senior management has embraced the quality movement as an important but not driving force of the business. This often has happened in companies whose product or service quality has never lost (or gained) them a market share. For example, food and beverage companies and pharmaceutical companies, along with many service organizations (such as insurance companies or financial services institutions), may not have competed on the basis of product/service quality, but they have seen the improvements in the companies who have become passionate about quality and they want these improvements for themselves.

As one executive said, "We make a popular, high-margin product. We've been spared the intense competition that is quality-based or cost-based. But the downside of that history is that over the years we've become wasteful, inefficient, and downright sloppy in many areas of the company. And we have been slow to adopt techniques and technologies that could make us more efficient. I need to streamline my operations every bit as much as the next guy. The only difference is that I have the luxury to streamline without having to make massive layoffs." Other executives are not so lucky; periodic layoffs have become their most routine way of managing their budgets.

Typically, the quality program in these situations may not have been sufficiently focused for it to "take root" and actually change the mindset of a sufficient number of people. Worse yet, the program might have started with fanfare, hoopla, and a lot of lip service. In such situations, TCM can be an effective way to focus and revitalize a performance improvement program without its having the appearance of being little more than just another fad. TCM can help make this possible in two important ways.

First, business process analysis provides a technique for defining the processes, breaking them down into activities, and identifying opportunities to eliminate waste, increase quality, decrease cost, reduce cycle time, and add flexibility. If cost reduction or headcount reduction is imperative, the business process analysis technique analyzes the activities so that the reductions are most likely to be sustainable. It does so by addressing the root causes of the activities and by making sure that the impact on upstream/downstream activities has been communicated and understood by all parties.

Business process analysis is not a technique unique to TCM. However, since it is the foundational step for activity-based costing and for improved performance measurement and improved decision support, it can be effectively positioned and employed within the context of a TCM project.

Second, TCM can be useful when a company is unaware of the magnitude of improvement possible in its operations. A Performance Management system that is directly relevant to the organization's critical success factors, and that includes comparison in performance against other organizations, can play an important role in defining and monitoring performance objectives.

TIME-BASED COMPETITION

The third strategic emphasis in American businesses today is *time-based competition.* Once again, the automotive industry, responding to offshore pressures, has introduced the new rules of competition. These new rules (rules generally called "time-based competition) are now being adopted in one industry after another.

Time-based competition focuses on the customer, embraces quality improvements, and strategically manages costs. In addition to addressing these issues, however, it adds speed as the most versatile competitive weapon. The breadth of possibilities for time-based competition is practically endless:

- Time to process a claim in an insurance company.
- Time to transfer funds in international banking.
- Time to design a new model of automobile.
- Time to develop new software applications.

- Time to communicate an order from a customer to the person responsible for filling the order.

The benefits to be achieved under the time-based competition paradigm can be significant. You can:

1. Increase your productivity.
2. Convert invested resources to cash more quickly.
3. Increase the prices you charge.
4. Decrease your risks.
5. Increase your market share.

If you approach your corporate improvement program with a focus on time, you can pay for the program with item 1 and still enjoy the benefits of items 2 through 5. On the other hand, if you approach your improvement program with only item 1 in mind, productivity improvement is all you'll get. (Your competitors will still clobber you.)*

TCM can help support this time-based competition strategy in four important ways. First, business process analysis is the primary technique for analyzing cycle time for all business processes and for identifying opportunities to streamline them. Linking this with ABC techniques applied at the process level combines the cost, time, and quality variables of a business, thereby associating a quantifiable financial impact for time.

Second, keeping the organization focused on the time objective may require a change in the measures used to monitor performance. Obviously, measures need to be implemented that reflect the time dimension of performance. Just

* This description of time-based competition is adapted from a speech by George Stalk, "Connecting the Organization to Compete on Time," 1991 Annual Meeting of Operations Management Association: Waco, Texas.

as important, however, you may want to eliminate some of your traditional measures that focus exclusively on productivity or utilization.

Third, it is also critically important that your capital budgeting techniques not be used in a way that sabotages the goal of compressing time. To increase your ability to respond quickly to a customer, you may want to explore the possibility of building extra capacity at key points in your service delivery processes. Rarely could this kind of investment pass an ROI test in which the return is measured only in cost savings. Justifying this investment in additional capacity may require you to update your techniques for capital investment justification.

Finally, under time-based competition, there is intense pressure to speed the development of new products and services, and the life cycles of individual products and services are forever getting shorter. The time in which it is possible to recoup the development cost is shortened. Life-cycle costing and target costing can provide the analytical framework for supporting the design decisions that essentially dictate the ultimate profitability of a product or services.

The message of this text is clear: You shouldn't have to manage your 1990s business with a 1940s cost accounting system. Today's business environment is dramatically different from the one that existed when most traditional cost management systems were developed. The cost structures have changed. The strategic imperatives have changed. In particular, the quality movement has proven that the key to improving performance (including cost performance) is to focus on your business processes and on your customers.

The cost management innovators have proven another point during the past few years: TCM techniques provide improved information that can truly help your company make progress toward its strategic goals.

Business process analysis is the foundation for recognizing opportunities for improvement, particularly in overhead areas of your business. Activity-based costing provides a much-needed increase in the accuracy of the cost calculations used in some of the most important decisions that a business makes—decisions about product offerings, product promotion and pricing, outsourcing, and customer strategies.

Continuous improvement demands that a company's performance measurement system support its strategic goals and its success factors. Continuous improvement also demands that the cost input for capital budgeting and new product development be supported by relevant cost information.

Part I of this book has sketched Total Cost Management and its component principles to show how TCM can help you sustain your competitive advantage in the complex global marketplace. Part II now describes the details, or the "how-to" of Total Cost Management.

Appendix to Part I: Self-Diagnostic Checklist

	Symptom	*TCM Issue*	*TCM Principal / Technique*
PERFORMANCE IMPROVEMENT OPPORTUNITIES	Unsatisfactorily long lead times	There may be activities that add cycle time but add no value	Cycle time/cost analysis within business process analysis
	SG&A costs are high and/or increasing as a percent of total costs	#1: There may be opportunities to reduce this overhead cost without reducing services valued by customers #2: Many of the SG&A costs may be incurred to promote, sell, and deliver products/services to customers. If so, product/service costs used for internal decision making need to reflect these "below the line" costs	#1: Business process analysis Activity-based process costing #2: Activity-based process/ service costing
	Slow inventory turns	Costly investment in stagnant resources	Business process analysis focusing on working capital management Activity-based process costing
	SG&A costs are high and/or increasing as a percent of total costs "Spaghetti" flow of work	High content of non-value-added costs	Business process analysis Activity-based process costing
	High and/or rising overhead costs	There may be activities being performed that add cost to the process but do not add value to the customer	Business process analysis Activity-based process costing
	You have implemented ABC and are confident that your product costs now accurately reflect all overhead activities. The cost of some products is unacceptably high, but the analysis does not suggest opportunities to improve the costs.	Improvement projects that focus exclusively on product cost calculations provide incomplete solutions	Activity-based costing coupled with business process analysis

COST ACCOUNTING IMPROVEMENT OPPORTUNITIES

Symptom	*TCM Issue*	*TCM Principal/Technique*
Labor is low percentage of total cost, but overhead is applied based on labor content	High probability of distorted product costs	Activity-based costing
Difficult products/services are not premium priced	The actual cost of the product/service may be obscured, and your product profitability analyses may be inaccurate	Activity-based costing
Recent history of winning a larger share of orders for low-volume products or losing important bids for high-volume products	Overhead allocation system may be systematically undercosting low-volume products and overcosting high-volume products	Activity-based costing
Material is high percentage of total cost	Material acquisition costs may be assigned to products using an illogical technique	Activity-based costing
Make/buy decisions are based on product cost information	Viable/profitable products/services may be unnecessarily eliminated from your operations	Activity-based costing
The product/service offering has become more complex, with many new products, services, and features coming available frequently	The greater the proliferation of products/services, the higher the likelihood that traditional cost accounting provides an inaccurate assessment of individual costs and profits	Activity-based costing
High-volume and low-volume products are produced together.	High probability of distorted product costs	Activity-based costing
You want to concentrate marketing efforts on your most profitable combinations of products/customer segments, and it is not clear which combinations are most profitable.	Analyzing activities by customers and/or customer segments is just as important as analyzing by product	Activity-based customer costing

	Symptom	*TCM Issue*	*TCM Principal / Technique*
CONTINUOUS IMPROVEMENT OPPORTUNITIES	Product life cycles are decreasing	The time is shortened in which to recoup product development costs. Your current analyses for predicting payback may be inadequate.	Continuous improvement; Life-cycle costing
	Capital projects that support strategic goals (e.g., improve quality or increase flexibility) frequently fail ROI tests	Traditional ROI techniques provide little support for evaluating benefits other than cost savings.	Capital investment evaluation
	Capital investments are based on labor savings plus incremental labor-based overhead	Economically viable projects may be routinely rejected.	Continuous improvement; Capital investment evaluation
	Performance measures over-emphasize department-level financial results and offer few insights into operational performance	The performance measures need to be related to the critical success factors of the business, and need additionally to be balanced between financial and non-financial measures.	Continuous improvement; Performance measurement

PART TWO

TCM PRINCIPLES

Introduction to TCM Principles

In this second part of the book, we will take a closer look at TCM's three major principles: *business process analysis, activity-based costing,* and *continuous improvement.* We will explain the derivation of each of these principles, then show how it works and provide practical suggestions for how best to apply it.

The sequence in which we describe these principles is important. We begin with business process analysis (BPA) as the foundation for all of the TCM techniques. In the three chapters devoted to BPA, you will see how to understand and document business processes as well as how to use that analysis to improve the quality, speed, and cost of the processes themselves.

We then progress to five chapters on activity-based costing where we will show how to expand business process analysis to calculate the costs of processes, products, services, and customers.

Finally, in the last two chapters of Part II, we show how you can use the process/activity view of costs to support your continuous improvement objective. This involves improving performance measurements and improving the information used to support specific decisions about:

1. investments in quality improvement programs;
2. decisions about new product/service development; and
3. decisions about acquiring new capital assets.

SECTION 1

Business Process Analysis

CHAPTER 4

The Whys and Hows of Business Process Analysis

Fundamental to Total Cost Management is the belief that an in-depth understanding and continuous improvement of business processes provide the keys to effective management of costs. The tools and techniques for studying these business processes are collectively called *business process analysis* (BPA).

WHY DO A BUSINESS PROCESS ANALYSIS?

The two principal ways to viewing an organization are from the functional view and from the process view. The *functional view* relies on the organizational chart as the primary model of the business. All resources belong to individual departments. Functional specialization and expertise are the major considerations in forming departments, which in turn are related through a hierarchy of reporting structures. Improvement programs focus on increasing the efficiency and effectiveness of specific functions and specific organizational units.

By contrast, the *process view* focuses on the work itself rather than on the organizational structure for managing the work. The process view identifies, at the highest level, the major elements of work that employees must perform for the business to function. These high-level elements are called *processes.* Exhibit 4-1 depicts an enterprise-level process model of a business.

At the enterprise level, the inputs are capital, human resources, materials and information, and technology. The six enterprise-level processes include:

1. the executive processes;
2. the support processes;
3. the process of gaining new business;
4. the process of designing new products and services;
5. the operations processes; and
6. the process of supporting the installed customer base.

The conduct of these processes are influenced by competitive and regulatory factors as well as by the stakeholders' interests. The outputs of the business processes (i.e., products, services, communications, and the like) go to the organization's customers as well as to end consumers.

Processes are broken down into *sub-processes* which further break down into *activities.* The collection of activities that make up a process then become the focus of virtually all analysis.

The process view provides such a powerful way of analyzing a business because *it is the way that a customer views a business.* A customer interacts with an organization *through its business processes*—entering into contracts, receiving goods and services, paying for these goods and services, and requesting after-sales support. Only by taking the same perspective about

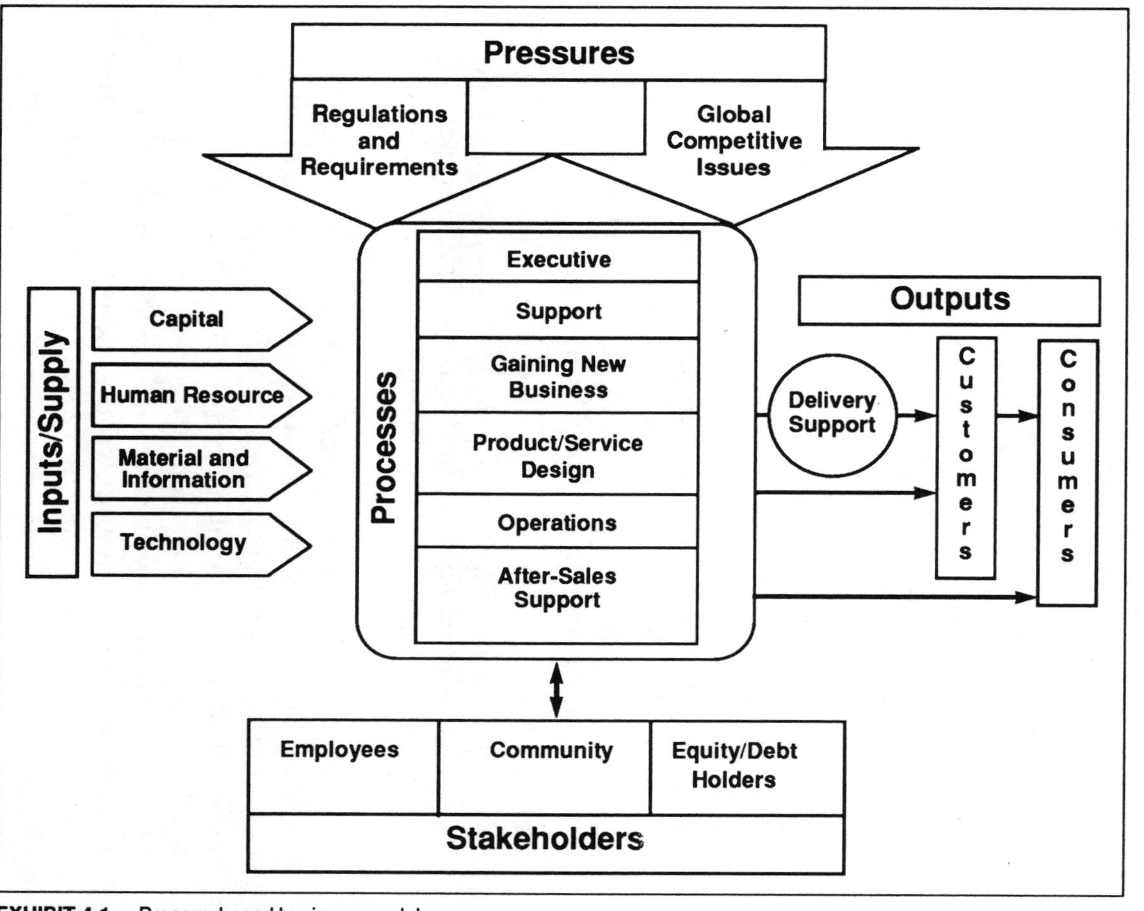

EXHIBIT 4-1. Process-based business model.

our businesses that our customers take, can we assess the "value" of the work we do.

This process view provides the foundation for Total Cost Management. The reason that TCM emphasizes the process view over the functional view is that the process approach enables an organization to design the work around a management goal or a customer requirement without necessarily changing the structure of the organization. The process view thus gives the company clearer insights into its effectiveness in satisfying customer needs and clearer insights as well into accomplishing its work.

There are two main reasons for performing a business process analysis:

1. A *business process analysis may be used as an end in itself* to guide cost and cycle time reduction programs, process quality improvement, or other efforts to improve organizational performance.
2. A *business process analysis may be used as a preliminary step for completing other TCM techniques*, among them activity-based costing, performance measurement improvements, or decision support improvements.

Whichever of these two reasons you may have for performing a business process analysis, the techniques involved are essentially the same. Every process, sub-process, and activity takes input, performs some form of conversion on that input to produce output, and transfers that output to a recipient or "customer." A business process analysis essentially identifies processes and breaks them down into activities; this, in turn, establishes a basis for managing costs from a variety of angles or objectives.

Before considering either the methods or the goals of business process analysis, however, let's focus briefly on the two reasons already noted for performing BPA.

Reason One: BPA is an End in Itself

Companies often find themselves in the position of needing to reduce costs—whether to satisfy specific financial constraints or to accomplish additional work without adding resources. Alternatively, companies may need to simplify and streamline their operations to reduce cycle time, increase responsiveness, improve quality, free capacity, or reduce working capital. Or companies may want to achieve improvement objectives without trading one performance dimension for another. They aren't willing, for instance, to sacrifice quality, cycle time, or responsiveness in their pursuit of cost reductions or working capital reductions.

Moreover, companies do not intentionally pursue temporary "fixes" for their performance problems. Yet, it is common to hear of organizations in which costs "creep back" not long after a significant cost-reduction effort. Executives lay off employees only to hire them back quickly as contractors. They may reduce costs by eliminating certain activities only to have those activities reappear elsewhere in the organization. They may eliminate a support service in an administrative department only to have the cycle time increased in the line department that had to absorb the service. In these cases, the logical flaw is that managers have eliminated activities without identifying the customer and/or the root cause of the activity. Only by breaking the dependency between an activity and its root cause and only by eliminating all requirements for the activity's output, can a company sustain its cost reduction efforts.

A business process analysis is the key analytical approach that supports managers in achieving these performance improvements. It does so by connecting process/activity identification, customer requirements, and analyses of value, cycle time, cost, quality, organization, and the root causes of problems.

A business process analysis is accomplished through very heavy involvement from the employees actually performing the activities. Their input is sought in:

- Defining the activities;
- Validating their own input requirements;
- Estimating cycle times;
- Identifying root causes; and
- Making value assessments.

The more empowered these teams of employees are, not only to offer input, but also to develop and implement improvements to the business processes, the more dramatic their role is in the improvement effort.

Customers also play a key role in a business process analysis. External customers are the parties who purchase the organization's output. These customers' current and future requirements are the basis for defining the value of the organization's goods and services. The analysis then focuses inward both on the chains of activities that produce the goods and services, as well as on the ones that provide support activities within the organization. When the output of a process is received by someone inside the enterprise, that person is called an *internal customer*. For instance, the managers who receive periodic accounting reports are internal customers of the process that produces the reports.

A primary technique within *business process analysis* is *process value analysis* (PVA). Applying PVA challenges each activity in terms of its role in satisfying its internal and external customers' needs (i.e., creating value). This challenge starts with the requirements of the external customer and moves backwards through each chain to document the relationship of all activities to their customers. As part of this process, BPA team members categorize each activity as either *value-added* (one that customers consider important to be performed) or *non-value-added* (one that customers consider unimportant or not worth paying for). Non-value-added activities are ones that do not affect the quality, performance, or functionality of the output.

Upon completing the value analysis and identifying root causes of non-value-added activities, organizations have a basis for making significant and sustainable improvements in cost and peformance by identifying activities that could be eliminated, combined, done in parallel, bypassed in particular instances, changed in sequence, changed in location, changed in mix, simplified, automated, integrated, or minimized. Moreover, once the list identifying activities to eliminate or change has been developed, the business process analysis can guide the implementation plan to ensure that all affected parties participate in the process redesign effort. Additionally, there is the significant benefit of having the entire organization focus on its ability to provide value to a customer.

Here's a small sample of results that process value analyses have achieved for various clients:

- A 50 percent reduction in cycle time;
- Average processing lead time reduced from 40 to 5 days;
- Errors reduced from 25 percent to 2 percent;
- Labor costs reduced despite a 40 percent increase in volume;
- A 90 percent increase in the ideas generated and implemented by employees;
- A 30 to 50 percent increase in capacity;
- A 30 to 50 percent reduction in overhead cost;
- A 50 percent reduction in finished goods inventory;

- A 40 to 70 percent reduction in space requirement; and
- A 70 percent reduction in work-in-process inventory.

In all of these instances, the dramatic results could not have been achieved using the functional view of the business. The process view provided the connection to the customer, and then the processes were analyzed and redesigned to optimize the value to the customer.

Reason Two: BPA is a Preliminary Step for Other TCM Techniques

Even if your primary objective of a TCM effort is something other than process improvement or redesign, a business process analysis still serves as the starting point for many of the other techniques. (All of these other techniques are explained in detail in later chapters of this book. They are mentioned here only to establish their relationships with business process analysis.) These techniques are:

- Activity-based costing;
- Performance measurement; and
- Decision support.

Activity-Based Costing *Activity-based costing* is a technique for calculating "object" costs. (The objects in question may be products, product lines, services, customers, customer segments, channels of distribution, or anything else of interest to management.) ABC costs are calculated so that overhead and SG&A costs assigned to an object reflect the overhead services actually performed for (or consumed by) that object. After the costs are determined, the most revealing analysis is assessing the profitability of individual objects.

Business process analysis starts by dividing processes into activities; these activities then become the focal point for identifying process improvement opportunities. Similarly, activity-based costing first organizes all costs that you want to trace to objects into *activity cost pools* based on the BPA. Each activity cost pool is then assigned to objects based on the number of times that activity was performed for the object or some other basis that reflects the object's demand for the activity.

Technically, you can calculate activity-based costs without first analyzing the process costs of the business and these costs' underlying activities. If you take this approach, however, you will lose much of ABC's potential power. Without business process analysis, activity-based costing can tell you what certain products, services, or customers cost; yet it cannot provide insights about possible corrective action if, like many people, you suffer "sticker shock" when you see the ABC results. BPA allows you to understand why an object costs what it does *and* to understand the corrective action you should take.

On the other hand, if you begin by documenting the business processes and their underlying activities and then use that analysis as the starting point for assigning costs to objects on an activity basis, you will be able to move back and forth between obtaining an accurate calculation of object profitability and identifying alternatives for improving that profitability. Exhibit 4-2 illustrates the interaction between business process analysis and activity-based costing.

Performance Measurement The second technique that commonly interacts with BPA is *performance measurement.* Traditional performance measurement systems use the functional view, rather than the process view, for capturing and reporting performance. Departmental profit and loss statements are prepared each month and compared against departmental budgets. They are summarized for higher management by "rolling up" the figures through the organizational hierarchy.

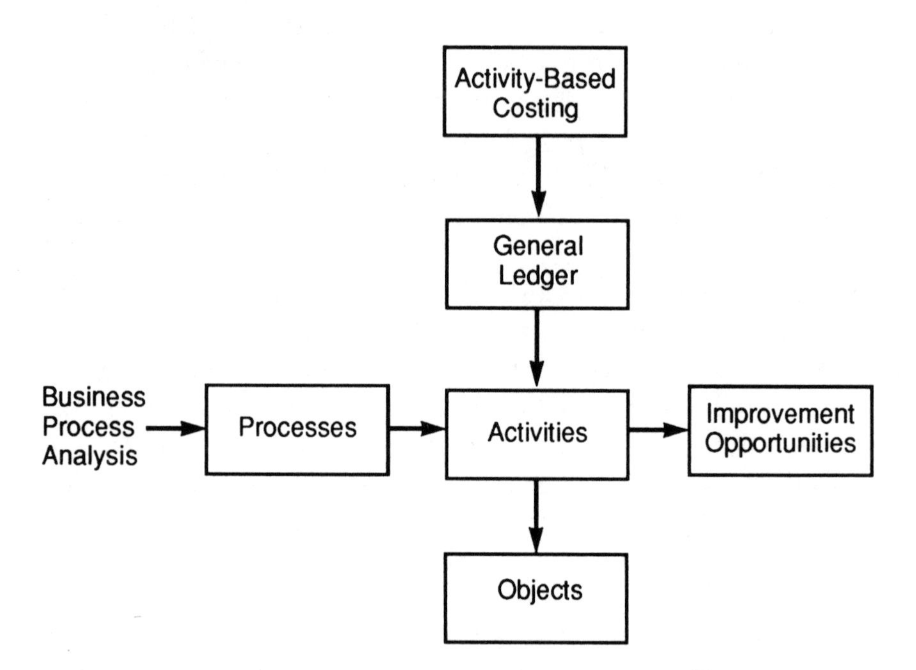

EXHIBIT 4-2. Relationship between activity-based costing and business process analysis.

*Adapted from diagram in The CAM-I Glossary of Activity-Based Management, Edited by Norm Raffish and Peter B.B.Turney, (Arlington: CAM-I, 1991.)

However, the factors critical to the success of the business are much more likely to be related to its processes than to its organization chart. Moreover, the critical processes usually include activities or impacts from many different organizational units. It may be critical, for instance, for a company to perform well and to improve its performance continuously in such dimensions as:

- The time between receiving a customer order and delivering the goods/services to the customer.

- The time required to define, design, and produce a new service.
- The compliance of the product/service with its specifications.
- The accuracy of the product/service specifications with the real needs of the marketplace.
- The short-term financial flexibility of the company, as indicated by its working capital levels.
- The ability to introduce new products/services to the market in an effective way.
- The ability to realize and maintain an acceptable margin on products/services.
- The ability to attract new customers.

An individual department cannot achieve any of these examples of "critical success factors" in isolation. In fact, each of these factors is associated with a high-level process best managed and monitored by concentrating on its sub-processes and activities.

Does this mean that managers are no longer responsible and accountable for performance? Absolutely not! Part of the process improvement discipline is to make sure that every process has an "executive owner" who has overall responsibility for the performance of that process. In this way, the process view does not imply an abdication of clear responsibility for performance. It does mean, however, that reporting on processes cannot be achieved by rolling-up through the organization chart. An improved performance measurement system needs a business process foundation.

Decision Support Likewise, the third category of TCM techniques that interact with BPA—techniques for improving decision support—all rely on an enhanced understanding of what causes cost in an organization. The process-view is fundamental to understanding the dynamics of time, quality, and cost.

Improvements to capital asset evaluation/justification techniques focus on ways to model the financial benefits of improved performance on strategic dimensions (i.e., quality, time, responsiveness, and flexibility). The process view provides a basis for assessing the likely impacts of the proposed capital acquisition on these strategic dimensions.

Life-cycle costing and target costing are the techniques for better managing the profitability of products and services by focusing on the decisions where costs are determined, rather than waiting to manage costs until they are incurred. Again, improving these cost-determining decisions is directly related to understanding the interrelationships documented in the business processes. These concepts will be covered extensively in later chapters of this book.

SOME SCOPE ISSUES YOU MUST CONSIDER BEFORE GETTING STARTED

Once your company's management decides to document the firm's business processes, an obvious issue arises—namely that of scope. "Do I really have to identify and analyze *all* the processes of my organization," you may ask, "before I can get on with improving my operations, calculating product/service or other costs, or developing my new performance measurement system?"

The answer to that question is yes—at least in terms of *identifying* the processes. You really do need to identify all processes of the organization—at a high level. Then, depending on the specific objective (or objectives) of your TCM project, you may want to limit the number of processes you then document to the activity level.

If, for instance, the primary objective of your project is to calculate the costs of serving different segments of customers, then you may concentrate your activity analysis on the processes of gaining new business, delivery support, and after-sales support. Or if, for instance, the primary objective of your project is to calculate activity-based product costs, and if you want to consider only manufacturing costs and not SG&A costs for the initial project, you need to document only manufacturing and manufacturing support processes to the activity level.

On the other hand, if your objective is to develop an enterprise-wide, comprehensive new performance measurement system, the business process analysis step would need to include the whole organization. Keep in mind that it is necessary to document processes down to the activity level in order to analyze and subsequently improve performance.

The other scope decision you will have to make is how extensive an analysis to perform on each activity. In this chapter, you will see a wide array of different "attributes" evaluated at the activity level. For instance, you may assess such attributes as cycle time, value-added/non-value-added characteristics, quality categories, customer connections, root causes, and output measures. The particular attributes you need to collect and evaluate will be determined by the specific objective(s) of your project.

THE STEPS IN PERFORMING A BUSINESS PROCESS ANALYSIS

How do you actually perform a business process analysis? The general steps include:

- Developing a business process model (see Exhibit 4-1).
- Developing a process-activity definition.
- Performing a process value analysis.
- Developing an improvement plan.

We will discuss each of these steps one by one. This chapter will explore the first two steps; Chapters Five and Six will explore the last two steps.

Step One: Develop a Business Process Model

A business is a series of interrelated processes called a Value Chain. (Michael E. Porter, *Competitive Advantage: Creating and Sustaining Superior Performance*, New York: The Free Press, 1985.) An essential ingredient to understanding the business is recognizing the interrelationships between the processes.

The objective of the business process model is to identify the major process flows within an organization. The business process model is essentially a flow chart of specific high-level processes linked together to show process flows, which can be further broken down into sub-processes and their supporting activities. The business process model provides an overall view of the organization, thus showing a company's major processes and the relationships among them.

When viewing most businesses from a high-level process perspective, it is likely that you will find most or all of the following major processes:

- Gain new business (attract new customers and earn additional business from existing customers).
- Design new products, services, and processes.
- Produce products and/or execute services.
- Provide services to the installed customer base.
- Set the leadership framework for the business.
- Support the day-to-day needs of the business.

Whether the enterprise is a retailer, manufacturer, distributor, service bureau, professional service firm, or some other service-oriented business, the model above can serve as a generic starting point. Each business should assess the generic model for appropriateness and "goodness" of fit. Once this is done, the major processes in turn can be broken down into supporting sub-processes. This first level of breaking down processes is much more specific to each individual company.

Exhibit 4-3 shows examples of sub-processes for the generic model. Note: keep in mind that this exhibit shows a typical model, not a description suitable for every company. Each individual enterprise will have its own variants on the model.

As you define your sub-processes, it is important to identify the process boundaries. For instance, if the sub-process is *order processing,* you should state the beginning and end points of the process. The beginning point may be "Receipt of an order from a customer," and the end point may be "Receipt of the goods by the customer." Specifying the boundaries clarifies the content of each sub-process.

Step Two: Developing a Process/Activity Definition

Once you have constructed a high-level business process model and have identified the sub-processes, your next step is to break down each targeted sub-process into its activities. The steps required to define a sub-process' activities are to:

- Identify the output (products and services) for the process.
- Identify the customers (internal and external) for the products and services.
- Identify the work performed in the creation of the output.
- Identify the process input.

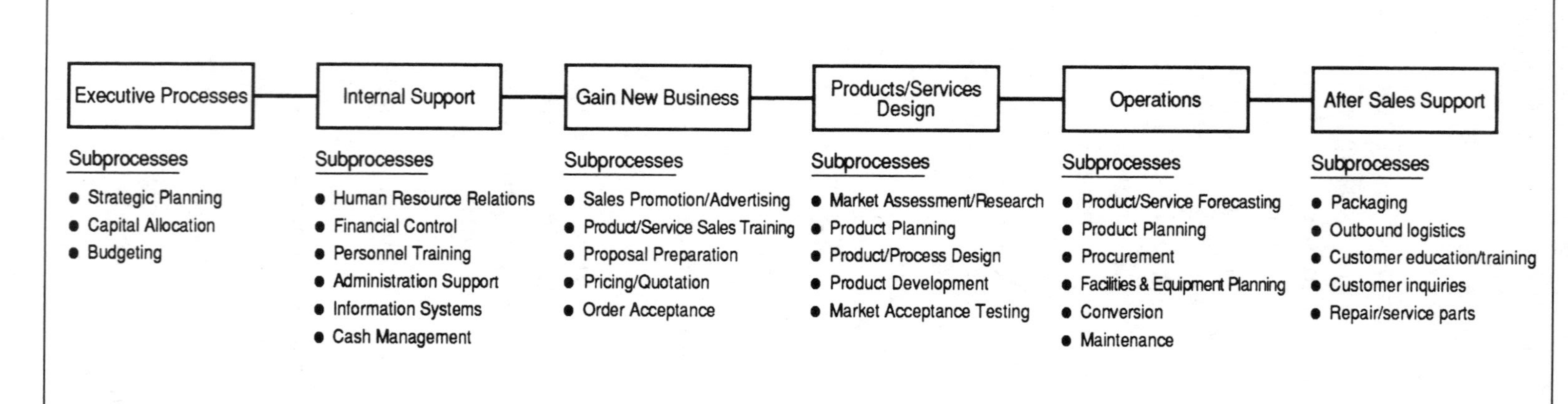

EXHIBIT 4-3. Typical business process model (with sub-processes).

The following is a description of each of these steps.

Identify the Output for the Sub-Process Once you have selected a sub-process for further analysis, the initial step in the activity definition is to define the sub-process output. The output is any product or service rendered from the sub-process. It also includes transactions, information, or paperwork created along the way. In defining the output, you should give special attention to acknowledging the creation of multiple products or services (i.e., co-products or by-products)—particularly if object costing is one of the TCM project goals.

Identify the Customers An important element of the business process analysis is its pervasive emphasis on customers. Both internal and external customers are identified for the sub-process output. This customer definition is critical because it provides the foundation for determining which of the activities performed comply with customer requirements (and, therefore, are value-added) and which ones are performed for reasons other than to satisfy customer requirements (and, therefore, are non-value-added).

Performing an evaluation of the primary output will determine if the output is truly customer-driven. A critical but constructive approach is best suited for this analysis, since output has often been provided for no other reason than that "we've always done it that way." This is particularly true for support and administrative services. Chances are that some outputs can be eliminated because they provide little or no value to the recipient. Typical examples are redundant reports, information that is never read and never used for decision-making purposes, or "just-in-case-I'll-need-it-sometime" materials.

Exhibit 4-4, "Aircraft Maintenance Process Overview," shows an example of the different types of customers often found in a particular process. This example, taken from an airline maintenance process, shows the process outputs and inputs.

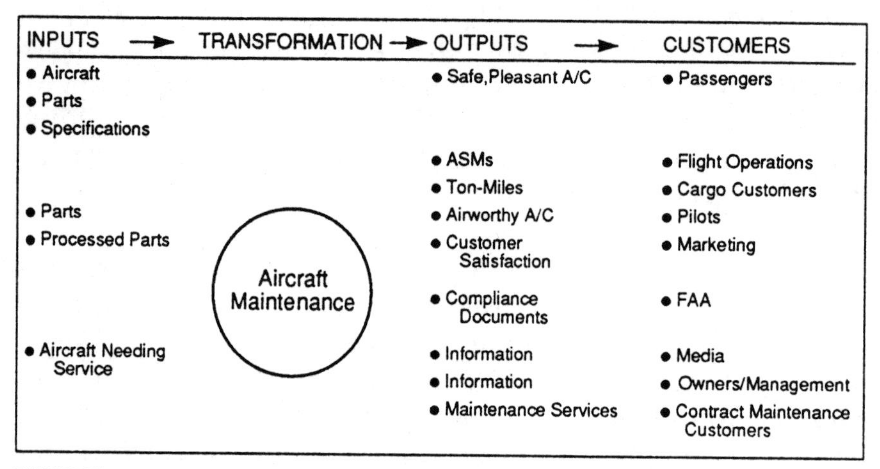

EXHIBIT 4-4. Aircraft maintenance process overview.

Identify the Activities After you have defined the sub-process outputs and customers, you then identify the activities that produce the outputs. In this step, the challenge is to document—generally through some form of flow-charting—the activities at the level needed to provide a meaningful depiction to the company. Activities defined too narrowly or in too much detail may complicate the overall analysis without adding useful information. Activities defined too broadly will fail to reveal opportunities for improvement.

For instance, in the example of ordering materials, the activities included:

- Issue purchase specifications.
- Obtain/request bids from vendors.
- Select vendors.
- Issue purchase order.
- Follow up with vendors.

The activities did not include such detail as:

- Retrieve purchase specifications from files.
- Insert purchase order into envelope.

Another challenge is to define the activity sequence within the sub-process. This becomes important when there are concurrent activities being performed by the same resource, with eventual costs being shared.

The intent of defining activities is *not* to perform a micro motion study, as some industrial engineers would do to build standard cost data. Rather, the intent is to develop an understanding of the major work performed in the natural course of doing business. The activity definition is therefore not a task-level definition.

During an interview with a data entry clerk, you may hear something like this: "Well, first I turn on my computer. Then I go get a batch of transactions to enter." While the clerk's response is correct, it is too high a level to be of much use. The interviewer may need to respond with, "Where do you get the batch of transactions, and how long does it take?"

A comfortable level of activity definition is more of an artform than a science, but it has major ramifications later in designing an ABC system and in developing a focused cost or performance improvement plan. The decision on how deep to drill the well is important because of the inherent complexities that will result when the analysis is replicated or automated in an integrated business process improvement and activity-based costing system. The most useful level of detail for your organization is something best determined in a pilot project before management makes plans for enterprise-wide implementation.

One approach is to identify activities at the level of detail that is most useful for performing a process value analysis; then combine activities into activity groups for performing activity-based costing. (We will address this topic more explicitly in our chapter on activity-based costing. For now, we will focus on defining activities for the purpose of Step Three—Process Value Analysis.)

Here are some additional tips for the step of identifying activities.

Tip #1: Check for completeness. In practice, activities are easy to overlook. The tendency is to fail to include the "side paths" in a workflow.

The next two exhibits provide an example of overlooking activities. Exhibit 4-5, "Panel Line Process-Initial Chart," shows the activities that a BPA team first identified when analyzing the processes for making the exterior components for white goods (that is, the side panels of washing machines, dryers, refrigerators, and so on). A knowledgeable engineer—a veteran of eight years' work in this area of manufacturing—provided this set of activities. The activities he designated essentially represent the value-added activities in this line of manufacturing.

To see if any activities might have been overlooked, we put a visible mark on some of the raw material coming into the process. We then followed this marked sample through the workpath. Exhibit 4-6, "Panel Line Process-Revised Chart," shows the results of the activity definition after we performed

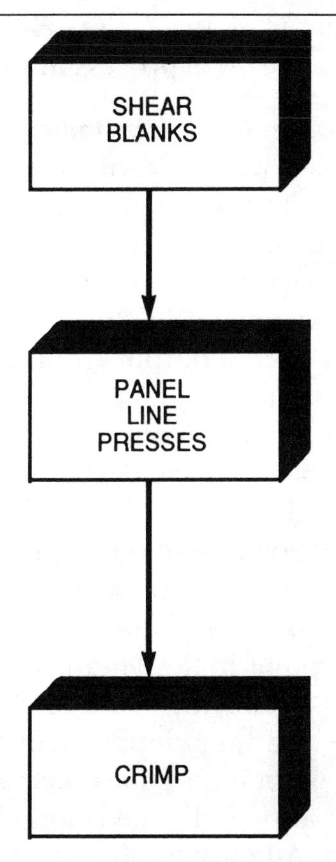

EXHIBIT 4-5. Panel Line Process–Initial Chart

a series of interviews, observed the assembly line in action, and basically walked the product through the process.

What we found was an additional 69 activities performed within the process, all of which were impediments to a smooth work flow—and all of which were non-value-added activities. The exhibit is especially dramatic in showing the opportunity for process improvement. Initially, the engineer didn't believe the findings; he literally repeated a walk-through of the marked material to see for himself. After doing so, however, he became a champion of the cause. He is now the project leader for the plant's business process improvement program.

Tip #2: Use facilitated group sessions rather than individual interviews. This is another way to verify the accuracy and completeness of the charting process. The group should include at least one representative from every area through which the work passes. If one person identifies an output that he or she creates, then the next person in the flow has to speak up to acknowledge receipt of that output from the first person. The second person also has to articulate how the work done in the previous activity is valuable to him or her.

Facilitated group sessions are particularly helpful in identifying non-value-added activities that build up as work passes from one department or functional area to another.

A familiar story is that new procedures may have been put into place as a result of a bad hand-off from one department to another. At some point in the organization's history, output got lost or damaged in moving from one area to another. In response, both the sending department and the receiving department started maintaining logs (i.e., a sending log and a receiving log); they also performed outgoing inspection and incoming inspection. All of these logging and inspecting activities are non-value-added work. Although non-value-added work can be performed at any point in a process, it is most likely to build up at organizational transfer points. That is another important reason why the entire process—not just the work performed in a particular functional area—must be documented. Much non-value-added work is likely to go undetected if the work flows are documented only within a department or functional area.

Tip #3: Check for multiple paths in the work flow. If all of the work does not flow exactly through the same path, it's important to document the points at which the work can split. It's also important to document the percentage of work that flows

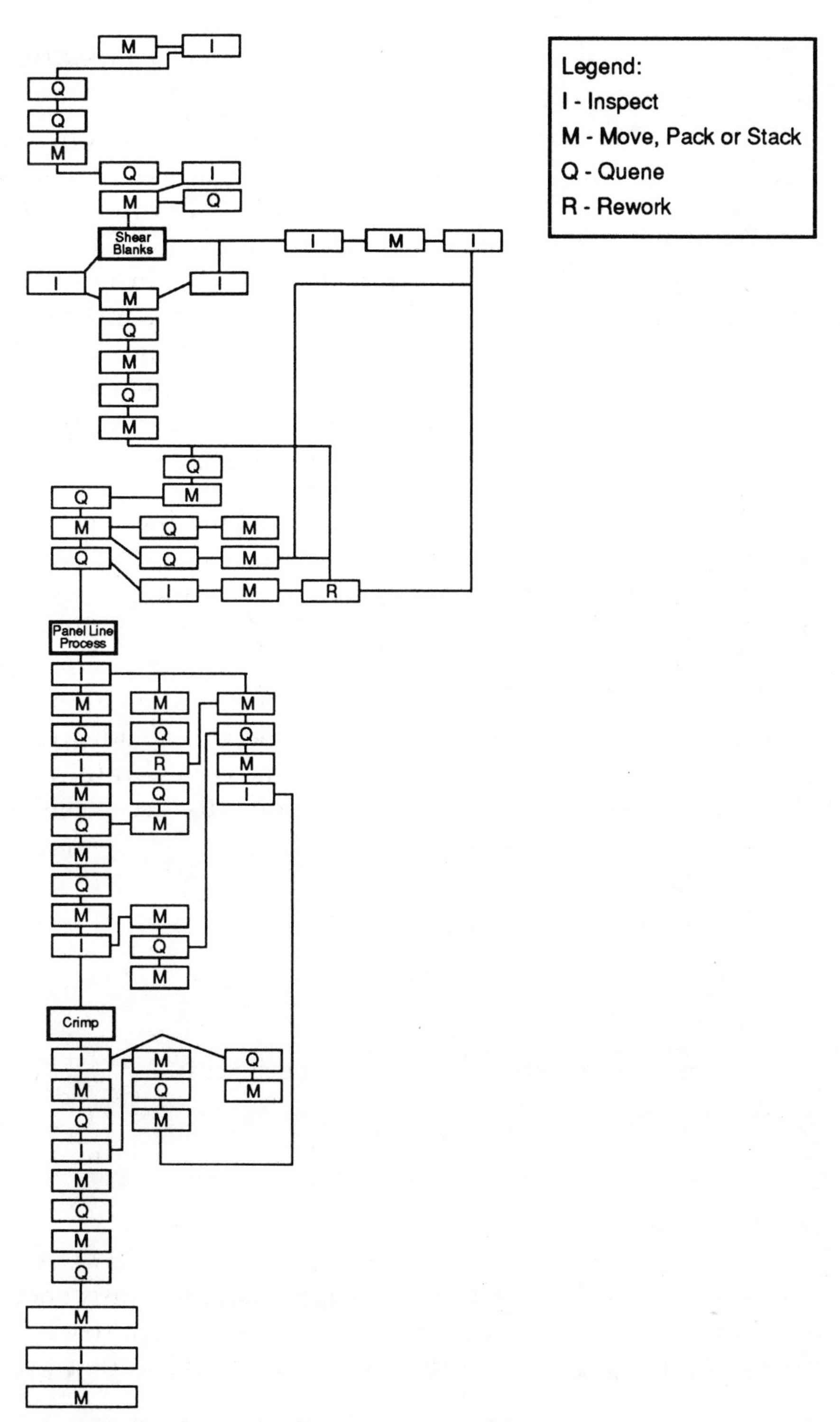

EXHIBIT 4-6. Panel Line Process-Revised Chart

along each path. An example of a split-point may be alternate paths based on a quality review. Good product flows down one path and unacceptable or questionable product flows through a different path. There may also be instances in which the product is graded, with the subsequent path depending on the grade. This is almost always true in the apparel industry, where markets exist for "first quality," "seconds," and "pound goods." Other industries may have their own version of grading. This documentation will be important for assessing the potential magnitude for improving the process.

Tip #4: Choose one or both of the two main approaches to activity identification. In practice, there are two primary approaches to breaking down activities from processes into sub-processes. These approaches can be used either separately or together in defining activities.

The first approach is "top down." It is a continuation of breaking down the processes into subprocesses. Under this approach, you can break down major activities until you achieve a sufficient level of detail. Techniques for accomplishing the breakdown include:

- One-on-one interviews;
- Facilitated group sessions;
- Activity charting;
- Normative models of previous experiences;
- Questionnaires;
- Sampling; and
- Storyboarding.

The advantages of the top-down approach are consistency and simplicity. The disadvantage of the top-down approach is the risk of missing some activities, especially those that are general in nature or are already performed in several existing processes, where the tendency may be to "pick it up later."

The second approach is the "bottom-up" method, where the intent is to establish the activities, sub-processes, and processes entirely from a bottom-up approach. The bottom-up approach is more likely to identify all the activities, but there tend to be many cycles of fine tuning or rework loops to connect those activities into a business process model.

A third approach—a hybrid of sorts—can be used effectively to take advantage of the strengths of each of the preceding two methods. This hybrid version begins with the business process model defined down to the sub-processes. It makes a first pass at the development of the underlying activities. It then reviews the sub-processes and the activities to check for missing activities and the proper placement of the activities relative to the sub-processes. This review may need to be repeated a few times before the definitions are finalized.

You saw an example of this hybrid approach in the Panel Line Process example. The bottom-up approach came into play when the work was physically observed rather than being described by a worker or manager.

Exhibit 4-7 shows these three approaches.

Identify Process Inputs The last step in activity definition is to define the inputs to each process. You can determine the inputs by collecting historical data, by making physical observations, or by interviewing employees. Reviewing documented procedures will also help in identifying the inputs. In administrative or service processes, you may need estimates of the amount of resources.

In all cases it is helpful to document the number of workers (expressed as full-time equivalents or FTEs) that are employed in the activity and the process. It is important to identify the process inputs in order to prioritize potential improvement efforts.

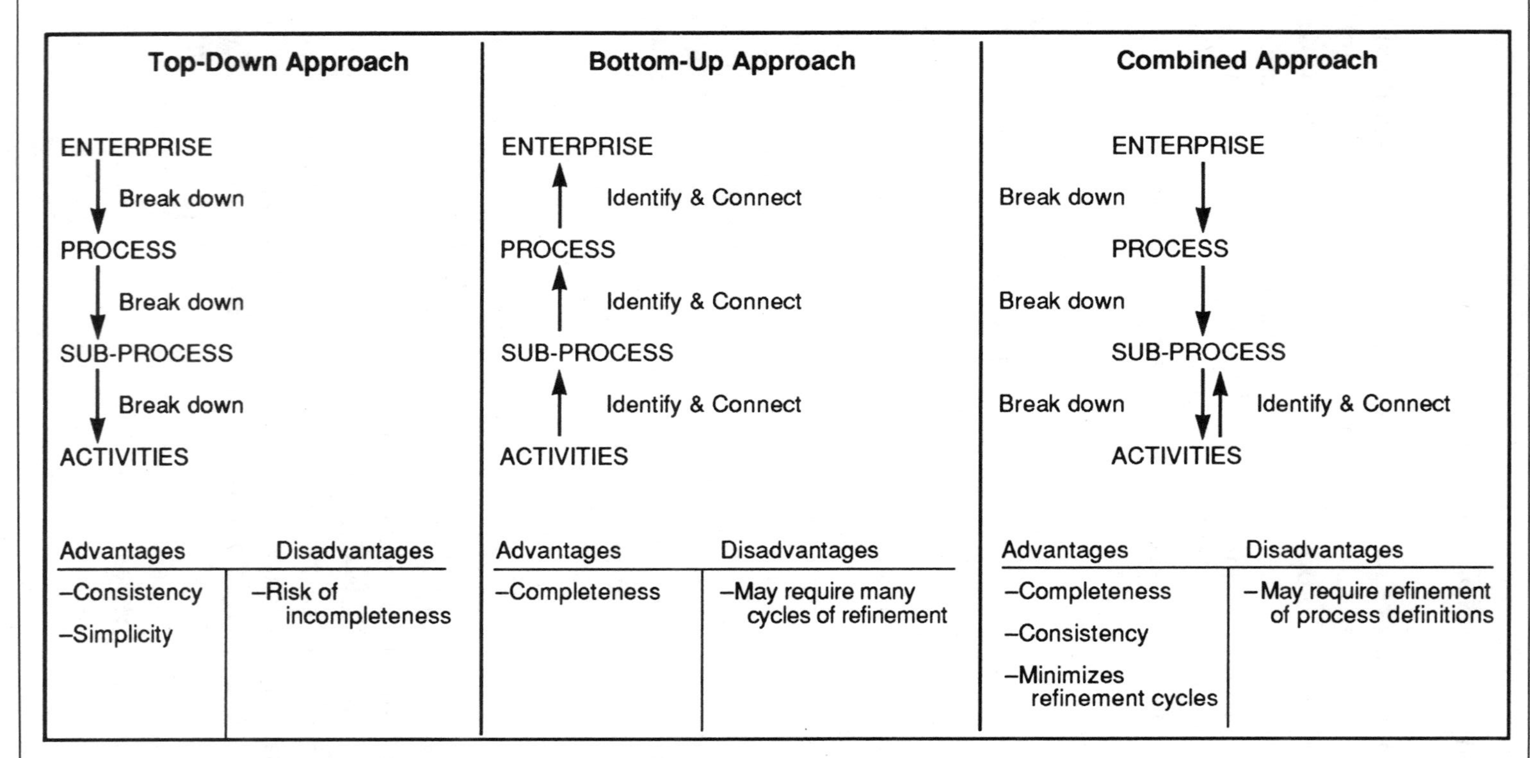

EXHIBIT 4-7. Process identification approaches

A FULL BUSINESS PROCESS MODEL

What follows is an example showing the breaking down of a process from the high-level process itself into sub-processes and then into activities.

Start by looking at Exhibit 4-8. This diagram shows the high-level process of managing materials. This particular example is from a client in the manufacturing sector, but it could just as easily describe a distributor, a hospital, or any other organization that handles large volumes of materials. One major factor that may differ from one industry to another is the technique used to accomplish the first sub-process—namely, identifying the materials needed. Once you know the quantity and timing of your material requirements, your organization will need to acquire those materials by performing the next four sub-processes:

1. Identify vendors;
2. Negotiate terms;
3. Order materials; and
4. Receive materials.

Notice how these activities cut across functions and organizational units.

Depending on the nature of the materials and the stage of the quality and time-based management initiatives, your organization may need to perform some or all of the remaining seven sub-processes:

1. Inspect materials;
2. Accept/reject materials;
3. Store materials;
4. Report on materials in stock;
5. Scrap materials;

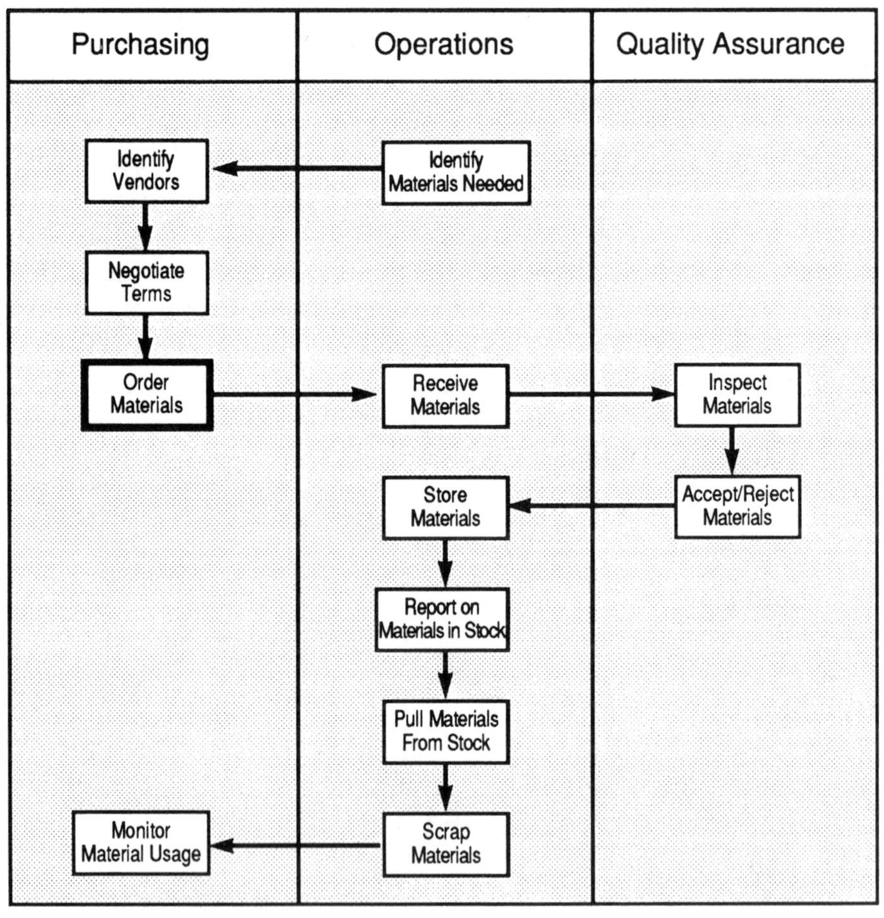

EXHIBIT 4-8. Materials Process (Process ➡ Sub Process)

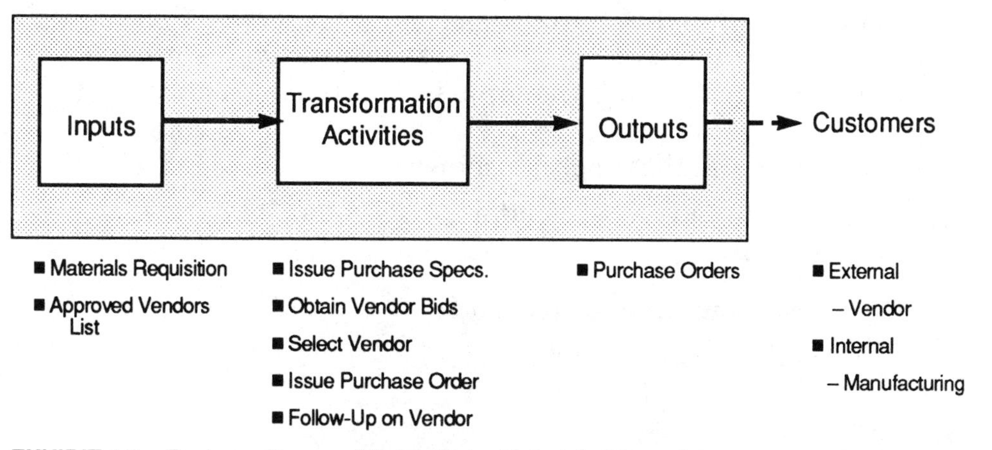

EXHIBIT 4-9. Business Process Model: Order Materials (Example)

6. Pull materials from stock; and
7. Monitor material usage.

The material ordering sub-processes from Exhibit 4-8 is further specified in Exhibit 4-9. The inputs to this sub-process are:

1. material requisitions; and
2. an approved vendors' list.

Production planning is the supplier of the material requisitions. Purchasing is its own supplier of an approved vendor list, and the output of the sub-process is purchase orders. There are two "customers" who receive this output. The vendor receives the purchase order, but the Manufacturing Department is also an internal customer in the sense that the issuance of a purchase order is an internal service that supports the manufacturing processes. Five activities are performed in transforming the inputs to outputs. They are:

1. Issue purchase specifications;
2. Obtain bids from vendors;
3. Select vendors;
4. Issue purchase order; and
5. Follow-up with vendors.

CONCLUSION

This concludes our discussion of step two in performing a business process analysis; we now move on to step three—performing a process value analysis—which begins our next chapter.

CHAPTER 5

Performing a Process Value Analysis

Once you have identified the activities within your business, you begin step three of business process analysis. The purpose of *process value analysis* is to identify opportunities to improve the performance of a business in such a way that the improvement lasts. Management may initiate an improvement because of specific symptoms or it may simply recognize some sort of lethargy within the organization. For instance, administrative overhead costs may be increasing; profit margins or market share may be eroding; response time to customers may be uncompetitive; the quality of the output may be unsatisfactory; a facility may be experiencing capacity problems. Any number of problems may spur executives toward taking action. Alternatively, the initiation of a process value analysis may have a more direct stimulus: a corporate directive for a budget reduction, for example.

In all of these instances, process value analysis is an appropriate technique to use for identifying improvement opportunities if the initiator suspects that:

- Some of the work being done may be unnecessary or redundant.
- The time and/or cost required to complete the work seems disproportionately high relative to its value to the organization.
- A process seems more complex than it needs to be.
- The resources of the organization seem to be tied up in unprofitable activities.

A distinguishing characteristic of process value analysis is that it is driven by customer input. (This is true whether the customer is external or internal.) The major opportunities for improvement come from activities that add time or cost to a process without adding any value in the eyes of the customer. Process value analysis helps you:

1. identify such activities; and
2. extricate them from your organization by analyzing them by "root causes" and addressing those causes.

This focus on root causes is also an important characteristic of BPA because that part of the analysis concentrates on inputs, not outputs, of the process.

In process value analysis, a project team collects, organizes, and presents information to guide the development of an improvement plan. The fundamental data needed for the analysis include cycle time, cost, and customer assessment of value. In this chapter, we will discuss each of these elements and show how to combine them in an overall analysis. In our next chapter, we will describe how to use this analysis to develop a process improvement plan.

SELECTING A PROCESS TO ANALYZE

If your improvement project already focuses on upgrading a particular process, this selection step will be unnecessary. You may have already identified the process you need to analyze in your statement of the project's objective. For instance, you may be striving to speed the processing of automobile collision claims in an insurance company, to reduce the cost of processing customer orders in a distribution company, to reduce the cost and time required to pay an invoice, or to attain some other specific cost-reduction goal. In each of these cases, you have already identified the process to be analyzed.

On the other hand, if your objective is more general—overall cost reduction, for instance—you may need to perform a selection or targeting step to determine which processes are the best bets for improvement. Here are some guidelines to help you make that selection.

Guideline #1

The more people and the more functional areas participating in a process, the higher the probability that the process contains a high proportion of non-value-added work. This is because non-value-added work tends to accumulate as work crosses organizational boundaries, and there is more of a tendency for repetitive activities when crossing functional boundaries.

Guideline #2

Similarly, the more approval levels required in a process, the more likely that non-value-added work has crept into it. A common example of redundant approvals is when a purchase requisition for capital equipment needs to be approved—even

			Number of Recipients				
PRIORITY	PROCESS	TYPE	ORG. 1	ORG. 2	ORG. 3	ORG. 4	ORG. 5
4	A	A	2	3		4	
1	B	CS	5	4	2		1
5	C	D	1	1	2		1
3	D	CS	3	3			3
2	E	A	3	5	2		2

Type A: Administrative
Type CS: Customer Service
Type D: Distribution

EXHIBIT 5-1. Process Targeting–Tabular.

though the capital budget was already approved and included the specific item.

Guideline #3

In many companies, administrative and support processes have a higher percentage of activities that are non-value-added than do processes directly engaged in making a physical product or delivering service to a client. This is largely because so many operational improvements have already been made through just-in-time programs, quality management programs, and the natural focus an organization has on the product/service producing areas.

Guideline #4

Look for the processes that require the greatest cycle time to produce the output. The longer the cycle time, the greater the likelihood that it contains non-value-added steps.

Guideline #5

Investigate the processes that are considered to be complex. If a process has a high perceived level of complexity, it probably contains many non-value-added steps.

You may find it helpful to summarize the information used to select processes for analysis and to present the summary in tabular or graphic format. (See Exhibits 5-1 and 5-2.) The tabular format of these exhibits displays each type of process and then shows the number of people within each functional organization who receive the work. If the work comes into an organization repeatedly, the receiver is counted repeatedly as well. If the work is passed around within the organization (for instance, for review or signature), then each pass would be reflected in the number recorded.

Other Considerations

In the exhibits, the project objective is "overall cost reduction." The ranking of the processes for selection is derived from the following logic. The company could probably achieve similar cost savings in Process B and Process E. Process B was selected

PRIORITY	PROCESS	ORG. 1	ORG. 2	ORG. 3	ORG. 4	ORG. 5
4	A					
1	B					
5	C					
3	D					
2	E					

Administrative Process

Customer Service Process

Distribution

EXHIBIT 5-2. Process targeting–graphical.

over Process E, however, because Process B was a customer service process. Management believed that improving Process B would improve the delivery of service to the customer in addition to reducing cost. Process A and Process D appeared to have similar potential for cost savings. Process D ended up ranked above Process A because Organization 4 was just beginning a seasonal "peak period" of work. One rule for selecting a process for improvement was that the process improvement team must include representation from every department that participated in the process; for this reason, management decided to delay analyzing Process A until it could convene a complete process improvement team. Process C shows up last in the ranking because the process had recently been redesigned. Management, therefore, believed that most of the inefficiency had already been squeezed out of the process.

DETERMINE CYCLE TIME

Once you have selected a process for analysis and have identified its activities, your next step is to collect cycle time data. *Cycle time* for the process is the amount of time required to complete the entire process. You should collect information about *average cycle time* and *maximum cycle time.* Here are some examples of cycle time:

- The time it takes to pay a single invoice.
- The time it takes to perform an end-of-quarter closing of the books.
- The time required to communicate to a warehouse a customer order that has unique packaging specifications.

Cycle time analysis is typically performed by following the work through the required activities in the process. Imagine placing a visible mark on a product, placing paperwork in a special folder, or tagging a computer transaction to facilitate watching it move along the processing route. By these means, you capture the cycle time for each activity in the *activity definition.* When the process is waiting for equipment maintenance, set-up, or other downtime, the cycle time of the work shows up as in a *state of queue.*

The following two examples show the results of documenting cycle times. The first example shows an administrative process; the second, a manufacturing process.

Example 1: Exhibit 5-3 documents the process of confirming an order from a customer who has requested particular optional features. Documenting this process used the following guidelines to define the activities and to estimate the times. The information was collected through a combination of group meetings, following a sample order through the process, and validating against a sample of actual orders.

Guideline #1—A separate activity was identified any time the customer order changed functional organizations.

Guideline #2—Each activity was segmented between time actually spent working on the order and categories of time when the order was not being worked on.

Guideline #3—The processing times were based on estimates volunteered by the people who performed the work.

Guideline #4—The move and queue times were also based on information from the mail room about pickup and delivery schedules for inter-office mail.

Guideline #5—The times for all of the activities were combined; the total time was then compared against the average total time for a sample of similar orders. The individual activity times were fine-tuned so the total was in line with those in the sample.

In this example, the customer order first came to the clerk in the Customer Service Department who was responsible for order entry. The clerk logged the order and sent it to the Credit Department for a credit check. When the customer service clerk received the approved order back from Credit, he

EXHIBIT 5-3 Cycle times.

Activity: Confirm a Customer Order

Processing		*Non-Processing*
.50	CS: Initiate paperwork	Queue 3.0 Move 4.0
.25	CR: Confirm available credit	Queue 1.0 Move 3.0
.10	CS: Request a ship date	Queue 3.0 Move 4.0
.50	EN: Confirm technical viability	Queue 16.0 Move 8.0
1.50	PP: Confirm components	Queue 8.0 Move 2.0
.25	PP: Schedule assembly	Queue 24.0 Inspect 1.0 Move 2.0
.10	PP: Firm ship date	Move 4.0
.10	CS: Confirm ship date to customer	Move 4.0 Mail 8.0
Total 3.3		Total 95.0

$$\text{Cycle Efficiency} = \frac{3.3}{98.3} = 3.4\%$$

ERNST & YOUNG

routed it through Engineering to make sure it was technically possible to make the item with the particular combination of options the customer had requested. Engineering then sent the order to Production Planning, where someone checked component availability. Once all the components were confirmed, the order was passed to the person who maintained the schedule for assembling custom orders. The assembly schedule was updated once a week. Once the schedule had been planned, the supervisor had to sign off on it before commitment dates could be given to customers. When the supervisor's signoff was complete, the order went back to the Customer Service clerk, who prepared and mailed an order confirmation to the customer.

Notice that the estimates have been summed for the *processing times* and the *non-processing times.* A *cycle efficiency* has also been calculated using the formula:

$$\frac{\text{Total Processing Time}}{(\text{Total Processing Time} + \text{Total Non-Processing Time})}.$$

In the case of the order entry example, the cycle efficiency is 3.4 percent. At first glance, this may look like an absurd efficiency rating, but a rating that low actually is not unusual for an administrative process. When companies first begin documenting process cycle times in this fashion, typical cycle efficiencies have been less than 5 percent for service, support, and administrative processes, less than 10 percent for discrete manufacturing, and greater than 30 percent for process manufacturing.

Cycle efficiency thus gives an indication of how much improvement is possible in a process and what approach should be taken to accomplish the improvement. In later chapters of Part II, we will discuss the importance of cycle efficiency and how to improve it. For now, our focus is simply the task of documenting it.

Example 2: Exhibit 5-4 shows a portion of the chart for a manufacturing process. The process in question is the manufacture of a component used in a common household hand tool (e.g., hammers, pliers, and the like). The chart's format is the same as the one used for the administrative process. In addition to queue, move, and inspection times, such charts also typically show setup times and average rework times.

Start the Activity Model

The final step in documenting process cycle time is to organize the information for graphical presentation—a task that is actually the first step in developing a cumulative model of the process. The cumulative activity model will be enhanced as more attributes are documented in the process value analysis. The completed model will become an important input to the effort to streamline and improve the process.

In modeling the cycle times, a horizontal bar is drawn to measure the total cycle time for the process. Then each activity (broken into its individual segments) is plotted on that bar proportionately to indicate the cycle time for each activity/segment. Exhibit 5-5 shows the timeline for the example of confirming the shipdate for a customer order.

ESTIMATE COST FOR EACH ACTIVITY/SEGMENT

After identifying activities and estimating cycle times, your next step in completing a process value analysis is to estimate the resources required for each activity/segment in the process being studied. A key decision in this step is to specify what unit will be used to measure the resources.

If the process being analyzed is labor-intensive, then *headcount* (measured as full-time equivalents) is a simple indi-

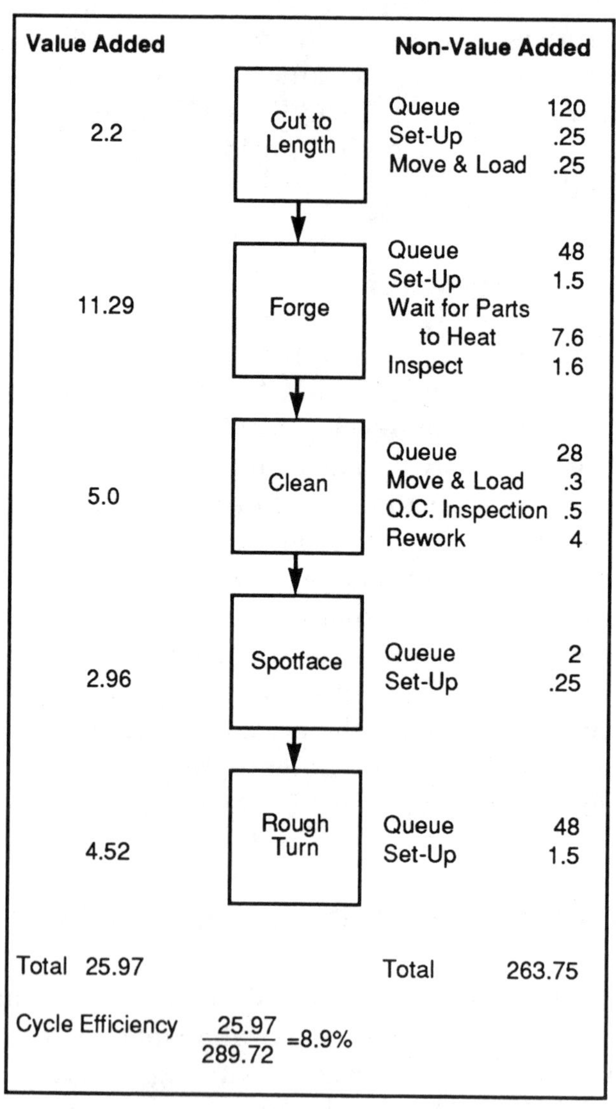

EXHIBIT 5-4. Activity Identification and Cycle Times

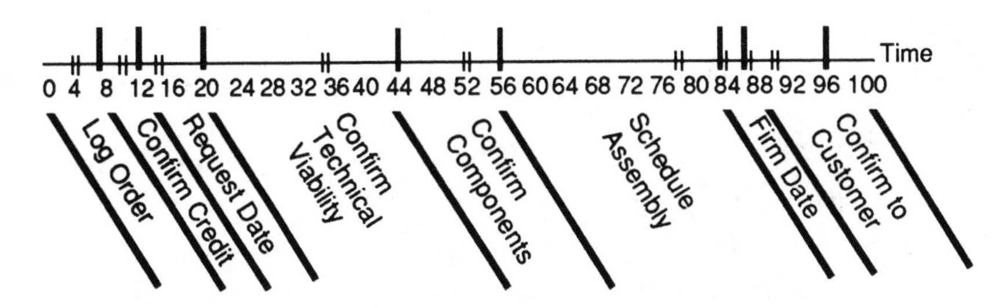

EXHIBIT 5-5. Time Line of Activities

cator of the resources. Headcount has, in fact, turned out to be an appropriate unit of measure for a surprising number of PVA studies. At first glance, this may seem contrary to the increasing automation we find in industry. But in many businesses, the processes most in need of improvement are "white collar" processes that remain labor-intensive.

If headcount is not an appropriate measure, then the monetary value of the resources needs to be estimated. (We will discuss the technique for calculating a monetary value for activity segments in Chapter 8 on activity-based process costing.)

Another decision you must make is the extent to which resources will be estimated for queue time and other non-processing time. Some PVA project teams choose to show a cost for queue time because they want the analysis to reflect their belief that "wasted time eventually is wasted money for the company"—even when it is not practical for them to calculate a precise cost. These teams may decide to calculate an imputed interest cost to reflect the cost of the delays. It is a measure of economic cost and should be calculated in most cases.

Some PVA teams may decide against including estimates for the cost of non-processing time in the charts and diagrams. The team members may believe that trying to estimate those costs would add little marginal value to the analysis. One team member commented, "I am convinced that we can make the point to our management about the financial impact of delays without actually trying to quantify that impact at this stage of the project."

If the ultimate objective of the project is to calculate activity-based product/service costs, then you probably will want to quantify the resources consumed in queues and other delays. If two similar products or services have costs that appear to be similar, but if one of them encounters many long delays in its production cycle and the other does not, you would want the relative costs of the two products or services to reflect the cost of the delays. In Chapter 9 on activity-based object costing, we will discuss how to make this kind of estimate.

Update the Activity Model

Once you have estimated the resources for the various activities/segments, you can add the cost dimension to the activity model. The technique for doing this is to show the cumulative cost of the process as it builds from activity/segment to activity/segment.

Exhibit 5-6 charts the resources and the cumulative resources required for the example we saw earlier (the process of confirming the ship date for a customer order). In this case, the project team decided to estimate the resources in units of *full-time equivalents* (FTEs). They also chose to attribute a portion of the cost of the inter-office mail operation to the "move" segments of the work. No cost was assigned for "queue" segments.

Exhibit 5-7 has updated the activity model for the process to reflect the resources as well as the cycle time. The horizontal axis shows the average time required to perform the process for a single customer order. The vertical axis shows the cumulative number of FTEs consumed by the process at each activity/segment.

MAKE VALUE-ADDED ASSESSMENT

In analyzing a business process, your next step is to perform a "value-added assessment" for each activity/segment in the process. This step is essential for developing a process improvement plan because the approach for improving an activity will depend on its *value-added assessment.*

In making a value-added assessment, you must categorize each activity/segment to reflect whether it "adds value" in the eyes of the customer. Activity segments that do add value in the eyes of the customer are classified as *value added,* or VA. Activities that do not add value in the eyes of the customer are classified as *non-value-added,* or NVA. Once the value-added assessments are made, improvement efforts concentrate on:

1. finding ways to eliminate the NVA work from the process; and
2. finding ways to improve the efficiency and effectiveness of the VA work.

		Resources	*Cumulative Resources*
CS: Initiate paperwork	Queue	0	0
	Process	3.0	3.0
	Move	.2	3.2
CR: Confirm available credit	Queue	0	3.2
	Process	2.0	5.2
	Move	.2	5.4
CS: Request a ship date	Queue	0	5.4
	Process	1.0	6.4
	Move	.2	6.6
EN: Confirm Technical viability	Queue	0	6.6
	Process	1.0	7.6
	Move	.2	7.8
PP: Confirm components	Queue	0	7.8
	Process	3.0	10.8
	Move	.2	11.0
PP: Schedule assembly	Queue	0	11.0
	Inspect	.2	11.2
	Process	1.0	12.2
	Move	.1	12.3
PP: Firm ship date	Process	1.0	13.3
	Move	.2	13.5
CS: Confirm ship date to customer	Process	1.0	14.5
	Move	.2	14.7
	Mail	0	14.7

EXHIBIT 5.6 Charting the resources.

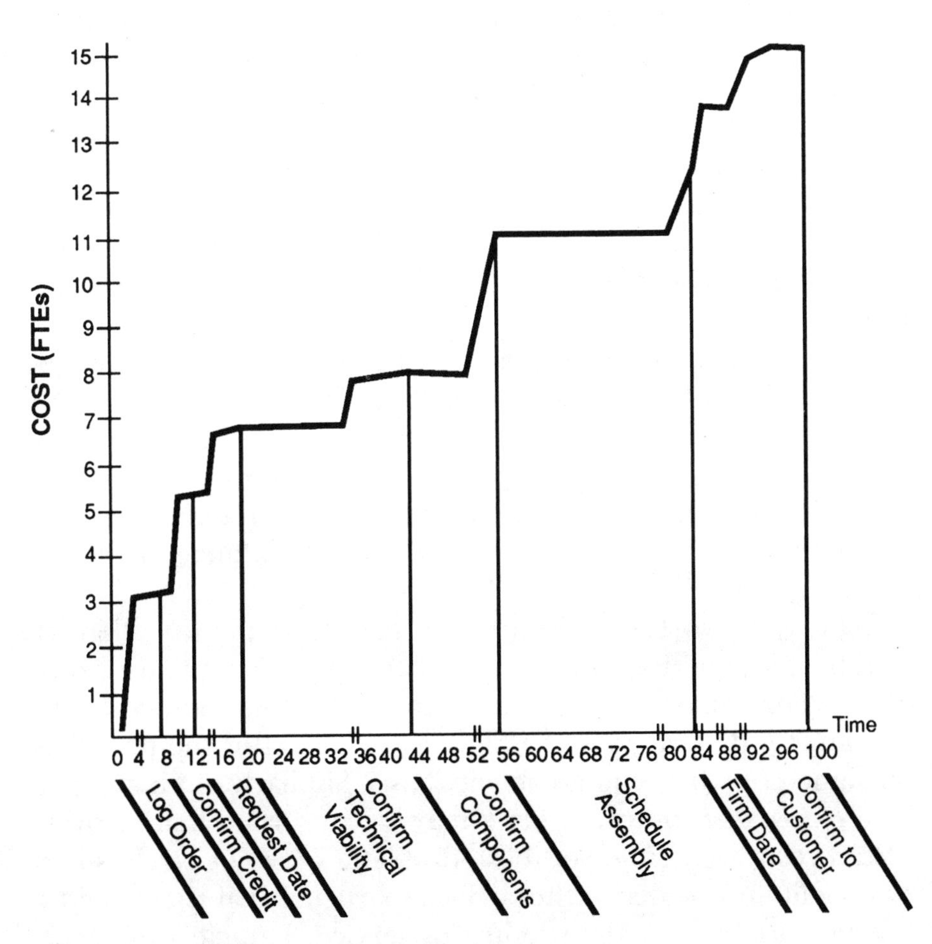

EXHIBIT 5-7. Activity model with time and cost.

There are a variety of techniques for determining *customer-perceived value.* You may use surveys, questionnaires, benchmarking, interviewing, or focus groups to solicit information about external customers. You would typically use structured interviewing to solicit information about internal customers. Whichever technique you choose to use, it is important to hear this information directly from the customers. The definition of customer-perceived value drives the entire logic flow for improving performance.

A Background Note

This concept did not originate in the world of cost management; value-added assessment is a fundamental concept from quality management. Anyone from a company whose quality management program has permeated the entire organization will recognize it at once. The concept has been embraced and has become an integral part of Total Cost Management for two reasons.

First, it works! TCM project teams frequently identify problems that they do not necessarily view as quality problems. For instance, they may discover that the total cost of a product line is entirely too high, especially after the team has assigned overhead on an activity basis. Similarly, an insurance company, distributor, or bank may be concerned that its overhead costs are rising, yet these problems may not be classified as quality problems on the surface (particularly if there is little or no variability in the product or service characteristics actually delivered to external customers). But value-added assessment has proven to be an effective technique for improving not only the quality of an operation, but its cycle time and cost as well. Even if business problems are initially discovered and classified as cost problems, value-added assessment is a fundamental method for finding solutions.

The second reason that value-added assessment is an integral part of TCM is that applying the concept prevents a company from unknowingly sacrificing quality or time in its effort to improve its costs. It does this by focusing on eliminating the costs/activities that are not value-adding to the process output.

CAUTION: PROCEED WITH SENSITIVITY

Before proceeding with "how-to" details, we should pause for a moment to acknowledge that a value-added assessment can be an emotional issue for the people within an organization. This is an issue that demands sensitivity and forethought in language, underlying attitudes, and action. For obvious reasons, people find it unpleasant and unnerving to have their work labeled as "non-value-added." They may be performing their work exactly as management has asked it to be done. The thought of having it declared to be "without value" strikes at the pride that intelligent, conscientious workers feel about their work. Not even a fool would want a job that he or she believed was worthless to the employer.

In truth, very few activities—even ones that are clearly non-value-added—can be eliminated with the wave of a wand. These activities came into being within organizations to address specific needs; thus the link must be broken between the activity and the root cause before you can effectively eliminate them. To achieve real improvements, you will need information, cooperation, innovation, enthusiasm, and a desire to change from all people who are in any way involved with the process.

The key philosophical point to embrace, believe, and communicate is that business processes, themselves, are the focus of the improvement effort. The language, attitudes, and techniques used in the improvement effort must manifest a genuine respect for the people currently engaged in those processes.

How to Distinguish VA from NVA Translating the value-added concept from theory to practice forces the project team to develop an operational definition for the value-added categories. Here are some of the common questions teams use to test whether an activity is value-added:

- Given a choice, would your customer be willing to pay for this activity?
- If you quit performing this activity (or, indeed, if you eliminated this entire process), would the customer care or even notice?
- If you quit performing this activity, would the output from the process still meet the customers' requirements?

Mark Beischel, Senior Manager at Ernst & Young, offers this suggestion for how to determine if an activity is VA or NVA:

> "Ask at each process step if eliminating it would detract in any way from the customer's satisfaction with the product. For example, if material handling, rework, machine setup, and process queues are eliminated, would customers be upset? Hardly. If the packaging or the painting step was eliminated, however, customers would quickly switch to another supplier."[1]

Another, even more specific, suggestion is to look for the "re" prefix in the activity name—names like rework, review, repair, reconcile, recheck, or rewrite.

---

[1] Mark E. Beischel "Improving Production with Process Value Analysis" *Journal of Accountancy* September 1990 pp 53-57.

How Many Categories Should be Used? Some project teams choose to use three categories rather than two to record the value-added assessment. James Harrington, an Ernst & Young principal, recommends these three categories:[2]

- *Real-value-added activities* (RVA) are those activities that, when viewed by the end customer, are required to provide the output that the customer is expecting.
- *Business-value-added activities* (BVA) are those that add no value from the customer's vantage point, but are required by the business.
- *Non-value-added activities* (NVA) are those that are not required by either the customers or the business.

Examples of a business-value-added activity include checking the credit rating of a potential customer, processing a payroll, and preparing tax returns. Examples of non-value-added activities include storage of inventory or movement of paperwork.

One client was enthusiastic about the potential power of process value analysis to help the company improve its performance. But the client believed that it would create a more positive environment by using vocabulary that emphasized the type of customer rather than the activities' worth. That company called this attribute the *customer type* and broke it down further into three categories—P, I, and N—where:

P indicated an activity that was valued by paying customers;

---

[2] H. James Harrington *Business Process Improvement: The Breakthrough Strategy for Total Quality, Productivity, and Competitiveness*, McGraw-Hill, Inc. New York 1991.

I indicated an activity that was valued only by internal customers and non-paying external customers (e.g., the Internal Revenue Service); and

N indicated an activity that was valued by no customer.

The decision about how many categories to use depends on the emphasis in the project. Teams that choose to use two categories stress the point that "a customer is a customer" whether that person is inside or outside the organization. Teams that choose to use three categories want to distinguish between the needs of the two types of customers.

Update the Activity Model

Once you have assigned a value-added category for each activity/segment, you can add the value dimension to the activity model. The technique for doing this is to code each activity/segment in the model with a different pattern or color to indicate its value-added category.

Exhibit 5-8 shows the completion of the activity model for the example of confirming a ship date for a customer order. In the exhibit, real value-added activities are shown in black, business value-added activities are shown in gray, and non-value-added activities are shown in white.

Having coded the activity model by this means, it is extremely valuable for a project team to keep the graphical portrayal of the process in front of them as they continuously develop a plan for improving the process. The model plays a powerful role in keeping the team focused on the activities that offer the greatest opportunity for improvement. It also helps simplify the team's task by minimizing the energy spent pursuing improvements that have potential for only trivial impact.

These models are also extremely effective in presenting the results of the process analysis to people outside the project

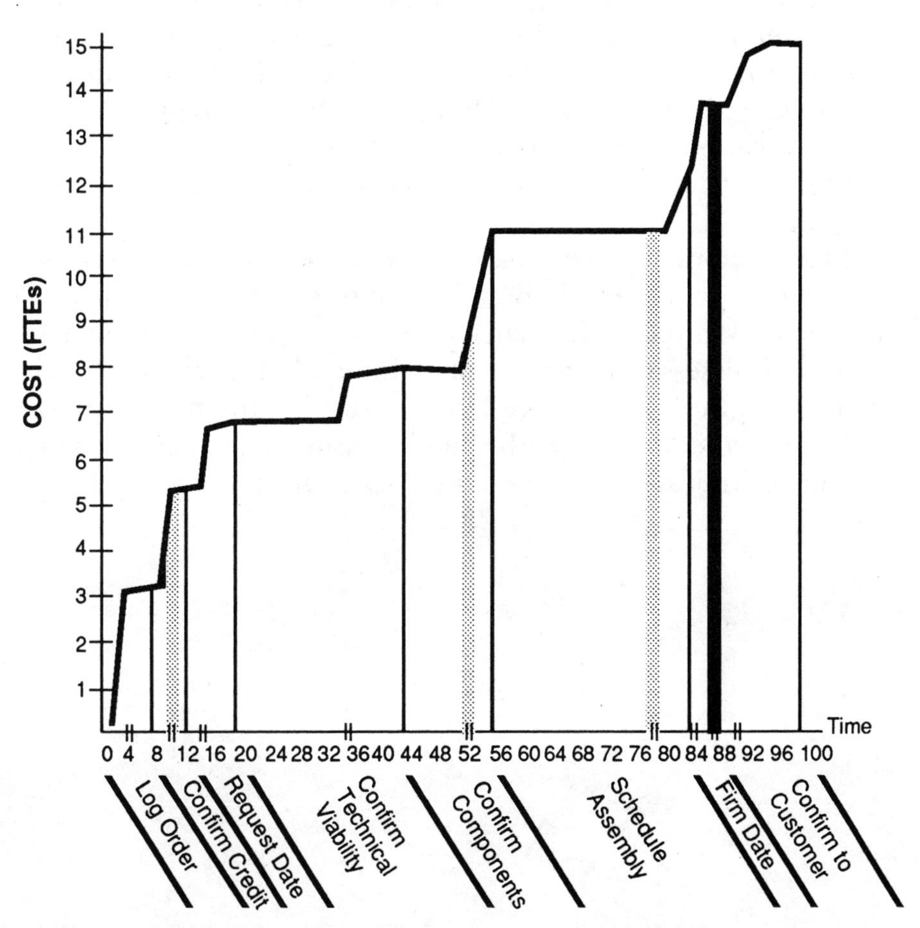

EXHIBIT 5-8. Activity model with time, cost and value-assessment.

team—especially to senior management. During the first presentation of the activity models in one company, a senior executive immediately grasped the dynamics and summarized his understanding with this comment, "Oh yeah! We need to figure out ways to quit doing that red stuff. And we can't afford for the yellow stuff to be disproportionate to the green." From that point on, the company quit using the words "value-added' and spoke only of "green," 'yellow," and "red" activities. Their communication was crystal clear. More importantly, the graphical models facilitated all conversation to focus on issues and solutions.

In actual practice, you may need to experiment in selecting the technology that works best for you in physically producing your activity models. In many processes—particularly white-collar processes—the width of value-added activities is so small that graphics packages cannot display them. You may find it expedient to draft the models and simply use a color marker to indicate the value-added categories.

CHAPTER 6

Using Process Value Analysis to Guide Improvement Efforts

Once you're finished performing a process value analysis, you arrive at step four of the business process analysis, namely, using PVA to guide improvement efforts. This step has two main sub-steps: first, identifying problems; and second, solving the problems by recommending solutions and developing an implementation plan.

IDENTIFYING PROBLEMS AND THEIR CAUSES

The first task in achieving process improvement or cost reduction is to identify problems within the process and then to identify those problems' *root causes*. The information already assembled by means of activity definition and process value analysis will be a primary input for these next tasks.

First, a brief recap. *Activity definition* included the following information:

- A high-level portrayal of all business processes and their relationships to each other.
- Descriptions of the processes being analyzed, including definitions of inputs, outputs, boundaries, customers, and customer requirements.
- Identification of the activities that comprise the process.
- A flow chart showing the relationships among the activities.

Process value analysis has added the following information about each activity:

- Cycle time.
- Resource requirements.
- Value-added/non-value-added assessment.

This information is now ready for use to begin the development of a process improvement plan. The plan begins by identifying process problems, then uses techniques to determine the root causes of those problems.

Identifying Problems

Teams made up of managers and workers within the process define specific problems. The information from the activity definition and the process value analysis is particularly useful to them for uncovering a variety of problems. The most common are gaps, waste, inefficiency, and instability.

Gaps The most important analysis is to determine if any *gaps* exist in meeting external customers' needs. In asking this question, you must include administrative services as well as the products and services specifically sold to customers. Such administrative services include any correspondence or communication with the customer—including order processing, invoice processing, product delivery, and related matters. You then analyze unmet needs of internal customers in the same way.

Identifying gaps leads an organization to focus its attention on requirements that are truly important to the customer. You identify gap problems by comparing the output of a process with its customer requirements.

Waste You can identify *waste* problems—the presence of non-value-added activities—by locating all the non-value-added activities on the activity model. (Note: If you did not seek direct input from customers at the time you defined the processes, you will need to validate your assumptions about the customer's requirements before you can identify gaps and/or waste accurately.)

Inefficiency You can best identify *inefficiency*—the result of complex methods causing long cycle times—by examining the sequence of the work flow. Even if the activities are all value-added, their sequence may make the overall process inefficient. You can also detect inefficiency by identifying any activities whose cost is disproportionately high relative to its value.

Instability High variability in the input, output, timing, and/or quality may indicate the presence of *instability*. Generally speaking, an unstable process is costly in two ways. First, the process itself is costly. Second, an unstable process requires more management resources than it should to monitor, expedite, and coordinate activities. You can identify instability problems by examining the flow charts and questioning the constancy of inputs, outputs, and timing. The presence of bottlenecks may also be an indicator of instability, as is the presence of points on the flow chart where the work flow for good output is different from the one for poor output.

Identifying Root Causes

Once the problems of a process have been defined, the next task of the project team is twofold: first, to find the root cause of the problems; second, to develop an action plan to solve them.

Before proceeding with other aspects of identifying root causes, however, we should digress briefly to discuss an issue of terminology. Much of the recent literature on cost management—particularly as it concerns activity-based costing—uses the expression *cost driver* to denote the factor or event that causes cost to be incurred or causes activities to be performed. By constrast, Ernst & Young has opted to use the expression *root cause* to denote such a factor. We have made that decision for two reasons.

First, the word "driver" has been used by so many different people with so many different meanings that it leads to wide misinterpretation. Many of those meanings require quantification for use in activity-based costing calculations. We have seen people fail to identify important structural causes of problems because of a fixation on naming quantifiable "drivers."

Second, we have found the expression "root cause" to facilitate clear and uncomplicated communication with senior management, whereas we have seen the expression "cost driver" to be perceived as jargon that actually impedes that communication.

Therefore, for the purposes of identifying and solving process problems, we will use the expression "root cause" throughout this book. In Chapters 8 and 9 on activity-based costing, we will define terms (including a whole family of "driver" terms) that are used for specifying technical calculations. For now, however, we will focus on identifying the underlying causes of problems.

Returning now to the principal subject under discussion: the most effective way to identify a problem's root causes is to use a structured process for brainstorming by the people involved in that process. The structure is based on the four categories of process elements that can be changed:

1. the input (i.e., materials and information);
2. the people;
3. the methods; and
4. the technology.

The structuring technique is to draw the main skeleton for a "fishbone diagram" on a flip-chart or similar device in the brainstorming room. Exhibit 6-1 shows the framework. The discussion and analysis then focus on responding to the question, "What is it about the methods (or technology or input or people) that might be contributing to the problem?" The companion question is "Why does that happen?" In fact, it is helpful to develop the practice of asking the "why" question five separate times. This technique helps assure that you do not mistake the symptoms for the causes. The responses to these questions are then posted onto the diagram using horizontal lines connected to the appropriate process element.

Particularly, when examining whether the method is a cause of the problem, you may find it helpful to consider James Harrington's description of why non-value-added activities may be present in processes. Non-value-added activities may exist because the process is inadequately designed or because the process is not functioning as designed. This includes activities such as moving, waiting, setting up for an activity, storing, inspecting, and doing work over. These activities should not be necessary to produce the output of the process, but they occur because of poor process design. Non-value-added activity may also be caused by factors outside the process itself. It is also important to question whether the entire process might be non-value-added.

Here are two examples of identifying root causes.

EXHIBIT 6-1.

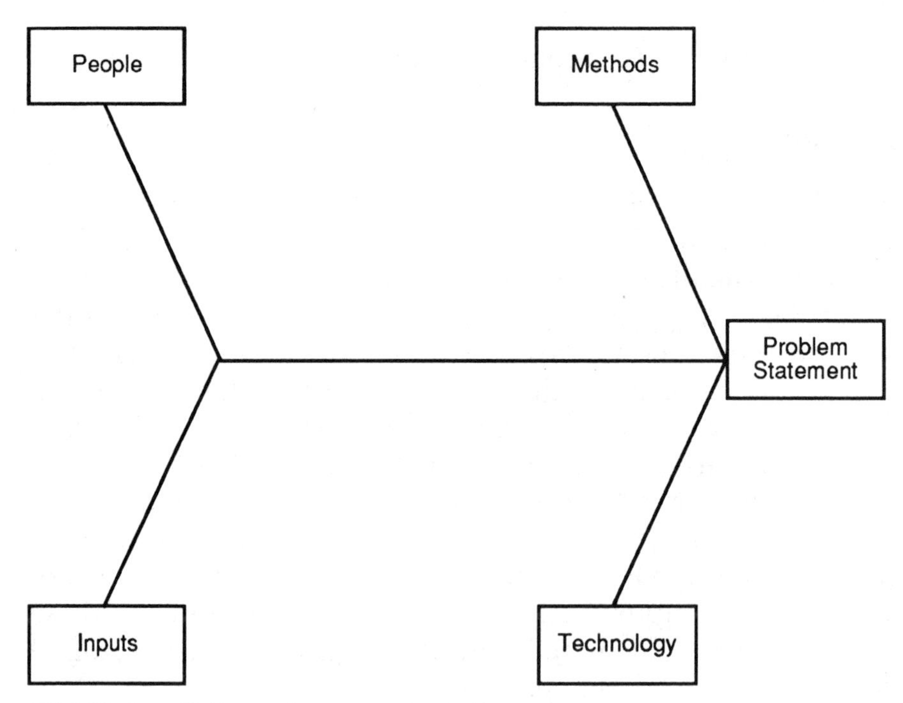

EXHIBIT 6-1. Fishbone diagram: main skeleton.

Example 1: Each order in an order entry process had to go through an engineering review before it could be accepted. One of the problems identified in the order-entry process was that "a high proportion of orders are rejected for having an invalid combination of options and features."

By brainstorming about possible causes of the problem, the process improvement team suggested a variety

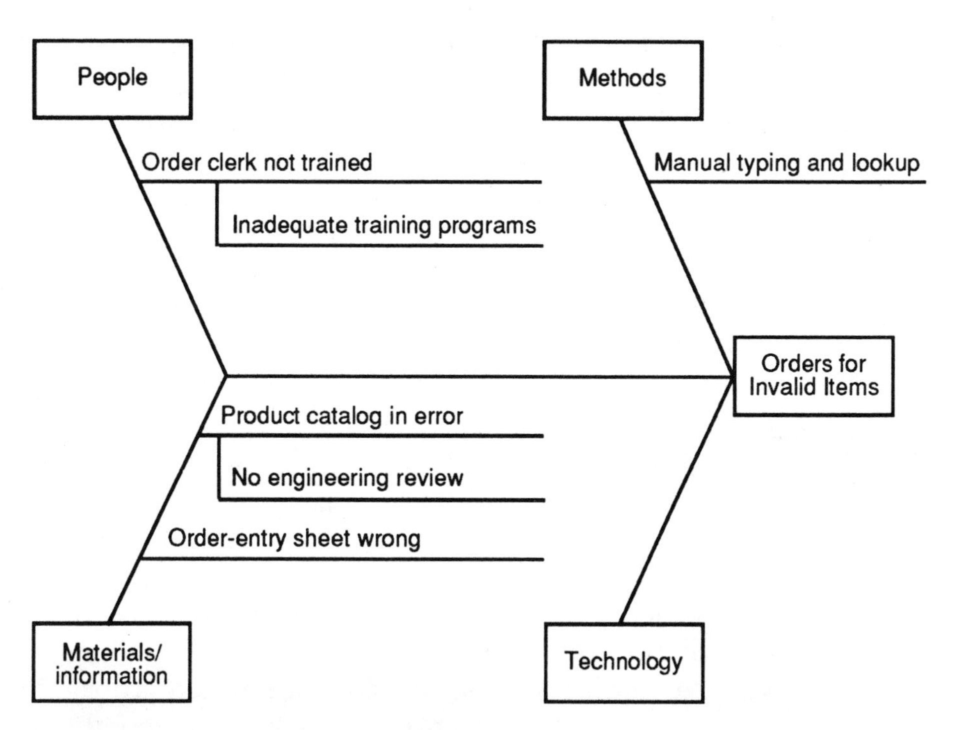

EXHIBIT 6-2. Fishbone diagram: detailed analysis.

of contributing factors. Exhibit 6-2 shows these factors. After examining a sample of rejected orders, the team began to concentrate on solving a fundamental flaw with the process input: the fact that the product catalog contained errors. The marketing group had assembled a matrix of product options and had published it without first subjecting it to an engineering review. Although the catalog was visually appealing, and though 90 percent of combinations were valid, the company simply could not make the items in the remaining 10 percent of the cells.

The team recommended that the catalog be corrected immediately and that future catalogs undergo an engineering review before publication. As a result of implementing this recommendation, the company managed to cut rejected orders by 50 percent. Moreover, the number of people needed to communicate with customers to resolve problems about their orders dropped 22 percent. These were only the tangible benefits of the process improvement effort; the intangible benefit of more satisfied customers was not quantified.

Example 2: The second example shows the results of a process value analysis performed for a producer of chilled beverages. The scope of the analysis included all production activities and production costs within a single plant. Exhibit 6-3 summarizes the costs of the non-value-added activity segments by category. The total cost of storing inventory, for instance, was $1,167,000.

Again, a brainstorming session identified root causes for each of the categories of non-value-added activities. Exhibit 6-3 also charts the relationship between root causes and the NVA category. For instance, the "purchase of raw material in large-sized drums" was named as a root cause of material losses, storage requirements, and testing requirements.

It is important to note that one root cause may affect multiple non-value-added activities and that a single activity may have multiple root causes. Exhibit 6-4 derives from the process value analysis for the beverage company. The analysis now includes recommended actions to address each of the

ROOT CAUSE ANALYSIS–EXAMPLE
TOTAL $ 000s

	NON-VALUE-ADDED COST						
	Mat'l Loss	Move	Store	Test	Downtime	Cleanup	Total
	$ 687	$2,160	$1,167	$ 250	$ 713	$ 547	$5,524
ROOT CAUSES:							
Distance from Supplier		X					
Freight Rate		X					
Inconsistent Raw Material				X			
Drummed Material	X		X	X			
Changeovers	X				X		
Lab v Prod. Test Equipment	X			X	X		
Cleanup Policy					X	X	
Number of Container Types	X						
Fill Weight Policy	X						
Equipment Reliability					X		
Domestic/Foreign Mix		X					
Number of Products	X		X	X		X	
Base Mfg. Agitator Design	X			X	X	X	
Inconsistent Calibration Outside	X			X	X	X	
Product Viscosity	X			X			
Blend Process Controls	X						

EXHIBIT 6-3. Root cause analysis: categories

root causes. In this particular example, the annual cost savings from these recommended actions were estimated to be $1.8 million.

Root Cause Categories

After naming the specific root cause of each activity, you may find it helpful to organize these root causes into categories. Typical categories include company policy, incompatible technologies, system requirements, and process organization. Estimating the monetary value of the categories is particularly beneficial in overcoming resistance to changing such root causes as company policy or control procedures.

SOLVING THE PROBLEMS

This brings us to our next major juncture in using business process analysis. Once you have identified the process problems and their root causes, you will be ready to develop a plan of action for improving the process itself.

There are two key steps in developing such a plan. The first is to develop approaches to address each of the root causes of the problems you have identified. The second is to sequence these approaches into an action plan.

Developing Solutions

In this discussion, we will offer some guidelines and suggestions for how to accomplish each of these steps. Obviously, developing innovative solutions will vary in accordance with every problem and with every environment. No canned solutions exist for the problems that may be identified in a process value analysis. The following discussion is, therefore, not

ROOT CAUSE	RECOMMENDED ACTION STEPS	APPROXIMATE SAVINGS $ 000's
Inconsistent Raw Materials	Monitor Vendors for Tighter Tolerance	$ 300
Equipment Reliability	Institute Preventive Maintenance Program in Fill/Pack	$ 500
Numbers of Products	Analyze Cost/Profitability of Low Volume Products	Not Quantified
Process Controls Calibration	Program Timing of Stop Product Controls Hire Instrumentation Technician	$ 300
Downtime/Cleanup Time	Consider 40 Hour Run Times	$ 100
	Standardize Production/QA Test Equipment	$ 200
Net Fill Weight Policy	Adopt More Stringent Fill Policies	$ 100
Number of Container Types	Standardize Types/Vendors	$ 100
Operator Reliability	Enhance Operator Training Change Sick Leave Policy	$ 200
	Total	$ 1800

EXHIBIT 6-4. Root cause analysis: suggested actions

intended as a comprehensive guide, but rather as an overview intended to help you avoid overlooking some avenues that might lead you toward effective solutions.

The solution to a process problem can lie in five possible areas. Recall for a moment our first view of a process:

Suppliers→Input→Process→Output→Customers

Inputs, which come from suppliers (internal or external) go into the process. The process itself is a set of activities. Those activities are executed through people and through technology. By these means, the input is converted to output, which goes to customers (internal or external).

The five possible elements that you could change are:

1. the output;
2. the input;
3. the set of the activities;
4. the people; or
5. the technology.

Note that changing either the output or the input requires collaboration, cooperation, and consensus with the customers and suppliers respectively.

Each of these five approaches to solution development will be discussed. We describe the five types of changes as though they are independent. In practice, however, the ultimate solution to a problem often consists of a combination of one or more of these elements.

Changing the Output If you have identified the problem as a gap (i.e., a customer's unmet need), then one of the changes you need to make is in specifying the output itself. Once the output has been redefined, however, the ways to produce the new output will be through changes to the input and/or the activities, people, and/or technology. We are, therefore, not going to elaborate here on how to change the output.

One other point to keep in mind about the output when you are working on improving a process: make sure you do not unknowingly change the output as a result of the other changes you make to the process. Your testing/evaluation of the changed process must include a verification that the output still meets all the requirements of the customer.

Changing the Input A project team will often identify something about the input as a problem's root cause. The quality of the input may be poor; the flow of the input may be erratic; the input may be overly complex; the cost of the input may be too high; the lead time for the input may be too long. The list of things that may be wrong with the input is endless.

Improving the input through collaborative efforts with suppliers and through vendor certification programs has become strategically important for improving process reliability and product quality. That same strategy is equally applicable for non-manufacturing processes. But the same constraint also applies. You must involve the suppliers of your input in your effort to effect improvements.

> *Example 1*: Recall the earlier example in which a team analyzing an order entry process identified the product catalog errors as a root cause of customers' requesting invalid combinations of features. The order-entry project team did identify the solution to their own problem as improving the quality of the input they received. They wanted to receive orders from customers that did not contain invalid items. But to effect that change in their input, they had to collaborate with the marketing and engineering people to correct the underlying flaw.

Example 2: A related example—one involving a different company from that in Example 1—shows an opposite story. This incident also concerns an improvement project for an order-entry process.

Orders came into the process from the company's sales representatives; no orders were received directly from customers. When the project team developed the activity model, one of the first activities identified was the validation of all data on an order. It was apparent that the activity was both time-consuming and expensive. Additionally, it was classified as a non-value-added activity.

The team decided to eliminate that activity from the process; they simply agreed among themselves that they would not perform that activity in the future. They did not ask why the orders contained errors. More importantly, they did not communicate with anyone in the sales department to let them know that orders would no longer be validated. They simply quit doing it.

The net effect of their "improvement" was an immediate deterioration of service to the customers. Customers did not receive the products they thought they had ordered, and they had no advance warning that any problem existed. In truth, the project team did not solve the problem of poor quality input; and it certainly did not achieve a cost reduction. Their change to the process simply let the problem leap-frog the order-entry department and go straight from the sales department to the customer. The moral of the story: Avoid this sort of perfunctory response to seeing a non-value-added activity and you'll also avoid the problem this company encountered. Using process value analysis will protect you from getting into this sort of trouble.

Changing the Activities Changing a process can range from minor tinkerings to complete overhaul. Total Cost Management, like any approach, is unable to anticipate the breadth and number of specific situations you may encounter. Consequently, the following discussion emphasizes some of the guidelines you may use to modify a process.

- *Eliminate unnecessary administrative steps.* For example, question any document log in use.
- *Question every approval/signoff step* and keep only the ones that are genuinely required for the process to function.
- *Question every inspection step.* Develop ways for the person who originally does the work to assure its accuracy and completeness before releasing it.
- *Question the sequence of the work.* As work changes hands, see if activities can be bundled.
- *Look for ways to shorten the distance* when the workflow covers a long geographical span.
- *Question the necessity for all written correspondence* in the process.
- *Eliminate redundancy.*

A final note on process improvement. The real experts in the process are the people who work in it day in, day out. They are the ones who will be able to suggest the most important changes to the process.

Changing the People Another of the common "root causes" of process problems is that the people performing the activities may lack proper training. In fact, it is often unclear what skills are, in fact, necessary to perform an activity until you have analyzed a process.

The recommendation for training may be for people to acquire specific new skills. This is particularly true when the scope of work performed by any one person ends up enlarged. Some companies have become so serious about developing a versatile work force that their compensation systems have been changed to a "pay for skills" basis.

Many times the process analysis reveals that instructions informing people how to perform a process do not exist. Everyone who does the job is following his or her own method to one degree or another. In situations such as these, a dual recommendation often results: first, formalize the process instructions; second, conduct meaningful training on the new procedures.

In other situations, people are using equipment or technology with only a surface understanding of the capabilities at their disposal. This is as true in administrative processes as it is in the seemingly more technical areas of the business. In many cases, the "people changes" that are needed are more concerned with underlying attitudes and dynamics than with technologies or procedures. It may be important for people to develop new understandings and appreciation of how they impact customers. Priorities may need to change. People may need enhanced skills to interact effectively across organizational boundaries. People may need to develop team-building skills and problem-solving skills. People may need to increase their capacity to absorb change and initiate change. The organizational structure itself may need to change as a means of improving the performance of the processes.

Changing the Technology Finally, you can improve a process by changing the technology used to perform the activities in the process. The range of options here is wide. You may decide to automate certain activities; you may replace equipment to increase reliability and efficiency and to reduce variation; you may change the technology along with a total redesign of the process; or you may develop and/or implement new information systems. In particular, information technology can be a great *enabler* of change in optimizing value-added work and eliminating the non-value-added work.

Consider our original order-entry example, for instance. One obvious way to reduce cycle time in the process was to replace inter-office mail with electronic mail for all "internal move" activities, and to use fax technology instead of mail to communicate the planned ship date for the order.

Implement the Solutions

Once you have proposed ways to address each of the root causes of problems that you have identified, you need to organize those proposals into an action plan. Sequencing the proposals—that is, prioritizing your course of action—is key to developing that plan.

Prioritizing Actions A variety of different criteria may be used for prioritizing the implementation of the recommended solutions. The first rule for selecting which recommendations to implement is, of course, to make sure your improvement objective is clear. For example, if your prime objective is to reduce cycle time, you may select a different set of actions to implement than if your objective were to remove costs from this year's budget.

Strategies for Prioritizing Here are three additional approaches to prioritizing. (These three approaches are not mutually exclusive. Your own implementation priorities may be based on a combination of these and other factors, such as the availability of necesary resources):

- Effort to implement.
- Quality category.
- Improvement hierarchy.

Effort to Implement. You may want to categorize your improvement opportunities by making a high-level estimate of the relative time and resources required for implementing each recommendation. The typical categories are *simple, moderate,* and *complex.*

Simple: Project teams often develop a lively terminology to describe the recommended improvements in this category. Typical names include "low-hanging fruit," or "no-brainer" opportunities. These names apply to changes that can be made with a quick fix—typically a simple procedural change—that impacts very few people and requires no new technology. Typical of such improvements are:

- Eliminating any bureaucratic non-value-added activities (i.e., ones whose elimination would have no external impact).
- Utilizing an improved technology that already exists in the company.
- Eliminating any redundant activities.
- Changing the sequence of activities to make its flow more efficient.

A huge benefit can come from gathering this low-hanging fruit for immediate implementation. A TCM project is often the first time process value analysis has been performed for any of the administrative processes in the business. In such cases, improvements categorized as "simple" can be significant. Implementing them results in two kinds of benefits. Not only can you take a giant step forward toward achieving a corporate goal; you may also be able to use the savings from these improvements to develop and implement solutions for the more difficult problems.

Moderate: Recommendations categorized as moderate in effort usually require procedural changes from people or functions outside the project group. They may also require collaboration with suppliers and/or customers. Or they may require the acquisition of new technology.

Complex: Recommendations categorized as complex typically involve simultaneous changes in the activities, people, and technology. The solutions are frequently structural rather than procedural. Generally, they are longer-term with significant capital investment required.

Quality Category. Another structure that can be helpful in prioritizing recommendations is the categories associated with the *costs of quality*. (In Chapter 12, we will devote a full section to calculating and reporting quality costs. For now, we are mentioning this concept only to define the priorities.) The essence of the cost of quality message is this: The earlier in the process you solve your quality problems, the less costly you will find them. Preventing poor quality is preferable to allowing it to occur at all. If you cannot prevent all quality problems, then you should search for incidents of poor quality as soon as they could occur. This is far less costly than letting them slide downstream. Finding and dealing with a problem that remains inside your company is less costly than having a customer experience the problem. The most expensive place possible for a problem to occur is in the hands of your customer.

Improvement Hierarchy. A final technique for sequencing improvement efforts utilizes the collective wisdom of *just-in-time* (JIT) projects. The advice from the just-in-time veterans is the adage: "Simplify, Automate, Integrate." This adage has been validated time and time again in process improvement projects. Sequence your improvement efforts so that you simplify a process before you automate it; then automate it before you attempt to integrate it with other processes.

By examining activity models, the economics of this adage becomes evident. Assume, for instance, that you are working to improve the process illustrated in the activity model (shown in Exhibit 6-5). The background of the exhibit shows the

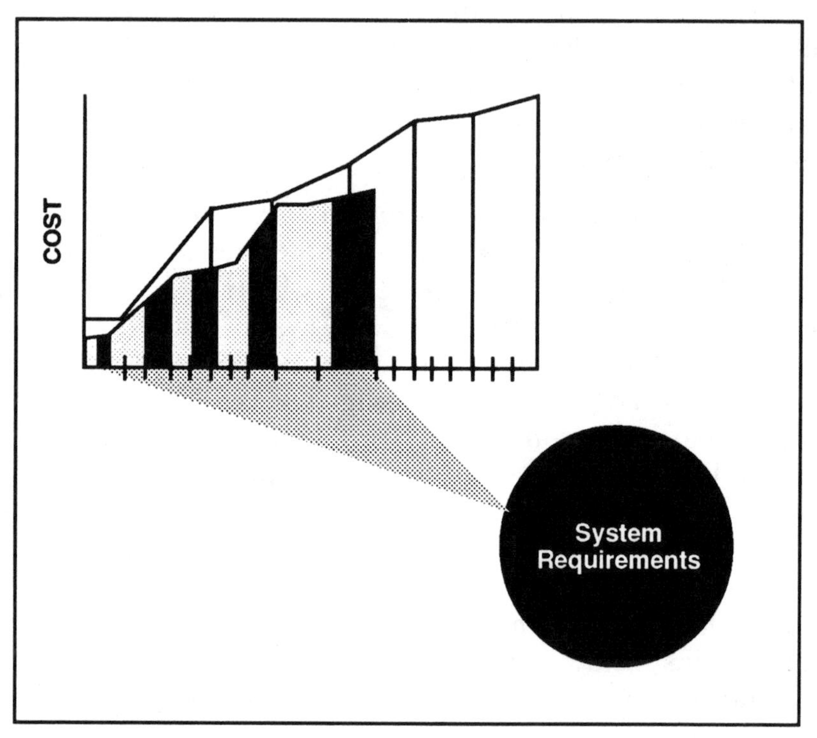

EXHIBIT 6-5. Value–driven systems.

process before it has been simplified; the foreground shows the process after it has been simplified. Which version of the process would you rather automate?

If you automate it before simplifying it, you will essentially be making many non-value-added activities permanent. You may find a way to perform these activities faster, cheaper, or both; but you have institutionalized their existence. (Automating an unwieldy process has been called "paving a cowpath.")

On the other hand, if you work first to streamline the process—thus eliminating all the non-value-added activities possible—your automation effort will be simpler. You will also end up with a more effective automated process than would have been possible had you automated it first. Particularly when you are automating information systems, it is important to determine the system requirements from a streamlined view of the process. Ernst & Young calls this developing "value-driven systems."

Likewise, it is important to delay elaborate integration of processes—particularly the development of computer-integrated processes—until the processes are truly efficient, effective, and stable. Integrating two problem-riddled processes will inevitably result in a certifiable mega-mess.

CONCLUSION

Business process analysis is the fundamental technique for understanding, analyzing, and improving the performance of an organization. It focuses on the flow of the work rather than emphasizing the organizational structure used to manage the work. It requires that you explicitly consider your customers' needs. It helps you structure the definition of business problems in such a way that you can identify and address their root causes. It provides a basis for improving quality, reducing cycle time, and reducing costs.

Business process analysis is a technique with double benefits. It allows you to achieve both short-term and longer-term results by identifying opportunities for significant improvements. At the same time, it also serves as the foundation for the other accounting techniques that can keep your company on the track of continuous improvement.

Let's now turn to those other techniques.

SECTION 2

Activity-Based Costing

CHAPTER 7

Activity-Based Costing—What It Is and Where It Came From

Activity-based costing (ABC) has received tremendous attention lately in the business press, in the academic literature, and in industry seminars. Much of this attention has focused exclusively on the process of calculating more accurate product costs. The Ernst & Young approach to ABC recognizes the importance of improved product costs, and the techniques we describe and illustrate in this book show how to use ABC to improve your product costing. Through the experiences we've gained while helping numerous clients conduct activity-based costing projects, however, we have significantly broadened our view of ABC's power beyond pure product cost determinations. Throughout all chapters devoted to ABC in this book, we will be sharing this broadened view.

Our discussion of activity-based costing includes five chapters:

- Chapter 7 outlines the theory and principles of ABC.

- Chapter 8 describes and illustrates the technique for developing activity-based process costs.
- Chapter 9 describes and illustrates the techniques for developing activity-based costs for products, services, customers, and other cost objects.
- Chapter 10 discusses how to use the results of ABC in making significant managerial decisions.
- Chapter 11 discusses the key issues you must address in implementing activity-based costing.

Before we begin, a brief note: Although ABC is a technique relevant to the full spectrum of industries, it has its roots in the manufacturing sector. In describing the evolution of ABC's principles, we will first tell the story of its "birth" in the world of manufacturing; we'll then explain how its application has grown in other industries.

ABC BUILDS ON A FOUNDATION OF BUSINESS PROCESS ANALYSIS

Business process analysis embodies the concept that a business is a series of inter-related processes, and that these processes consist of activities that convert inputs to outputs. Activity-based costing manifests this concept and, for that matter, builds on it by organizing all cost information on an activity basis. The fundamental belief behind this costing approach is that cost is *caused* and that the causes of cost can be managed. The closer you come to relating the costs to their causes, the more helpful your accounting information will be in guiding the management decisions of your business. In implementing this concept, you will see strong integration between business process analysis and activity-based costing.

The business process analysis chapters in this book have shown how to develop activity models by using headcount (as an example) to indicate the resources required for the various business activities. The following activity-based costing chapters will show how to determine the costs of the activities using the technique of *activity-based process costing*. We will then show how to use the results of the activity-based process costing to:

- Calculate improved costs for products and other cost objects;
- Support cost reduction efforts; and
- Support business process improvement efforts.

The process of using one technique as the foundation for another then continues as we proceed into later sections of *Total Cost Management*. In the continuous improvement section of this book, for instance, we will show how to use the results of business process analysis and activity-based costing to:

- Support improved performance measurements;
- Develop improved techniques for evaluating proposed investments of new capital assets;
- Extend the product costing improvements through life-cycle costing and target costing; and
- Evaluate a company's achievements and opportunities in its quality program.

DIVERSITY-COMPLEXITY: THE ROOT OF TODAY'S COSTING PROBLEM

Many problems in today's costing environment stem from the high level of diversity and variety in the current products and processes. Few companies operate in the Henry Ford mold—"Any color as long as it's black." Rare is the company that has a high level of stability in its operations or processes.

If product variety were absent, the business environment would be simple. A production line could be fine-tuned to provide a continuous stream of a single product. Only a minimum of staff would be necessary to provide support services for this environment. No production planning staff would be required. Essentially the only decision required for production planning would be setting the plant's work hours. Expediting or rescheduling a particular order would be meaningless. There would be no setups or changeovers. There would never be a question about interrupting long, efficient production runs to accommodate a small order. Production could occur at such a constant speed that there would be fewer opportunities for the products to suffer damage as they went through the plant.

In a world like this, you could do product costing literally on the back of an envelope. You would simply divide the total production costs by the total production volume to calculate a unit cost. This product costing technique would be the same whether the factory was labor-intensive or highly automated. In either case, all costs would be incurred for the purpose of producing the sole output. The distinction between direct labor and indirect labor would be meaningless.

Similarly, if a factory had no variability in its processes, its simplicity would be powerful. Machines would not break down. Bottlenecks would not develop. All output would be perfect. Incoming material would not be late. Best of all, there would be no need for the large numbers of staff and complex systems currently required to deal with constant disruptions.

But this single-product, stable-process environment bears no resemblance to reality in most of today's businesses. The multiple-product, variable-process environment requires most companies to need extensive support services simply to keep everything coordinated. These support services, in turn, require a large amount of managerial time and attention. If the products themselves are complex—with large numbers of components and many levels of raw materials, components, and sub-assemblies—then the factory and its support staff can grow to a massive level of complexity. Such complexity is generally costly; it is at the heart of many overhead problems.

THE "HIDDEN FACTORY"

Jeffrey Miller and Thomas Vollmann, researchers at Boston University, provided a truly seminal notion that later developed into activity-based costing. In an article entitled "The Hidden Factory," (*Harvard Business Review*, September–October, 1985), Miller and Vollmann addressed the question, "What causes overhead?" At the time of this article's publication, manufacturing managers were struggling with the issue of overhead costs. In fact, the problem of "high and rising overhead costs" ranked behind only quality as the primary concern of manufacturing executives.* Managers had much clearer visions of how to solve their quality problems than of how to solve their overhead problems. "The Hidden Factory" was the first significant attempt to conceptualize the causes of overhead in the modern manufacturing environment.

Miller and Vollmann articulated three important themes that influenced the future direction of cost management. First, the overhead problem is not a cyclical phenomenon. Their research showed that overhead costs had been rising in American industry (both in relative and absolute terms) for more than a hundred years. The dynamics of modern factories indicated that this trend will surely continue. In a relative sense, overhead replaces direct labor as the pace of automation increases. In an absolute sense, support costs are increas-

* See the *Summary Report* for the North American Manufacturing Futures Survey, Boston University Manufacturing Roundtable, 1983, 1984, 1985.

ing. These problems are not ephemeral. If we simply ignore them, they are not going to go away.

Second, Miller and Vollmann reached a significant insight about what causes overhead costs. "For managers," they wrote, "the critical step in controlling overhead costs lies in developing a model that relates these costs to the forces behind them." In two sentences, the authors then created a vision for how managers and accountants could view overhead costs: "Unit output drives direct labor and materials inputs on the actual shop floor that we all think of when we envision a factory. But in the 'hidden factory,' where the bulk of manufacturing overhead costs accumulates, the real driving force comes from transactions, not physical products."

In one of these authors speeches, he referred both to the "visible factory," where people took raw materials and converted them into finished products, and to the "hidden factory" where people shoved numbers in and out of computers all day. His point was important. The work of the hidden factory is essentially all non-value-added work.

Miller and Vollmann then defined four categories of transactions that account for much of the overhead costs in a manufacturing organization. These categories are:

- *Logistical transactions* which order, execute, and confirm the materials from one location to another.
- *Balancing transactions* which ensure that the supplies of materials, labor, and capacity are equal to the demand.
- *Quality transactions* which extend far beyond what we usually think of as quality control, indirect engineering, and procurement. (They include identifying and communicating specifications, certifying that other transactions have taken place as they should have, and developing and recording relevant data.)
- *Change transactions* which update basic manufacturing information systems to accommodate changes in

engineering designs, schedules, routings, standards, materials specifications, and bills of materials.

Finally, Miller and Vollmann described three general approaches for managing overhead costs more effectively:

- Analyze which transactions are necessary, and improve the methods used to carry them out;
- Increase the stability of operations; and
- Rely on automation and systems integration.

Miller and Vollmann's article ends with an important message:

> . . .[M]anufacturing managers will have to look beyond accounting conventions to analyze and categorize costs in a way that has functional meaning. We believe that the answer does not lie in inventing new accounting systems alone. This is a problem for the accountants to solve if they can; certainly it will help if they do. But no amount of bookkeeping magic will let manufacturing managers avoid one of the strategic necessities of the future: understanding how to manage the hidden factory.

EARLY EXPERIMENTS WITH "TRANSACTION-BASED COSTING"

The concepts embodied in the "hidden factory" became the basis for developing the accounting techniques now popularly known as activity-based costing. With this new emphasis on "transactions" as a cause of overhead, three notions caught the attention of cost accounting researchers.

First, large amounts of overhead costs were being allocated to products based on the products' direct labor content, sales, units produced, or some other volume measure. If in fact the overhead varied in accordance with some variable other than volume (as Miller and Vollmann's research suggested), then the product costs that manufacturers were currently calculating could be seriously in error.

The second notion was that if transactions caused overhead, managers could assign overhead costs to products in a way that reflected the relative demand of individual products for all the different types of transactions.

The third notion was that since computer-based processing systems performed a large amount of work in the "hidden factory," the history files within those systems contained a wealth of data that analysts could use to allocate the transaction costs to individual products.

Harvard Business School researchers conducted the first case studies that reflect "hidden factory" concepts to attribute cost to products through transaction data. The results of these early case studies were shocking. They identified many products whose costs far exceeded their selling prices. They also showed important high-volume products whose costs were significantly lower than previously thought.*

These early case studies brought home the strategic impact of costing inaccuracies. If the costs are wrong, then all decisions about pricing, product mix, and promotion could be undermining long-term profitability. Companies might be arriving at exactly the wrong conclusions in make-buy decisions; their marketing programs might be promoting products with negative margins and failing to promote products with positive margins; tactical plans might be based on erroneous assumptions about the relative profitability of the company's customers.

---

*R. Cooper and R. Kaplan, "How Product Costing Distorts Product Costs," *Management Accounting*, April, 1988.

ACTIVITY-BASED COSTING TAKES OFF

The name of this new accounting technique evolved quickly from "transaction-based costing" to "stragetic product costing;" ultimately it settled on "activity-based costing." By whatever name, the results of this early work caught the attention of manufacturing executives across North America and Europe. It made great press: "Manufacturing Executives Have No Idea What Their Products Cost—No Idea Where They're Making or Losing Money." Not only were these problems graphic, they were also real problems that managers truly related to. Perhaps most important, accounting innovators began proposing solutions that struck managers as reasonable.

It's not hard to guess what happened next. So many people jumped on the ABC bandwagon that it became a fad almost overnight. Activity-based costing became a popular theme among accountants and operations managers, practitioners and researchers, seminar promoters, and software developers. (We actually received T-shirts at a seminar that announced "COST ACCOUNTING—IT'S AS EASY AS ABC.") ABC was promoted with great eloquence as the cost accounting snake-oil of the late 1980s and early 1990s.

These comments are not intended to belittle the work of the early researchers and implementers! Indeed, we owe considerable thanks to the people who developed, experimented with, and publicly shared the results of their early work. We are proud to have been a part of this effort, and we owe thanks to the clients with whom we worked shoulder-to-shoulder on early ABC projects. We make these comments simply to give perspective to the current state of affairs.

Starting in 1988, accounting practitioners have done much work under the name of "activity-based costing." Some of this work has proved fruitful; some hasn't. Some has even taken a direction we believe to be misguided. In particular, we believe that while product costing is important, the preoccupation with product costing has overshadowed ABC's power to help you actually reduce overhead costs and manage the business more effectively. (You can actually accomplish both these objectives in an ABC project—but only if you conduct the project with the intent of accomplishing both.) Furthermore, we believe that ABC has become such a popular term that it is now important to sort out the substance from the hype; only then can companies benefit from the genuinely significant experiences of the ABC projects conducted to date.

ABC: SHEDDING LIGHT ON THE "ECONOMICS OF OVERHEAD"

One of the most important benefits of activity-based costing is the focus it provides a company's performance improvement efforts by estimating the costs for key causes of cost. Managers can use these estimates to prioritize and monitor improvements efforts as well as to cost products. When you know the cost for certain causes of overhead, you can make better decisions about which problems are the most important to tackle. Quality improvement programs catch and keep the attention of top management when the costs of poor quality become known. Likewise, simplification programs catch and keep the attention of top management when executives learn the costs of diversity and complexity.

A prime example of the type of hidden cost that ABC can help expose is "part proliferation." When a product is designed with many components, or when a new component part is designed when an already existing one would have sufficed, new parts have to be added to the support requirements for a plant. Exhibit 7-1 shows a partial list of the "overhead work" required to create and support an individual part number. Service proliferation is equally troublesome—cafeteria-style insurance plans, software packaging options, and health care services, to name only a few.

Engineering

- Designing requirements
- Detailed drafting
- Checking
- Storing documents
- Developing the bill of material
- Process planning
- Developing the routing
- Designing tools and fixtures
- Fabricating or buying the tools and fixtures
- Processing engineering change orders

Procurement

- Sourcing
- Validating/certifying
- Ordering
- Expediting
- Setting a standard cost
- Analyzing variances

Receiving

- Receiving
- Verifying parts
- Counting/checking
- Matching with purchase order

Incoming Inspection

- Inspecting
- Documenting out-of-spec incidents
- Taking action on out-of-spec incidents

Material Handling

- Moving material to stock or point of usage
- Documenting the movement

Stores

- Receiving
- Cycle counting
- Issuing
- Receiving/processing returns

Scheduling/Inventory Control

- Developing item-master information
- Analyzing inventory requirements
- Analyzing for scrap/slow-moving/obsolence problems
- Controlling the perpetual inventory balance
- Planning replenishments
- Scheduling
- Generating work orders or purchase orders

Master Scheduling

- Forecasting sales orders
- Calculating component demand

Production

- Setting up production equipment
- Training
- Tooling

Information Systems

- Storing the data
- Processing the data
- Maintaining history files

EXHIBIT 7-1. **Activities required to support a part.**

Operations managers within a company may have known for years that the more parts they had to manage, the more demanding their work became. But after using ABC techniques to estimate what it actually costs to add and maintain a new part, operations managers are equipped to get the organizational support they need to solve the problem. It is not surprising that manufacturers have estimated the annual administrative cost of each part number to be $10,000 or more.

Other significant causes of complexity that ABC can help expose include:

- Operations layout;
- Bill of material configuration;
- Long lead-time sourcing; and
- Process instability.

When companies began to explore the idea that transactions could cause cost—or, at least, that overhead cost may correlate strongly with the number of transactions—managers identified many examples. Exhibit 7-2 shows candidates that were identified as "potential causes of cost." A list like this is very useful in getting started as you think about overhead.

Yet you can interpret a list like this in two different ways. On the one hand, it can be a starting point for identifying the "root causes" of overhead. On the other hand, it can be used solely as a basis for attaching cost to product. Take, for example, the overhead costs associated with material handling. On the surface, it seems logical to use the "number of move transactions" as a basis for allocating material handling costs to product—that is, if product costing is your only objective. However, if controlling and reducing overhead cost is one of your objectives, you really do need to look beneath the surface to investigate why so much material movement is needed.

As we worked with one client who was analyzing material handling costs, the client identified two different "root causes"

- Number of labor transactions
- Number of material moves
- Number of total part numbers
- Number of parts received
- Number of part numbers in an average product
- Number of products
- Average number of options
- Number of schedule changes
- Number of accessories
- Number of vendors
- Number of units scrapped
- Number of engineering change notices
- Number of process changes
- Number of units reworked
- Number of direct labor employees
- Number of new parts introduced

EXHIBIT 7-2. Potential causes of cost*

for the high amount of material handling. In the fabrication area of the plant, the factory layout itself seemed to be the prime culprit. This part of the factory was organized into groups of similar machining equipment. Parts literally traveled miles and miles in a spaghetti-like fashion in order to be processed by the different machining functions. In the assembly area of the plant, the large number of components and complexity of product design required for making the end

* Robert D. McIlhattan, "How Cost Management Systems Can Support the JIT Philosophy," *Management Accounting*, September, 1987, p. 22.

product was identified as a "root cause" of the high cost of material handling. The client decided to treat "number of moves" as a symptom rather than a cause of an overhead problem. This decision then was reflected in the way that the client decided:

1. to assign the overhead to product;
2. to prioritize improvement projects; and
3. to develop new performance measures.

This story illustrates three central elements of Ernst & Young's approach to activity-based costing. First, the important benefits of ABC come from project team members truly understanding the dynamics of what causes overhead in their company. Business process analysis is the primary technique for gaining that knowledge. Once the members of a team have developed those insights, they can use them as a foundation for all sorts of accounting improvements—process costing, product costing, and performance measurements—to mention just a few. Without that understanding, an ABC project team could accomplish nothing more than just moving the numbers around.

The second point illustrated in this story is equally important. An ABC project cannot be successfully conducted as a "backroom" accounting project. An ABC project is one of the best possible vehicles for getting people from operations and from accounting alike to learn about each others' disciplines and challenges. Neither group working alone brings all the knowledge and skills needed to accomplish something meaningful in the project. Furthermore, once the analytical part of the project is completed, a broad support base is necessary to turn the results of the analysis into successful corporate action plans. Keep in mind, too, that only when the action plans have been implemented can the organization realize bottom-line benefits from activity-based costing.

The third point to note is that an ABC approach is much more of a mindset issue than it is a software issue. An approach that places a premium on understanding the cost dynamics will be far more valuable to you than the "system" itself.

AN OVERVIEW OF THE ABC TECHNIQUE

Activity-based costing occurs in two major phases. First, you determine the costs of significant activities. Then you assign the costs of the activities to products or to other "objects" of interest, such as customers or services. We refer to this first phase as *activity-based process costing* and to the second phase as *activity-based product costing* (or more accurately *activity-based object costing*). We use the term "activity-based costing" to refer generically to this overall process.

As previously mentioned, activity-based process costing serves two separate purposes. First, it develops the costs of the activities identified in the business process analysis. Second, it is a necessary intermediate step in calculating activity-based object costs. activity-based process costing is a major link between improving the accuracy of your costing and improving the performance of your business.

The prime objective in this costing technique is to assign costs that reflect or "mirror" the physical dynamics of the business. A phrase often used to describe the underlying concept of ABC is that "the business's resources are consumed in the conduct of activities, and activities are performed in the service of products." Activity-based costing tries to manifest this two-stage dynamic. As we saw in the chapter describing business process analysis, activities also provide the key to analyzing and improving business processes.

In trying to actually accomplish this goal of having the costing process mirror the physical dynamics, ABC utilizes a hierarchy of techniques. This hierarchy applies both to process and to object costing. The first preference for assigning cost is "direct charging." If, for instance, the sole purpose for a piece of equipment is to produce a particular product, then the costs related to that equipment should be directly charged to that product. Or if an individual loan officer is dedicated to servicing a particular type of loan, all costs associated with the loan officer should be charged to that particular type of loan. These costs should not be assigned through any form of allocation. If direct charging is not possible, then the second preference is to assign the cost on some basis that indicates the level of service provided—such as transaction counts. The technique of "last resort" is volume-based allocation.*

IS ABC APPLICABLE TO NON-MANUFACTURING ENTERPRISES?

Activity-based costing is as applicable to service organizations as it is to manufacturers. Moreover, it is as applicable in determining the costs of services, customers, or lines of business as it is in determining the costs of manufactured products. Both in service organizations and in manufacturing organizations, the problem is making management decisions that can make and keep complex, diverse organizations profitable. Having good information about the costs of processes, products, services, customers, and channels of distribution is critical for managers making those decisions.

On a practical level, the answer is not as universal. On one hand, activity-based process costing has been equally successful in manufacturing and non-manufacturing environments. However, in taking the costs from the process level to services, customers, and other objects, some environments have proven

---

* For a more detailed discussion of this hierarchy, see Michael R. Ostrenga, "Activities: The Focal Point of Total Cost Management," in *Management Accounting*, February, 1990.

more amenable than others to the technique. The key issue is whether any data exist that can be used to trace the activity costs to these other objects. In complex manufacturing environments, project teams can typically dig out a wealth of data to use in attaching activity costs to products. In fact, their challenge is often to make sure the level of detail in their product costing does not become overly complex. In non-manufacturing environments, or in costing objects other than products, the availability of data varies widely from one organization to another. After we have illustrated how the technique works, we will revisit the issues for non-manufacturing environments.

Let's now start exploring ABC in action.

CHAPTER 8

Activity-Based Process Costing

Before you begin the detailed work of an ABC project, you must undertake some preliminary planning and background steps.

DEFINE YOUR GOALS, SCOPE, AND OBJECTIVES

Teams undertaking ABC projects vary considerably in their experience with similar techniques. All teams, however, must start with the most fundamental and most important step: clearly defining the project's goals, scope, and objectives. Throughout the course of the project, you will be basing many decisions on this definition. Is your emphasis on business processes, on product profitability, or on customer profitability? Is your objective to cost individual products, product families, specific customers, or categories of customers? Is it your objective to cost services? If so, at what level of detail? Do you want to calculate the "cost per unit" of the cost object, or do you prefer to prepare reports showing the annual costs and profitability of the cost object? The more clearly and precisely you can define what you ultimately want to cost, the more focused your project can be.

Another important task in defining your focus is this: before you begin the project, compile a list of the types of management decisions you expect to make based on the results of your project. Be sure that your scope and objectives are in synch with this list.

In addition, you should be sure to thoroughly study the systems that your company uses at present to support the organization's processes and the systems employed for calculating costs. This step is important to make sure that all members of your multi-disciplinary team have a common understanding of the architecture underlying the current cost information.

(*Note*: Chapter 11 addresses a variety of additional issues that may or may not apply to individual teams' needs and concerns. Particularly if your team is relatively new to this sort of project, check ahead to that chapter for more detail on some of the implementation steps.)

The organization of a typical company's financial records reflects two dimensions:

1. the categories of cost required for external reporting; and
2. the organizational units incurring the cost.

Costs are accumulated in a company's general ledger. To enter any cost into this ledger, the entry must specify both of these two dimensions (i.e., the account and the organizational unit).

As emphasized earlier in this book, you need a process/activity view of costs, rather than this account/cost-center view, to cost objects on an activity basis. The first major step in activity-based costing, then, is to reorganize the general ledger costs to a process-activity orientation.

SPECIFY THE ACTIVITIES: CONNECTING BUSINESS PROCESS ANALYSIS AND ACTIVITY-BASED COSTING

In activity-based costing, costs flow from their general ledger organization to activities, then from activities to cost objects.

Based on your intended use of the information, you will need to consider many factors in specifying the activities. Rather than identify all these factors now, we will point out and illustrate how activity definition affects later steps in the ABC technique. After we have built the context for these considerations in this chapter, we will summarize them for you in Chapter 11 dealing with implementation issues.

There are two basic approaches for specifying the activities. Using one instead of the other depends upon whether or not you are building your ABC work on a foundation of a business process analysis. We will discuss each of these cases separately.

Building on Business Process Analysis

If you have already performed a business process analysis, then the activities (as defined for that BPA) should be the starting point to specify the activities for your activity-based costing. Typically, though, the definition of activities required for an effective business process analysis is more detailed than that required for calculating costs of products or other cost objects. In fact, it is important that your product costing techniques be no more detailed than necessary.

To find the appropriate level of detail for the business process analysis and for the activity-based costing, you may want to group some of the BPA activities together for purposes of doing the ABC work. If you decide to combine these activities, you will actually need to make two separate decisions. One is the composition of the group; the other is whether to perform the groupings (i.e., which activities to combine into the activity pools) before or after costing the activities. The major factor to consider in making this second decision is your assessment of how valuable the detailed activity cost information could be for you in your ongoing efforts to manage the process.

Exhibits 8-1 and 8-2 are based on a case in which a business process analysis is underway. The process depicted here is *material handling*—a process bounded from the time the material is received until it is issued to a production or a sales order. All of the work (except for the inspection activity) is performed within a single department—namely, the Receiving and Stores Department. (Personnel from the Quality Assurance Department perform this inspection activity.) Activities and cycle times have been identified, but the costs have not been calculated for the activities within the process. Exhibit 8-2 shows the general ledger accounts and amounts for the Receiving and Stores Department and for the Quality Assurance Department. Exhibit 8-1 shows the activities and relative times for the process.

In the analysis that we will develop as this chapter progresses, we will cost separately each of the activities in the material handling process in this example. That level of detail will allow us to illustrate how to develop cost-based activity models for the business process analysis. (In the BPA chapters, we illustrated only headcount-based activity models.) However, that level of detail is more refined than necessary for calculating product costs. We, therefore, will group the activities into activity cost pools before assigning them to products.

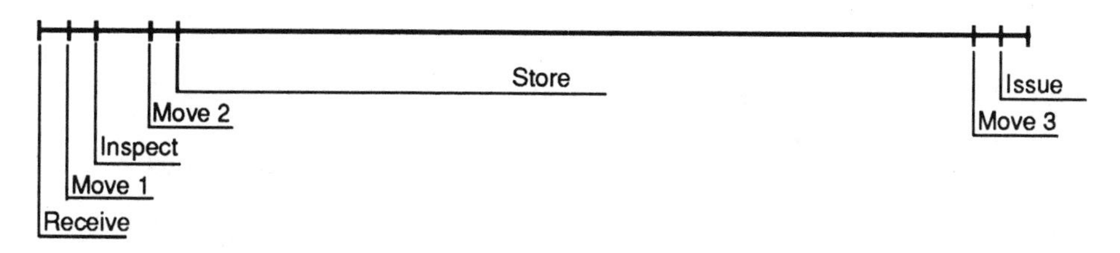

EXHIBIT 8-1. Time line for material handling process: Receipt-to-issue.

When You Do Not Have a Complete Business Process Analysis

Even though the Ernst & Young methodology strongly recommends that you perform business process analysis before launching an activity-based costing project, you may encounter situations in which that sequence is not possible. For instance, the scope of your completed BPA work may have included only those processes that had the most urgent need for improvement. Yet, all of the processes may need to be considered in order to calculate object costs. In such a case, you

	Quality Assurance	Receiving & Stores
Payroll	$ 210,000	$ 350,000
Payroll Taxes	21,000	35,000
Benefits	42,000	70,000
Travel	30,000	0
Supplies	6,000	10,000
Sub-total	$ 309,000	$ 465,000
Occupancy Charges	25,000	500,000
MIS Charges	8,000	40,000
Depreciation on Equipment	14,000	200,000
Total	$ 356,000	$1,205,000

EXHIBIT 8-2. General ledger costs for the Quality Assurance Department and for the Receiving and Stores Department.

will need to collect enough information about the remaining processes to specify the activities to use for ABC purposes.

The most effective way to collect this information is to conduct interviews with the managers of the functional areas. The purpose of these interviews is to gather enough information to identify the key services, the recipients of the services, and appropriate assignment bases. (See Chapter 11 for a list of sample questions.)

Note: These interviews are not a substitute for doing a complete BPA since they do not include validation of requirements, analyses of cycle time or root causes, or value assessment. You do, however, want to gain a thorough-enough understanding of the work in these functional areas so that the ABC architecture you design can easily accommodate future BPA expansions. This is important. After all, business process analysis rather than activity-based costing is the key technique for reducing costs. By having a broad view of the information you wish to gain from these interviews, you can avoid having to say to yourself six months later, "If only I had acknowledged even the possibility of future BPA work, I would have designed my ABC structure differently."

In the exhibit we saw earlier (Exhibit 8-1), we included all the Receiving and Stores Department's work in the material handling process. However, only a portion of the Quality Assurance Department's work relates to the material handling BPA process. By interviewing the department manager, the ABC team determined that the Quality Assurance Department actually performed multiple activities. Quality Assurance conducted the inspections for incoming material, but more importantly, the department was in the early stages of evolving to a total quality management view of its role. Some of the Quality Assurance Department personnel were working with key vendors on certification programs that would ultimately eliminate the need to inspect materials received from those vendors. Other personnel were working to reduce the variability in the output of major production processes. Still others were working on a variety of general improvement projects.

After talking with the manager of the Quality Assurance Department, the ABC project team decided to specify two activities for that department: inspection and prevention.

DEVELOP A COST FLOW ARCHITECTURE

Once you have identified the activities, you should start the process of reorganizing the classification of costs from their general ledger categories to the activity categories. You will do this in two phases of work. The first examination will be on a global level, in which you look for opportunities to compress the general ledger data. You will then build the details of a new costing architecture by examining the general ledger data on a cost-center by cost-center basis.

Global Examination

Begin with a high-level (or global) examination of the general ledger. As a preliminary step, review the entire chart of accounts. Make sure you understand the structure of the account numbering scheme as well as the contents of every account. Additionally, be sure to sketch out an organization chart based on the cost center information in the general ledger. You are likely to find differences between the functional organization chart and the one in the general ledger. The most common differences are functional areas that are separate for operational purposes but are combined for accounting purposes. You will probably find cost centers as well that have no corresponding functional manager. Typical examples of cost centers with no corresponding managers are the centers for balance sheet accounts and the ones for occupancy costs.

Once you have a clear understanding of the general ledger's structure, you are ready to begin developing the ABC cost flow architecture. We have a strong recommendation as you perform this work: Do not begin model development and do not enter data into any software package until you have completed sketching out the entire architecture. By following this advice, you should be able to avoid expensive cycles of rework. (Incidentally, one of the most expensive types of rework is intellectual rework performed by professional-level staff.)

Note Opportunities for Data Compression

Your next task is to look for opportunities to compress data. First, examine the accounts and identify any similar ones that you may want to combine for analytical purposes. For example, you may see separate accounts for various categories of employee benefits (e.g., insurance, vacations, sick pay, and payroll taxes). For activity costing purposes, you would probably want to combine these accounts. Likewise, if the company maintains travel costs in the general ledger by travel category (e.g., airfare, hotel, ground transportation, and meals), you should probably combine these accounts as well.

An important characteristic to look for in making these combinations is whether the individual accounts in the collection are typically incurred together or caused by the same factor. Finally, search to see if some accounts reflect only a trivial amount of cost. If you find such accounts, you probably want to combine them with larger accounts that represent similar cost categories.

Combine and Sequence Centers

In examining the cost-centers, you should consider two dimensions. First, examine the cost-centers in the same way you examined the accounts. Look for cost-centers that you might combine for activity costing purposes. In particular, look for cost-centers that show only a trivial amount of cost. If there are such cost-centers, assess whether there are logical reasons to combine them with other cost-centers that perform similar work.

Second, you will find it helpful to review the sequence of the cost-centers before you proceed. Since you will be examining the details of the general ledger information on a cost-center by cost-center basis, try to sequence them so that you consolidate the ones that are either functionally similar or else interact heavily with each other in performing important processes. To the extent possible, sequencing should reflect the process flow. Put the cost-centers with the largest costs on top.

Note Data Expansion Requirements

You should also question whether any account is maintained in the general ledger at such a summarized level that you should examine details from a supporting system. A typical candidate is depreciation expense. Many companies maintain depreciation at such a summarized level in the general ledger that you may want to examine the information in the Fixed Assets System to assess whether those details should be used in your ABC analysis.

Note Any Previously Made Allocations or Cross-Charges

Your final step before analyzing the general ledger information by cost-center is to examine any allocations or *cross-charges* or *cost transfers* that may have already been made. Most companies employ some form of cross-charging to reflect the cost of services provided by one cost-center to another. The level of sophistication in these cross-charging systems varies widely.

If these cross-charges have been based on actual services performed or actual demands, they are a positive contribution to the ABC effort. If, for instance, the charges for the services of a company's Computer Center or Management Information System (MIS) Department are charged to user departments based on actual CPU time usage, on dedicated storage devices, on the number of programming or report requests, or on similar measures, then that cross-charge will save you the step in your ABC work of having to decide how to charge those costs.

On the other hand, if you see large cross-charges that are truly calculated as arbitrary allocations bearing no relationship to demand for services of one department by another, be sure to flag such charges. If they are significant in amount, you would want to reverse such allocations for activity-based costing purposes. A typical example is the allocation of corporate expenses to operating divisions.

After reviewing the general ledger data in our ongoing ABC example, the project team noted the following findings:

- All of the payroll accounts (including wages, salaries, and overtime and shift premiums) have been combined into a single payroll summary account.
- All benefit accounts and travel accounts have likewise been combined into a benefit summary account and a travel summary account, respectively.
- Supplies are charged to departments based on actual requisitions.
- MIS costs are charged based on a formula that reflects actual demands or usage.
- Occupancy costs are charged to departments based on square footage of space occupied.
- Depreciation on capital assets is charged to departments based on data in the Fixed Assets System associating each capital asset with a custodial department.

After making this global assessment, the ABC project team decided that the use of summary accounts would be their only global change to the general ledger data.

COST-CENTER BY COST-CENTER EXAMINATION

You are now ready to begin the next step in performing activity-based costing—namely, examining the general ledger data by looking at the costs in the individual cost-centers. The main objective of performing this examination is to specify the rules for assigning costs to the activities. You will recall that the preferential sequence for cost assignment is:

- Direct assignment.
- Assignment on an activity or causal basis.
- Volume-based allocation.

Identify Candidates for Direct Charging of Costs

The first thing to question in an individual cost-center is whether there are costs dedicated to particular activities and/or particular products (or other cost objects). Examples of typical direct charge candidates are:

1. Costs that can be charged directly to processes/activities, such as:
   - depreciation;
   - maintenance;
   - process engineering;
   - supervision;
   - tools/tooling;
   - in-line inspection;
   - dedicated material handling; and
   - any dedicated human resources.
2. Costs that can be charged directly to products or product families, such as:
   - scrap;
   - dedicated tooling;
   - warranty cost;

- product engineering; and
- commissions.

Note: If costs are identified as directly chargeable to a product (or other cost object), you must decide whether you want to associate them as well with processes/activities. If you want your process costs to reflect the full costs of the process, you will want to count the cost as part of the process and tag it for direct assignment to the product.

A Comment on the Example

After reviewing the costs in the quality assurance and the receiving and stores cost-centers, the project team identified two direct charge candidates:

1. All travel expenses for the Quality Assurance Department were associated with the vendor certification program for a particular purchased part. All of these expenses, therefore, should be reflected in the prevention activity and tagged for direct assignment to the part as well.
2. After scanning the fixed assets records for the depreciation expense, the project team determined that all of the depreciation expense for the quality assurance cost-center was associated with equipment used to test incoming materials. All of it, therefore, should be charged to the inspection activity pool.

Review Remaining Costs for Assignment to Activity Cost Pools

Your next step is to review costs that cannot be directly charged to products. You must also determine a basis for assigning each of them to activities. The bases used to assign costs from the general ledger to activity cost pools are called *resource drivers.*

Note regarding terminology: The sentence above is our introduction to the technical use of the term "driver." A driver is a basis for cost assignment. Recall the theme from the previous section: "Resources are consumed by activities and activities are performed for products or other objects." The terminology for ABC is based on that theme. A "resource driver" is the basis used to assign costs from their general ledger orientation to activities (or, more precisely, to "activity cost pools"). As you will see in our next chapter, an *activity driver* is the term used to describe the basis for assigning costs from an activity cost pool to products or other cost objects.)*

You should consider two major characteristics when you specify resource drivers. First, a resource driver must bear a logical relationship to its activity. Second, you must have available (or be able to collect) statistics allowing you to associate the costs with the activities. Typical resource drivers include:

- Headcount;
- Square footage;
- Kilowatt hours;
- Number of terminals; and
- Managerial estimates of relative effort.

---

* So much inconsistent terminology developed as ABC techniques evolved that standardization of terms became important for clear communication. The CAM-I CMS project has published a glossary for activity-based costing with the intent to eliminate much of this inconsistency. Except for our use of the term "root cause," the language used in this book to describe the techniques of ABC are consistent with the CAM-I CMS Glossary.

	Quality Assurance		Receiving & Stores	
Payroll	$ 210,000	Headcount	$ 350,000	Headcount
Payroll Taxes	21,000	Headcount	35,000	Headcount
Benefits	42,000	Headcount	70,000	Headcount
Travel	30,000	Direct	0	Headcount
Supplies	6,000	Headcount	10,000	Headcount
Sub-total	$ 309,000		$ 465,000	
Occupancy Charges	25,000	Headcount	500,000	Sq. footage
MIS Charges	8,000	Headcount	40,000	No. of terminals
Depreciation on Equipment	14,000	Direct	200,000	Sq. footage
Total	$ 356,000		$1,205,000	

EXHIBIT 8-3. Identification of resource drivers for the Quality Assurance Department and the Receiving and Stores Department.

In Exhibit 8-3, we have added a notation for the resource drivers for each cost in the quality assurance cost-center and the receiving and stores cost-center.

COLLECT THE INFORMATION ABOUT THE RESOURCE DRIVERS

Once you have specified the resource drivers, you need to collect information about the quantity of each resource driver associated with each of the activities you want to cost. For example, if you specify headcount as the basis for assigning cost to activities, then you need to collect information about the number of people engaged in each of the activities. (The technical name we use for these quantities is the *resource consumption factor.*)

Exhibit 8-4 shows the resource consumption factors for the quality assurance cost-center and for the receiving and stores cost-center.

Quality Assurance

Activity	Headcount
Inspection	4
Prevention	3
Total	7

Receiving & Stores

Activity	Headcount	Sq. Feet	No. of Terminals
Receive	4	1000	2
Move-1	2		
Move-2	1		
Store	4	15000	2
Move-3	1		
Issue	2	750	1
Total	14	16750	5

EXHIBIT 8-4. Resource consumption factors

COST THE PROCESS/ACTIVITY

Assigning costs from the general ledger to activity cost pools is now mechanical. First, calculate a costing rate for each cost category. (We call this the *resource costing rate.*) In our example, for instance, the resource costing rate for personnel and supplies in the receiving and stores cost-center is $33,214.29 ($465,000 in costs divided by the total headcount in the cost-center of 14 FTEs).

Exhibit 8-5 shows the calculation of the resource costing rates for both the quality assurance and the receiving and stores cost-centers. Exhibit 8-6 shows the results of assigning the costs to the activities. Each figure was calculated by multiplying the resource costing rate times the companion resource consumption factor. For instance, in the Receiving and Stores Department, the amount of personnel and supplies cost assigned to the receive activity ($132,857) is based on the resource costing rate of $33,214.29 per FTE, and on the fact that there are four FTEs in the department that perform the receive activity.

If you are conducting this work of costing the activities as part of a business process analysis, you now have the information you need to develop the activity model for the process. Exhibit 8-7 shows the activity model for the process of material handling—from receipt to issue.

CONCLUSION

Completing activity-based process costing is a significant milestone in an ABC project. As a result of this work, you can see the complete costs of your business processes. Particularly for business processes that cross organizational boundaries, or for activities that share resources within or between departments, the activity-based costs can be eye-opening. Even in organiza-

Quality Assurance

	Amount	Resource Drivers	Total Factors	Resource Costing Rate
	(a)		(b)	(a/b)
All costs except travel,& depr	$ 312,000	Headcount	7	$44,571
Depreciation on Equipment	30,000	Direct		
Travel	14,000	Direct		
Total	$ 356,000			

Receiving & Stores

	Amount	Resource Driver	Total Factors	Resource Costing Rate
	(a)		(b)	(a/b)
Personnel & supplies	$ 465,000	Headcount	14	$33,214
Occupancy & Depreciation	700,000	Sq.Ft	16750	42
MIS Charges	40,000	# Terminals	5	8,000
Total	$1,205,000			

EXHIBIT 8-5. Calculation of resource costing rates for the Quality Assurance Department and for the Receiving and Stores Department.

Activity Costs

Quality Assurance Department

	Inspection	Prevention	
All costs except travel & depr	$ 178,286	$ 133,714	
Travel		30,000	(Part-1)
Depr on Equipment	14,000		
Total	$ 192,286	$ 163,714	

Activity Costs

Receiving & Stores Dept

	Receive	Move-1	Move-2	Store	Move-3	Issue
Personnel & suppl's	132,857	66,429	33,214	132,857	33,214	66,429
Occupancy & Depr	41,791			626,866		31,343
MIS charges	16,000			16,000		8,000
Total	190,648	66,429	33,214	775,723	33,214	105,772

EXHIBIT 8-6. Reorganization of costs from general ledger organization to activity organization.

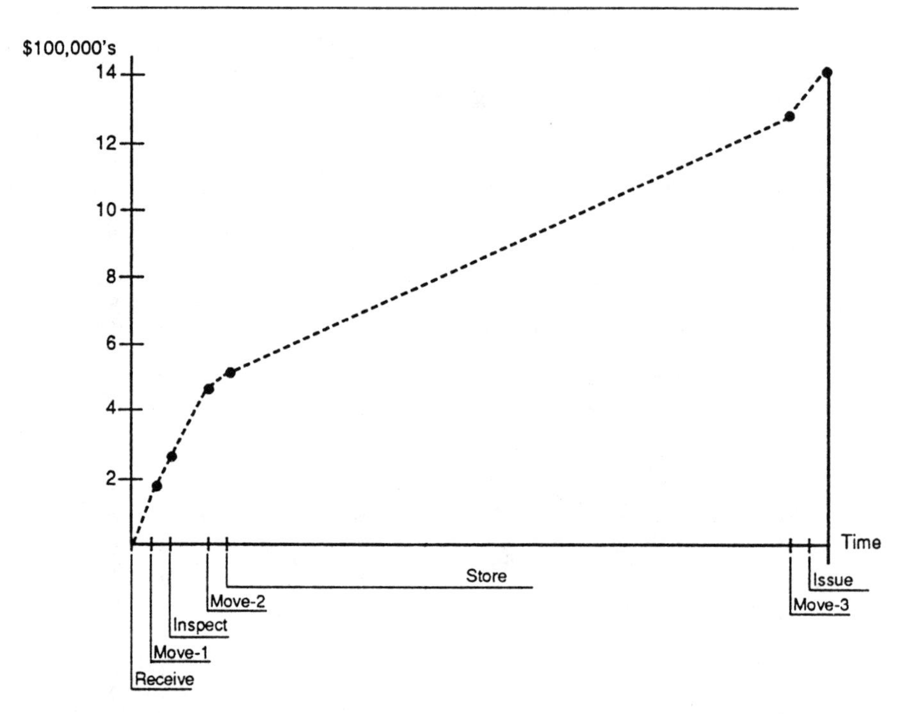

EXHIBIT 8-7. Material Handling Process: cycle time/cost profile

tions whose major ABC objective is product costing or object costing, we have never failed to see managers interpret the activity-based process costs as important, action-inspiring information.

CHAPTER 9

Activity-Based Object Costing

Once you have completed costing the activities by means of activity-based process costing, you are ready to begin the technique of assigning costs to products or other objects. The steps to go from activity-based process costing to *activity-based object costing* include the following:

- Forming the activity cost pools;
- Specifying the activity drivers;
- Gathering the data;
- Performing the calculations; and
- Presenting and interpreting the results.

We will discuss the "how-to's" for each of these steps in turn.

FORMING THE ACTIVITY COST POOLS

As mentioned in the previous chapter, the level of detail that is appropriate for activity-based process costing may be finer than you need for costing objects. You may want to consolidate some of your activities into more aggregated activity cost pools before you go further with your ABC project. (Again, we will make the recommendation here already made in our previous discussion on activity-based process costing: Avoid unnecessary cycles of rework in your project, be sure to sketch out your entire architecture for activity-based object costing before you actually begin making calculations and entering data into any database.)

Here are some factors to consider when making decisions about consolidating activities.

You will be using an activity driver to assign costs from each activity pool to objects. You need to define each activity pool with an eye to possible bases for later assigning the costs to objects.

Activities that have the same root cause are likely candidates for consolidating. You will achieve greater flexibility to move between analyzing costs and developing plans to actually reduce the costs if you combine only activities with the same root cause.

Identify all categories that you want to use for displaying your object costs, and do not combine any activities that belong in different categories. We recommend, for instance, that you not combine value-added activities and non-value-added activities into a single pool—even if you later assign them to products using identical assignment bases. We make this recommendation because it is informative to see the separation between value-added and non-value-added costs at the object level. It's also a good idea not to combine activities that are allowable product costs under GAAP with ones that are not allowable. Most ABC analyses include a comparison of the ABC costs with the company's traditional costs. To do an apples-to-apples comparison, you will need to be able to calculate a sub-total for your ABC product cost that includes only the costs allowable by GAAP. For instance, you would want to keep separate activity pools for production costs vis-à-vis the costs of distributing finished goods. Similarly, in an insurance environment, you would not want to combine claims costs with administrative costs.

Examine the results of the activity-based process costing to locate any activities that reflect a relatively insignificant cost. If any such activities exist, consider combining them with related activities.

> *Example*: In this chapter, we will continue using the example we developed in the previous chapter. In that example, we analyzed the costs in two departments (the Receiving and Stores Department and the Quality Assurance Department), and we organized the costs into eight activities (the seven activities from the business process analysis: Receive, Move-1, Inspect, Move-2, Store, Move-3, and Issue plus an activity for the Prevention work of the Quality Assurance Department).
>
> After reviewing the activity-based process costs, the project team decided that the activities were more detailed than necessary for calculating product costs. They, therefore, grouped the activities into four activity cost pools before assigning them to products. Exhibit 9-1 shows the grouping from the business process analysis. The Receive, Move-1, Inspect, and Move-2 activities were grouped together into a *receiving pool*. It was believed that the receiving of materials initiated this whole set of activities. Move-3 and Issue are grouped together into an *issue pool*. It was believed that the issuing of materials to orders initiated this pair of activities. Storage remained as a separate activity, as did Prevention. Exhibit 9-2 shows the consolidation of costs based on this grouping.*

---

* To keep the example simple, we will complete the product costing as though the costs in the Quality Assurance Department and the Receiving and Stores Department represent all the company's overhead costs.

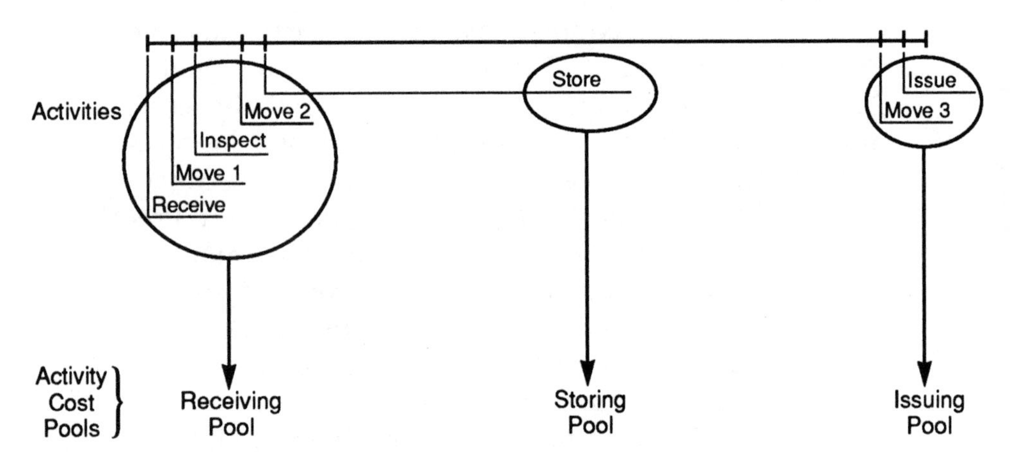

EXHIBIT 9-1. Grouping of activities into activity cost pools.

Product Information about Our Example

The company in our example makes four products. (Again, we have simplified the environment to present a complete example.) Exhibit 9-3 shows the bills of material for the prod-

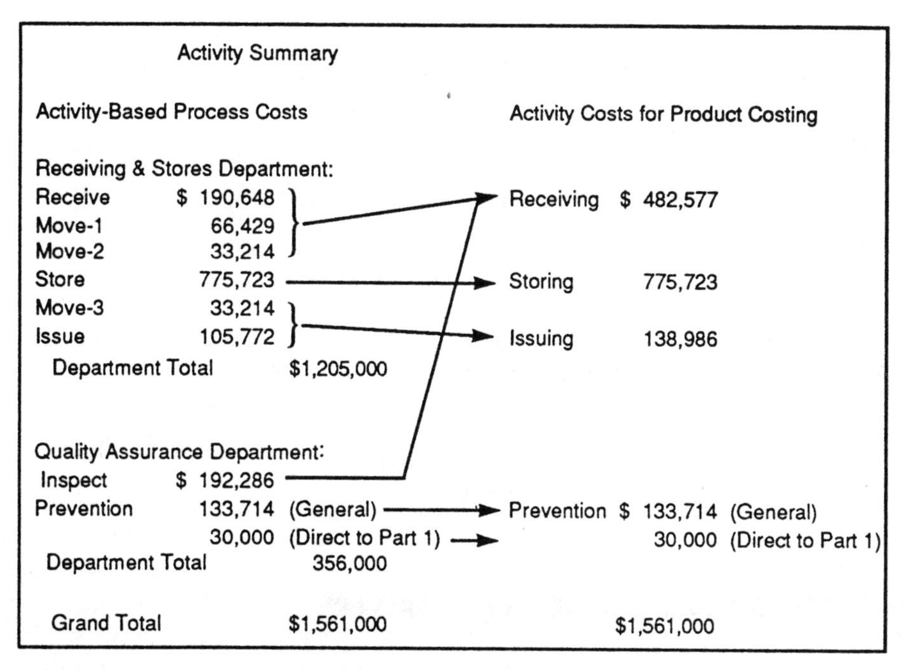

EXHIBIT 9-2. Consolidating activities for activity-based product costing.

ucts' component parts. The numbers in parentheses indicate the total annual production of the four products. For instance, total annual production of FG-1 is 1,000,000. The horizontal lines indicate components. FG-1, for instance, is assembled from two purchased parts (Part-1 and Part-3). The numbers to the right of the horizontal line indicate how many of the components are needed to make one of the finished goods. In our example, the manufacture of one FG-1 requires one Part-1 and two Part-3s.

Here are some general comments about the products:

- FG-1 and FG-4 are both high-volume products that the company makes on an almost constant schedule.
- FG-2 and FG-3 are low-volume products that are made as needed to satisfy specific customer orders.
- FG-2 uses the same components that are used in the high-volume products.
- FG-3, on the other hand, is made from components that are unique to that product.

Later analyses will show the implications of these characteristics on the products' costs.

SPECIFYING THE ACTIVITY DRIVERS

The second step to object costing is specifying the *activity drivers*. An activity driver is the basis used to assign costs from activity cost pools to cost objects. One of the factors that you had to consider in forming the activity cost pools was whether you could think of activity drivers that might be appropriate for the pool. By the time you reach the step of "specifying the activity driver for each cost pool," you have already given preliminary thought to possible drivers.

There are three critical characteristics for an activity driver:

1. An activity driver should reflect the demand that one object places on the activity relative to other objects.

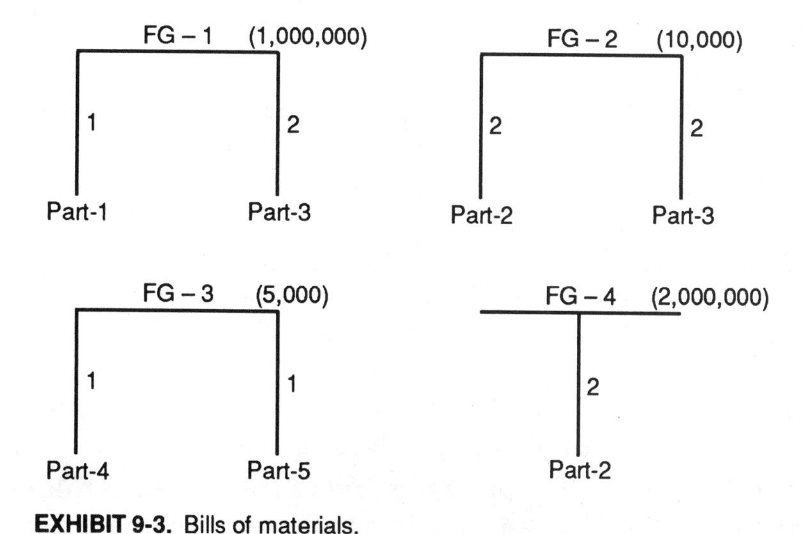

EXHIBIT 9-3. Bills of materials.

2. It should be reflective of or correlated to the root cause.
3. Quantifying the activity driver must be both possible and practical.

The following are some tips that may help you select activity drivers that have these characteristics.

Tip #1—Resist the temptation to name something as an activity driver just because related data is available. Always ask the question, "Does any one cost object require more of this activity than another—and if so, why?"

In one instance, an insurance company was performing an ABC analysis. The ABC team first proposed that "salaries for claims processing" be assigned to cost objects (in this case, different types of insurance policies) based on the "number of claims." But the claims manager argued that there was a very high level of variability in the amount of time required by different claims. The team developed a formula for classifying each claim's level of difficulty. The formula included such factors as the type of claim, the medium of submission (paper or electronic), and whether the claim was from an individual or an institution. The "weighted" number of claims was then used as the activity driver.

In Chapter 7, we mentioned a project in which we worked with a client to analyze processes and to cost products. Moving material within the plant represented a significant amount of overhead cost. We first imagined that a simple and logical activity driver in this situation would be the number of "move" transactions. The team, however, decided not to jump so fast. Once the team identified root causes through business process analysis, the client concluded that the root cause of excessive material movement was different in the fabrication half of the plant than in the assembly half.

Based on the root cause analysis, the team decided to keep separate the activity cost pools for material movement in fabrication and in assembly. For the material movement-assembly pool, the "number of components" was named as the activity driver. With this driver, a product containing 100 components would be assigned twice as much material movement cost as a product containing only 50 components.

Tip #2—When considering alternative activity drivers, weigh the relative cost of collecting the data against the relative precision each would offer. In the example just described, the project team considered two possible activity drivers for the material handling-fabrication pool. One was the "total distance between operations;" the other was "the number of move transactions." Even though they considered the "distance between operations" to better capture the correlation, no data was readily available for quantifying that driver. They decided that the "number of move transactions" sufficiently reflected the dynamics, and data to support it was readily available. This was an example of using a *surrogate driver* (i.e., a driver that adequately models the relationship even though it is not the root cause).

Exhibit 9-4 shows a sample of activity drivers that were considered during an ABC project with one client. As shown in the exhibit, the project team assessed each proposed activity driver on four criteria before they selected the specific ones they would use.

Tip #3—As your project team is making decisions about activity drivers, be sure you get input from people directly involved in the activities. Involve those people even if they are not permanent members of the team.

For example, we are aware of one company's ABC team that used personnel from accounting and manufacturing departments to help name activity drivers for some of the engineering cost pools. The team had been relying on a generic list of typical activity drivers that they had seen in a business publication. None of the typical drivers seemed to fit. When one team member asked a buddy in the engineering department about data availability, he discovered that this department tracked all its work using PC-based project management systems. There was a wealth of information very valuable to the ABC project already maintained at the department level and separate from the corporate data sys-

Possible Activity Drivers	Relates to Root Causes	Easy to Measure	Data Availability	Quantifiable
Distance between operations	3	3	4	5
Number of moves	4	3	4	4
Number of vehicles	2	5	5	5
Direct-labor hours	2	5	5	5
Available machine hours	4	4	4	4
Number of units produced	3	5	5	5
Number of good units produced	4	4	4	4
Budgeted machine hours	3	4	4	4
Number of inspections	3	2	3	2
Number of reworked units	2	2	2	2
Number of engineering changes	3	3	3	2
Number of parts to assemble	5	4	4	4
Number of rejected units	3	2	2	3

******Ratings range from 1 to 5, lowest to highest*

EXHIBIT 9-4. Activity driver selection criteria.

tems. In fact, searching for the best activity drivers is sometimes a bit like a treasure hunt. Good data often turns up in department-level or private files. Only by soliciting information about available data from the people actually engaged in the day-to-day work will you discover these sources of information.

What If You Have Activity Pools with No Natural Drivers?

You may end up with an activity cost pool for which you cannot specify an activity driver that clearly captures the relationship between the activity costs and the objects. If the objective of your project is to assign all costs to objects, then you may have to use some general-level basis for assigning the costs of that pool.

Early in our discussion of ABC, when we stated the conceptual objectives of activity-based costing, we outlined a hierarchy for assigning costs to objects. The first preference for assigning costs is *direct charging*. The second preference is to assign costs on some basis that indicates the level of service provided. The technique of *last resort* is volume-based allocation. When companies begin ABC costing projects, they usually have costing systems in which 100 percent of the overhead cost is assigned to objects using volume-based allocation (e.g., labor hours or sales revenue). In successful ABC projects, the percentage of overhead cost assigned through volume-based allocation can often be reduced to no more than five or 10 percent.

Full Costing Debate

In fact, accounting theorists debate whether costs that cannot be associated either directly or through an activity basis should be assigned to objects at all. One can make a strong argument for eliminating such costs from low-level objects and assigning them only at higher levels (e.g., product family or facility levels). The flip side of this argument is that ABC costs are most often used for intermediate-term decisions (e.g., pricing

Activity Cost Pool	*Activity Driver*
Receiving	Number of Receipt Transactions
Storing	Weighted Factor Including: Average Value of Inventory and Days' Supply
Issuing	Number of Issue Transactions
Prevention	Standard Labor Cost

EXHIBIT 9-5. Activity drivers used for assigning costs to products.

or planning the composition of a product line), and full costs are often preferable for such decisions. The choice that is appropriate for any particular situation will differ depending on the nature of the costs and the planned use of your ABC results.

Specifying the Activity Drivers for Our Example

We have four activity cost pools in the example we've been discussing. Exhibit 9-5 shows the activity drivers that will be used for assigning the costs to products.

Each of these activity drivers requires separate comment.

Receiving The costs of the *receiving activity* will be assigned to products based on the number of receipt transactions processed. Note that all the items received into the Receiving and Stores Department are purchased parts. Finished goods are not received into this warehouse.

Storing Within the *storing activity* are costs of housing, insuring, periodically counting, and generally protecting the inventory. The days' supply figure was taken from the company's "Obsolete and Slow-moving Inventory Report." It indicates how many days' worth of requirements would be covered by the current inventory level. Note that as in the receiving activity, all of the items stored in the Receiving and Stores Department are purchased parts.

Issuing The costs of the issuing activity will be assigned based on the number of issue transactions. An *issue transaction* indicates that materials are removed from storage in order to manufacture or assemble them into a finished good. The costs of the issuing activity will be assigned to the finished goods to which the material is issued.

Prevention The *prevention activity* represented a great variety of work, none of which was significant enough in cost to warrant further breakdown. Other than the travel cost that has already been earmarked (in the previous chapters) for charging directly to Part-1, the costs of the prevention activity will be allocated based on standard labor cost.

In this example then, $1,427,286 (or approximately 91.5 percent of the total overhead cost) will be assigned to products by direct charging or through activity-based assignment. The other 8.5 percent of the total overhead cost ($133,714) will be allocated on a volume basis. (The company previously had charged all overhead to product on the basis of labor cost.)

GATHERING THE DATA

Once you have finalized an activity driver for each activity cost pool, you then need to collect or develop data about each activity driver for each object. If, for instance, you have named "Number of Customer Inquiries" as an activity driver, you must then gather the information about how many customer inquiries there are for each object. (The technical name we use for these statistics is *activity consumption factors*.)

You may need to employ a variety of sources and techniques to gather the data. Data about *transaction counts* can often be extracted and summarized from the *transaction history files* that are a standard component of many computer systems. In other cases, you may need to develop the statistics by taking samples, making forecasts, or developing some specialized reports. This is especially true if you define any weighted factors. In our example, for instance, the activity driver for the storing activity was defined as a weighted factor that reflected both the average inventory levels and how quickly inventory moved through the system.

Keep in mind that the objective is to gather data that "fairly represent" the demands that one object makes on each activity relative to the other objects. Try to keep the data gathering as simple as possible. Opt for simplicity over excess precision. Sampling is often a cost-effective technique for estimating the required data.

Exhibit 9-6 shows the activity consumption factors for our example. In gathering the data, the team admitted that the days' supply figure was from a report that really showed only a snapshot of a single point in time rather than an average profile over the entire year. After running the report, they showed it to the manager in the Receiving and Stores Department and asked if the numbers felt "representative or typical," and the manager agreed that they did. The team decided to use the figures directly from the report rather than to define a much more complex formula that would approximate an annual average.

This example is typical of the decisions that have to be made during the data-gathering step. Many times a team will be able to define data collection methods where the extra precision in the data may not be worth the extra costs required to collect it. When such a situation arises, often the best solution is to use the less expensive data unless you can prove that it truly introduces significant distortion into the costing.

	No. of Receipt Transactions	Average Inventory	Days' Supply	No. of Issue Transactions	Standard Labor Cost
FG-1				100	$ 0.50
FG-2				30	0.15
FG-3				25	0.15
FG-4				125	0.20
Part-1	50	$ 22,500	3		
Part-2	125	66,000	2		
Part-3	25	40,000	6		
Part-4	15	3,500	18		
Part-5	10	2,000	25		

EXHIBIT 9-6. Activity consumption factors.

PERFORMING THE CALCULATIONS

Before you begin to actually assign costs to objects, you need to finalize your decisions about how to structure the calculations:

- Is it your intention to calculate a cost-per-unit of each object? Or is your emphasis total annual cost?
- Do you want to calculate any categories of sub-totals, and, if so, what groupings of cost categories do you want to make?
- If your focus is product costing, how much of the value-chain do you want to include?
- Is your emphasis only on the production costs or do you need to include the engineering costs and sales and marketing costs as well?

It is important to finalize these sorts of decisions before you design the actual sequence of work for costing of your objects.

In our example, we will initially calculate unit production costs. To keep the example simple, we will be combining all of the activity costs together for each product before calculating its unit cost. After you have seen the whole costing process, we will elaborate on options for presenting the results.

You now have all the data you need to assign the activity costs to products. In doing this, you will need to calculate an *activity costing rate* and then apply that rate to individual items.

Exhibit 9-7 shows the activity costing rates for the receiving and issuing activities and the percentage factors for the storing activity. For the receiving activity, for instance, the total cost is $482,577. The total number of receiving transactions is 225. The average cost per receipt, then, is $2,144.79.

Note: Another of the decisions you will need to make for your projects is how best to display the results of your calculations. On one hand, displaying the calculations to the *n*th decimal place creates an image of irrelevant precision. On the other hand, rounding the numbers as you present them can create an image of faulty arithmetic. Whatever decision you make about presenting the numbers, be sure that you do no rounding in your actual calculations of the numbers. Rounding errors can compound in an ABC project to such an extent

Receiving Costs

		No. of Receipts	ABC Cost
$ 482,577	Part 1	50	$ 107,239
	Part 2	125	268,098
	Part 3	25	53,620
	Part 4	15	32,172
	Part 5	10	21,448
	Total	225	$ 482,577

Activity Costing Rate: $ 2,144.79

Storing Costs

		Avg. Value	Days' Supply	Weight	Percent	ABC Cost
$ 775,723						
	Part 1	$ 22,500	3	67,500	12.22%	$ 94,772
	Part 2	66,000	2	132,000	23.89%	185,331
	Part 3	40,000	6	240,000	43.44%	336,966
	Part 4	3,500	18	63,000	11.40%	88,453
	Part 5	2,000	25	50,000	9.05%	70,201
			Total	552,500	100.00%	$ 775,723

Issuing Costs

		No. of Issues	ABC Cost
$ 138,986	FG 1	100	$ 49,638
	FG 2	30	14,891
	FG 3	25	12,409
	FG 4	125	62,047
	Total	280	$ 138,986

Activity Costing Rate: $ 496.38

EXHIBIT 9-7. Activity costing rates and assignments

that validating the accuracy of the work can become a real problem.

After you have calculated the activity costing rates, stop for a moment and evaluate the managerial usefulness of these numbers. They are not merely intermediate calculations on the journey to product cost. Particularly for activities that are related to transactions, reporting and monitoring the cost per transaction over time can be extremely valuable. In our example, for instance, the fact that the company averages spending over $2,000 every time a shipment of raw materials is received is valuable information for management. These activity costing rates also provide the foundation needed to change a company's performance measurement system and budgeting practices to an activity basis.

Once the activity costing rate has been calculated, it is applied to each individual object by multiplying it times the activity consumption factor for that object. In our example, the amount of receiving costs assigned to Part-1 ($107,239) was calculated by multipying the activity costing rate ($2,114.79) times the 50 receipt transactions that were processed for Part-1.

After you have calculated the costs for each product and for each activity, you will need to sum the activities to get a total for each product. Exhibit 9-8 shows the total ABC overhead costs for each item. It also has divided that total by the annual usage of the item to get a cost per unit.

CALCULATING THE COST OF A HIGHER-LEVEL ITEM

If you are costing products in a retail or distribution environment, calculating this unit cost may complete the process of

Total ABC Overhead Costs							
	Receiving	Storing	Issuing	Prevention	Total	Annual Usage	Cost Per Unit
Part 1	$ 107,239	$ 94,772		$ 30,000	$ 232,011	1,000,000	$ 0.23
Part 2	268,098	185,331			453,429	4,020,000	0.11
Part 3	53,620	336,966			390,586	2,020,000	0.19
Part 4	32,172	88,453			120,625	5,000	24.13
Part 5	21,448	70,201			91,649	5,000	18.33
FG-1			49,638		49,638	1,000,000	0.05
FG-2			14,891		14,891	10,000	1.49
FG-3			12,409		12,409	5,000	2.48
FG-4			62,047		62,047	2,000,000	0.03
Total	$ 482,577	$ 775,723		$ 138,985	$ 30,000	$1,427,285	

EXHIBIT 9-8. Total ABC overhead costs.

determining the overhead cost of a product. On the other hand, if you are calculating costs of higher-level items, then you must still complete a "cost rollup" in which the cost of each item reflects the costs of its components plus the costs of converting or assembling those components into the finished product. A cost rollup may also be necessary to cost other higher-level objects such as a product or service family or a segment of customers.

Once you have calculated the ABC unit costs, you can include those costs in the cost rollup using exactly the same logic that is used for the other cost elements in the rollup. Exhibit 9-9 shows the calculation of total costs for the four finished goods produced in our example company. Let's walk through the calculation of cost for FG-1.

- FG-1 is made from two components. Each FG-1 requires one Part-1 and two Part-3s.
- The material cost of a Part-1 is $2.25. We have just finished calculating the ABC overhead cost of a Part-1 to be $0.23.
- The material cost of an individual Part-3 is $3.00. Since FG-1 requires two Part-3s, the material cost of the Part-3s used to make an FG-1 is $6.00. Likewise, the ABC overhead cost of a Part-3 was calculated to be $0.193, and the ABC overhead costs of the Part-3s used to make an FG-1 is $0.39.
- The labor cost to assemble the components into the finished product is $0.50 per unit.
- The unit cost of the ABC overhead calculated for FG-1 was $0.05. You will recall that the one element of overhead that was not assigned through an ABC technique was the cost of the general prevention activities of the Quality Assurance Department. Those costs have now been assigned to the finished product based on the labor cost to make the product.

Activity-Based Costing

		Materials	Labor	ABC Overhead	Labor-Based Overhead	Total	FG Total
FG-1	Conversion		0.50	0.05	0.07	0.62	
	Part 1 (1)	2.25		0.23		2.48	
	Part 3 (2)	6.00		0.39		6.39	
	Total	8.25	0.50	0.67	0.07		$ 9.49
FG-2	Conversion		0.15	1.49	0.02	1.66	
	Part 2 (2)	6.00		0.23		6.23	
	Part 3 (2)	6.00		0.39		6.39	
	Total	12.00	0.15	2.10	0.02		$ 14.27
FG-3	Conversion		0.15	2.48	0.02	2.65	
	Part 4 (1)	3.50		24.13		27.63	
	Part 5 (1)	4.00		18.33		22.33	
	Total	7.50	0.15	44.94	0.02		$ 52.61
FG-4	Conversion		0.20	0.03	0.03	0.26	
	Part 2 (2)	6.00		0.23		6.23	
	Total	6.00	0.20	0.26	0.03		$ 6.49

EXHIBIT 9-9. ABC cost calculations for each of the finished goods.

We then calculate a total for each cost element:

Materials:	$8.25
Labor:	0.50
Overhead Applied through ABC Techniques:	0.67
Overhead Applied, Based on Labor Costs:	0.07
Total Production Cost of One FG-1:	$9.49

PRESENTING AND INTERPRETING THE RESULTS

One of the most important aspects of the process of converting to ABC is to make sure all the project team members thoroughly understand the results of the cost calculation, and then organize the findings in such a way that they can be used in key management decisions.

One of the first things a team usually does with the new ABC cost calculations is to compare them to the traditional costs and summarize the key differences.

For our example, Exhibit 9-10 shows the "traditional" cost calculation for each of the four finished goods. The differences between the costs calculated using ABC techniques and ones using the traditional techniques are typical of the dynamics many companies discover when they conduct their first ABC project. Exhibit 9-11 displays those differences.

The low-volume products (FG-2 and FG-3) are undercosted in the traditional system. They require much more overhead support than had previously been reflected in their costs. The most seriously distorted case is FG-3. Not only is FG-3 a low-volume product, but it is made from components that are unique to that product. The high-volume products (FG-1 and FG-4) have been, in effect, subsidizing the low-volume products; as a result, they were overcosted in the traditional system. The degree of error for high-volume products depends largely on how much they are subsidizing the low-volume products.

Traditional Costing						
		Materials	Labor	Overhead	Total	FG Total
FG-1	Conversion		0.50	0.87	1.37	
	Part 1 (1)	2.25			2.25	
	Part 3 (2)	6.00			6.00	
Total		8.25	0.50	0.87		$ 9.62
FG-2	Conversion		0.15	0.26	0.41	
	Part 2 (2)	6.00			6.00	
	Part 3 (2)	6.00			6.00	
Total		12.00	0.15	0.26		$12.41
FG-3	Conversion		0.15	0.26	0.41	
	Part 4 (1)	3.50			3.50	
	Part 5 (1)	4.00			4.00	
Total		7.50	0.15	0.26		$ 7.91
FG-4	Conversion		0.20	0.35	0.55	
	Part 2 (2)	6.00			6.00	
Total		6.00	0.20	0.35		$ 6.55

EXHIBIT 9-10. Traditional costs calculations for each of the finished goods.

	Trad Cost	ABC Cost	Difference
FG-1	$ 9.62	$ 9.49	$ 0.13
FG-2	12.41	14.27	-1.86
FG-3	7.91	52.61	-44.7
FG-4	6.55	6.49	0.06

EXHIBIT 9-11. The difference between traditional cost calculations and ABC cost calculations.

ABC IN NON-MANUFACTURING ENVIRONMENTS

In Chapter 7, we mentioned that activity-based costing is properly applied to cost many different types of objects: services, customers, geographic regions, lines of business, and channels of distribution as well as products. Most of our discussion since then, however, may give the impression that ABC is used mostly for costing products. Quite the contrary: ABC is being applied just as successfully in costing services, customers, regions, and other objects of management interest.

The following discussion shows how. Keep in mind that there's no new theory here; conceptually, costing non-product objects is identical to the technique for costing products. The important decisions are:

1. defining the object; and
2. specifying the drivers, particularly the activity drivers.

Here are two examples that illustrate some of the issues involved in costing objects other than products.

Example 1—Costing Individual Customers: A company was an early implementor of ABC concepts. As a manufacturer and distributor of toiletries, this company produced high-volume mainstay products and low-volume fashion items. Its three primary types of customers were:

1. grocery store and drug store chains;
2. the large national discount chains; and
3. specialty boutiques.

It operated from a single plant and a single distribution center.

The company wanted to get a better handle on product profitability and customer profitability. The major purpose of its ABC project was to develop an analytical basis for modifying its pricing strategy. The company had always premium-priced its fashion items. However, as the discount chains made new demands for price concessions, as well as demands for packaging and delivery specifications, management began to question the accuracy of all its costs currently used in pricing decisions.

As a consequence of analyzing the various operations, management concluded that within the manufacturing facility, the different products varied greatly in how much overhead support they required. Once a product reached the distribution center, the dynamics changed. Diversity of customer requirements rather than inherent differences among the products caused the high overhead costs in the post-production activities.

The ABC project team developed the costing architecture shown in Exhibit 9-12. The team assigned overhead costs incurred within the plant to products. They assigned selling and distribution costs to customers. Costs directly charged to customers included shipping costs and sales commissions.

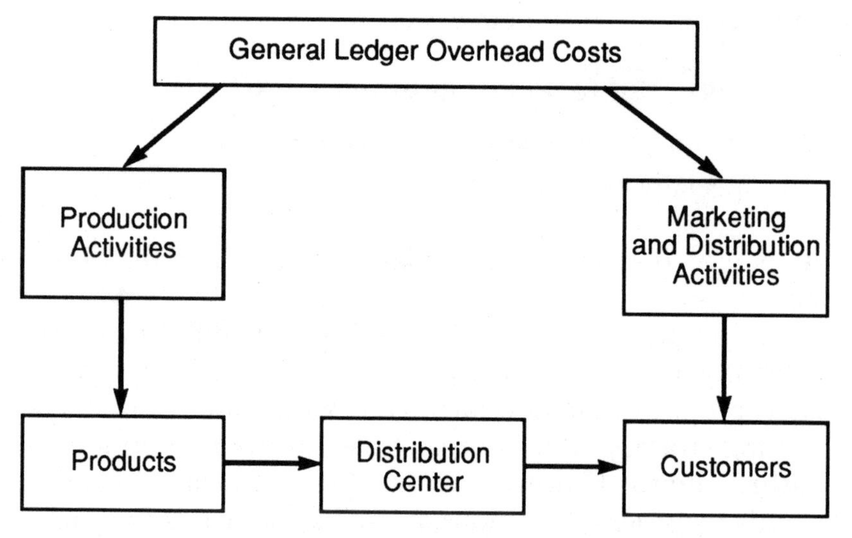

EXHIBIT 9-12. Customer costing.

Activity drivers used to assign the remaining costs to customers included such measures as:

- the number of orders;
- the number of order changes;
- the number of special packing requests;
- the number of pick tickets; and
- the number of expedite requests.

The team then calculated the total cost for each individual customer by combining:

1. the costs of the products that a specific customer purchased; and
2. the costs incurred in servicing that customer's orders.

Example 2—Costing Customer Segments: Another company, a distributor of industrial goods, used ABC to examine its costs in serving different segments of customers. The company wanted to re-evaluate its whole approach to marketing and servicing customers. The company was not so much concerned with the profitability of individual products or services; rather, it was reassessing which segments of customers it should be targeting and what levels of services it should be offering. It also wanted to give more focus to its promotion efforts by analyzing the relative profitability of the major markets it served.

The company was moving toward a close-to-the-customer strategy. It wanted to know which aspects of its current organization and infrastructure most profitably supported that strategy. Its objective in its ABC project was to analyze its costs and profitability as the foundation step to developing new strategies about its markets and services, and then to making changes in its internal structure to support the new strategy.

Defining the Costs Objects

After setting goals and objectives for the project, the first step in the ABC effort was to define objects to be costed—both the final objects and intermediate objects.

The *final objects* were defined as segments of customers, with each customer segment defined along three dimensions:

- sales volume;
- level of service; and
- industry classification.

Sales volume was organized into six categories of annual sales, and each customer was classified into one of the six categories.

The *level of service* delivered as part of the sales/service process differed significantly from one customer to another. For some customers, the sales/service representative simply visited the customer on a regular schedule; during those visits, the customer would order items as needed. In other cases, the sales/service representative interacted on a more formal level, working through the purchasing department buyers rather than through the individual consumption sites. Higher levels of service included the sales/service representative physically restocking the inventory in the customer's display units and offering product demonstrations and collaborative problem-solving services with the customer. Four "levels of service" categories were defined; again, each customer was classified into one of the four categories.

Finally, the ABC team defined the major characteristics of the industries in which their customers operated. Each customer was classified into one of the five categories. *Industry classification* schemes looked at common SIC codes and common business processes.

The ABC team thus defined a customer segment as a unique combination of sales volume category, service level category, and industry characteristics. Each customer was then classified into a particular customer segment.

SETTING THE SCOPE

The client wanted to analyze how much it "cost to serve" each of the customer segments. It, therefore, included almost all costs and key activities and processes of the business unit in the analysis. The only costs excluded were those not even indirectly related to serving customers—for example, tax accounting and financial reporting. The allocation of corporate costs to the business unit were also excluded.

THE APPROACH

Once these definitions were complete, the analytical work of the project was to organize all revenues and all costs that were within the project's scope into the previously defined customer segments. The basic logic for the analysis was to organize the costs from their general ledger format into activity cost pools and then from the activity cost pools to the customer segments.

Before the ABC team began defining the activities, the members explored with the company executives whether there might be activity-related dynamics that the executives considered particularly relevant to the strategy decisions they needed to make. One particular set of dynamics surfaced that were of major interest to the executives. In the past, the company had experienced a high level of personnel turnover among the sales/service representatives. The executives wanted a better understanding of:

- The relationship between sales/service representative turnover and customer turnover.
- The costs to recruit new sales/service representatives and to make them productive.
- The relative profitability of new and veteran representatives.
- The cost associated with a new representative becoming veteran.

ACTIVITIES

The team then defined categories of activities, with specific activities within each category. For instance, within the category of "sales/service representative activities" were such specific activities as:

- developing new customers;
- travel and waiting;
- face-to-face selling;
- replenishing stock;
- problem-solving during sales calls;
- order writing; and
- customer training.

Within the "order processing and collection-related activities" category were such specific activities as:

- customer order entry;
- accounts receivable posting—lockbox;
- accounts receivable posting—not lockbox;
- collections—internal;

- collections—outside collections agency;
- credit analysis—new customers; and
- credit analysis—existing customers.

For all activities that were performed by sales/service representatives, or which were performed to support the sales/service representatives, the ABC team defined separate cost pools for new and veteran representatives. For instance, there was a separate cost pool for "travel and waiting—new reps" and "travel and waiting—veteran reps."

DRIVERS

Once the activities had been identified, the ABC team needed to define:

1. resource drivers to convert the general ledger costs into activity cost pools; and
2. activity drivers to convert the activity cost pools into the customer segments.

The team used three basic techniques (sometimes in combination) to collect the driver data:

1. interviewing/surveys;
2. sampling; and
3. the use of existing data.

To estimate the relative effort required by different activities from the sales/service representative, a sample of sales/service representatives was selected to participate in a detailed survey. Each sales/service representative in the sample was asked to estimate the percent of time spent in each activity over the past year. Each was also asked to maintain a detailed record by customer and by activity for a period of one week. Sales managers were asked to complete a similar survey, with special emphasis on the support required by new representatives, veteran representatives, and vacant territories.

In other cases, existing data was available for such activity drivers as:

- *Customer Order Entry*: Number of customer order line items, by customer segment.
- *Accounts Receivable Posting—Lockbox*: Direct charges made by the bank for lockbox processing of accounts receivable.
- *Collections, Internal*: Number of collections on "collection status" as of a certain date.
- *Customer Support—Telephone Hotline*: Number of calls taken during a one-month period.

IMPACT OF FINDINGS

Once the ABC team had completed the calculations, the findings had far-reaching impact on the development of a new strategy for this business unit. Some of the findings and their impacts included the following results.

The accounts with small sales volume were highly unprofitable at every service level and in every industry. The strategy was revised to significantly de-emphasize all accounts that had only small sales volume potential.

The accounts with high sales volume were quite profitable, even though there was much diversity in the levels of service provided to these customers. The current strategy of diversity in service levels seemed to be effective, and no change was made to the form or the pricing of those different service levels.

Certain industries were only marginally profitable. After analyzing the composition of the activity groups, the new strategy emphasized ways to make these segments more cost-efficient.

The executives' concern about the impact of new representatives was confirmed in the ABC analysis. In fact, the impact was much more severe than originally estimated. The strategy revision included major new programs to:

1. increase the retention rate for sales/service representatives;
2. make new hires more effective more quickly;
3. further penetrate highly profitable market segments; and
4. redesign the sales and service business processes to improve quality and reduce cost.

CONCLUSION

Throughout this chapter and Chapter 8, we have covered the mechanics of activity-based Costing. In Chapter 8, we saw how to cost activities and processes, while in this chapter we've considered how to assign the costs from the activities to products or other objects. However, as we've stressed throughout this book, calculating more accurate costs does not in and of itself lead to improved financial performance. The new cost information must be incorporated into the organization's decision making. Chapter 10 illustrates ways to use the ABC results in significant managerial decisions.

CHAPTER 10

Using ABC Information

Companies typically commission ABC projects because the sponsors intuitively believe that the costs they use in making key decisions are either seriously inaccurate or altogether nonexistent. ABC project findings usually confirm the belief that distortion is not only present but is, in some instances, even worse than expected.

Once you have completed your calculations, you should turn your attention back to your key decisions and how the new cost information can affect them. The critical question is: "How do I use the results of our ABC perspective to improve the company's performance?" At the risk of stating the obvious, keep in mind that you must ultimately take action to reduce your total costs and/or increase your total revenue before the ABC project will have any effect on your bottom line.

Many people's immediate reaction to the ABC findings is to focus on the products, services, or customers that appear to be highly unprofitable and to investigate ways to remedy those problems. While it is prudent to take short-term action to deal with the most offensive situations, you shouldn't limit your action plan to addressing these particular problems. If used wisely, the ABC findings can guide a wide variety of actions—from short-term decisions about pricing or promotion to longer-term improvement projects to major decisions about your organization's infrastructure. What follows is a sampling of ways for you to utilize the results of your ABC analysis.

A CONCEPTUAL REMINDER

ABC costs are constructed with the objective of showing the "true" financial demands that a product, service, or customer places on an organization's resources. In an insurance company, for instance, the ABC analysis may show that policyholder communications for a single unit of a particular type of insurance policy cost $1. That $1 may include personnel and occupancy costs, equipment depreciation and computer services, and all other costs associated with providing the service. The costs are assigned from the activity to the policy type in a way that reflects the amount of policyholder communications required by that policy type relative to all other policy types.

In almost all cases, the ABC costs need to be interpreted as long-term, average costs. Rarely should they be interpreted as costs that vary with short-term volume.

It is appropriate to use ABC costs to:

1. gain an understanding of what causes costs in your company; and
2. assess the relative profitability of services, processes, products, customers, and so on.

It is also appropriate to use them to determine the areas most in need of improvement in your company. If, however, you begin to use the ABC costs to change the products and services you offer with an intent to reduce your overall overhead costs, you must develop a companion plan to make sure that the reductions in demand for overhead activities actually occur—and that the resources currently used to provide those activities are redeployed. In the absence of such a companion plan, the actions you take in response to the ABC findings are unlikely to have the positive effect on profitability that you seek.

DIRECT DECISIONS

The most prevalent use of ABC information is to help a company make decisions about the products and services it offers and about the markets and customers it serves. Sometimes there is a chicken-and-egg element to ABC analyses and the decisions they support. In many cases, an organization will conduct an ABC project as the basis for making a specific decision. In other cases, the organization will perform an ABC analysis because it is convinced that its current costs are seriously wrong, and one of its goals for the ABC project, therefore, is to analyze the results and determine which company decisions should change.

A typical example of the former case involved a client who manufactured two grades of the same product. The company manufactured its industrial-grade product from a more durable raw material and calibrated it to closer tolerances than the company's product intended for household use. The standard cost of the industrial-grade product was considerably higher than the standard cost for the household-grade product. The project's sponsor, however, suspected that the cost of these two products would be very close if overhead costs were calculated on more of a causal basis. The ABC project confirmed that suspicion. Based on the ABC results, the company decided to quit making the household-grade product and to sell the industrial-grade product in both markets.

Another typical example was a client who performed an ABC analysis in support of a strategic planning initiative. ABC was used to examine the costs of serving different groups of customers. The study helped management to identify profitable business segments; marketing then used the results to develop sales programs that were better targeted to different clusters of customers.

Whether conducted with a specific decision in mind or not, every ABC project we have seen has produced results that virtually demanded management attention. It is common, for instance, to discover a handful of products or services that cost many times more than their selling prices. In such a case you have to question whether you can afford to offer the product or service in the first place. Possible questions to consider include:

- Can I quit offering this service or product?
- Can I increase its selling price?
- Am I doing anything to promote this product or service actively?
- Even if I have to provide the product or service, would it be possible to subcontract it?
- Could I reduce enough non-value-added cost from the product or service to make it profitable?

Once you've identified issues requiring immediate attention, it's important to begin incorporating the ABC information into longer-term decisions.

USING ABC FOR FINANCIAL PLANNING AND ANALYSIS

In addition to supporting specific decisions, activity-based costs (particularly the activity-based process costs and the activity costing rates) can be used to help a company model its operations, analyze proposed changes, and strengthen its basis for managerial accountability. The following are examples of ways in which clients have used their ABC results.

Costing the Effect of Operational Change

One bank used the activity-based process costing methodology to demonstrate the effect of the cycle time reduction program in which employees were involved. Over time, the operational savings directly attributable to the program were tremendous. Because of the ABC approach, the savings were measurable for the first time.

Simulating Process Improvements

An airframe manufacturer used the ABC information to simulate the effect of process changes. The company used an activity-based process cost model to document the "as is" process. Proposed changes to the process and changes in the projected activity levels were then incorporated to create the "could be" model. The model was then used to project the financial effects of the proposed improvements.

Justifying Investments

A financial services processing center had been frustrated by its inability to meet return-on-investment thresholds in order to acquire new equipment needed to meet strategic goals. By using ABC to model the cost of 1) changing the process; 2) eliminating the causes of bottlenecks; and 3) reducing other non-value-added costs, the client was able to develop a framework for evaluating the change that mirrored the true dynamics of cost within the business.

Assigning Working Capital

Several divisions of a large insurance company used ABC and BPA concepts to determine how each process area should be charged with a cost of capital. The BPA focused on ways to reduce the working capital requirements.

Justifying Part Standardization

An electronics company experienced "sticker shock" when it used ABC to calculate the cost of carrying a part in its inventory system. As in many engineering-driven companies, proliferation of part numbers was common. The ABC findings influenced this company to start an immediate part number standardization program. It also developed a "behavior modifying" performance measure. This new measure was based on the number and percent of common parts (compared with the unique parts) used in the designs.

THE ROLE OF ABC IN YOUR CONTINUOUS IMPROVEMENT PROGRAM

One of the most important uses of ABC information is the focus it can provide to continuous improvement programs. ABC analyses, especially when coupled with business process analysis and root cause identification, can help you set the priorities and monitor the progress of improvement efforts.

By summarizing the cost of all activities that have the same root cause, you can easily see which operational issues are most important for the company to address. You may find, for instance, that the one factor that causes the highest amount of non-value-added cost is the number of parts you have to design, make or buy, market, and support. Or you may discover that a huge amount of non-value-added cost is caused by the layout of the facilities or by errors in key information or by high variability in the quality of a certain output. You will also see the relative impacts that non-value-added activities have on the profitability of specific products, services, and/or customers.

This information does not tell you how to correct a problem or how to make operational improvements. It does, however, add the structure and the relativity needed to set priorities and to set goals for specific areas of improvement. More importantly, when you use ABC within the framework of Total Cost Management, you will know where your most promising and most important opportunities lie. ABC information then comes back in to play as you monitor the results of your improvement efforts. You expect to see reductions in the cost of the activities when you target specific root causes for improvement. And you expect to see those reductions reflected in the cost of specific products and services.

ABC information can help justify decisions that would have been unthinkable without the emphasis on overhead costs. One of the most obvious places to witness an "overhead-driven" decision is in the packaging of commercial software for the personal computer. Rather than planning, producing, and distributing separate products for different-sized disks, manufacturers frequently include two sets of disks in the package—one on 3-1/2" disks and one on 5-1/4" disks. The extra material cost is more than made up in overhead savings.

One of the most fruitful areas for continuous improvement in manufacturing organizations lies in the collaboration between engineering and production specialists as they jointly make decisions about product and process design. The objective is called *design for manufacturability* or DFM. DFM manifests the belief that "design engineering is the most important leverage point for making improvements and that if design engineers truly understood the practical implications of manufacturing the products they designed, they would design the products differently." In a similar fashion, the results of an ABC analysis can be provided to design engineer-

ABC Statement of Operating Income Year Ending December 31,19XX		
REVENUE		$ 2,331
REAL-VALUE-ADDED COST OF SALES		
Materials	$ 364	
Conversion	516	880
REAL-VALUE-ADDED GROSS MARGIN		$ 1,451
BUSINESS-VALUE-ADDED COSTS		
Marketing	$ 232	
Distribution	349	
Administrative	120	
Research & Development	30	731
VALUE-ADDED OPERATING INCOME		$ 720
NON-VALUE-ADDED COSTS		
Production: Waste/Rework/Failures	132	
Marketing: Waste/Rework/Failures	41	
Distribution: Waste/Rework/Failures	62	
Administration: Waste/Rework/Failures	30	
Research & Development: Waste/Rework	8	
Excess Capacity Costs	0	272
OPERATING INCOME		$ 448
Ratio of non-value-added costs to revenue:	0.12	
Ratio of business-value-added costs to real-value-added costs:	0.83	

EXHIBIT 10-1. ABC statement of operating income.

ing teams to enable them to *design for profitability*. In effect, this use of ABC findings manifests the belief that "if design engineers truly understood the overhead implications of their design engineering decisions, they could design products that required less overhead support."

If the scope of your project is broad enough to allow you to generalize about the proportion of value-added to non-value-added costs, an effective way to keep the continuous improvement program supported by senior management is to restate the operating income of the company in ABC terms. Exhibit 10-1 illustrates such a restatement. Once the magnitude of the improvement opportunity has been estimated, senior management finds it hard to forget the message.

ABC IN "BRICK AND MORTAR" DECISIONS

The situations in which costs are most likely to be seriously distorted are ones in which an organization is trying to be "all things to all people," such as when:

- Service personnel perform a combination of highly structured and highly unstructured work.
- Delivery of service to high-volume customers is comingled with delivery of service to infrequent, low-volume customers.
- Production of high-volume products is comingled with production of low-volume products.
- Production of stable products is comingled with production of products that are constantly being changed by engineering.

In situations like these, the results of an ABC analysis may provide just the economic impetus needed to make a company question its all-things-to-all-people charter, and to also question whether the operations infrastructure is appropriate for its chosen strategy. Rather than simply embarking on a program of trying to make incremental improvements, a company with extremely high overhead costs and seriously distorted product costs may decide to change its operations infrastructure to gain more focus. Such a change may involve dividing a facility (both physically and organizationally) into sub-facilities or "plants within a plant" to allow each new organization to focus on a manageable number of requirements.*

WHAT YOU SHOULD *NOT* DO WITH ABC FINDINGS

It is possible to make some very short-sighted decisions based on the findings of an ABC project. You should avoid one particular genre of unfortunate decisions. Specifically, you do not want to undermine or lose ground in your company's efforts to improve quality or reduce cycle time by action that you take in response to the ABC numbers.

Often, ABC projects reveal that the costs of *batch-related activities* surpisingly are higher. An activity is batch-related if its cost varies with the number of batches processed instead of with the number of units processed. Service organizations often group work together in batches, especially when the work involves any kind of transaction processing, such as processing accounting entries or invoices. These batches of service work also require certain work to be performed at the batch level. Operations managers sometimes refer to these activities as the "get-ready" and "clean-up" activities. In a production environment, such activities include scheduling the

---

* The concept of focused factories and plant-within-a-plant come from: Wickman Skinner, "The Focused Factory," *Harvard Business Review*, May–June, 1974.

production, setting up the machines to produce the product, gathering together the components, inspecting the first units produced to make sure they are within specifications, and processing all the paperwork or computer transactions required for the batch. When the ABC analysis is completed and all costs are summarized for these activities that support batches of work, it is common to learn that they are significantly more expensive than previously thought.

Once you see how expensive these get-ready and clean-up activities are, you may respond hastily by suggesting that the work be processed in less frequent but larger batches. In fact, you may be tempted to pull out the formulas for calculating "economic order quantities" as you formalize your recommendation. If you find yourself leaning toward such a recommendation, stop! You are probably going in the wrong direction. In fact, you may be moving toward a recommendation that will ultimately set your company back in quality, time, and cost.

Operations personnel have spent the past 10 years learning to emphasize reduction of setup costs and to de-emphasize economic order quantitities. By reducing these setup costs, companies have simultaneously reduced their costs, increased their quality, and reduced their cycle time. They have set goals of "zero setup times" and "batch sizes of one," and they have had dramatic impacts as they worked to achieve these goals. They have also learned that increasing batch sizes has exactly the opposite effect. In terms of overhead costs, large batch sizes increase the likelihood for all four of the types of transactions (i.e., logistical, balancing, quality, and change) that cause overhead costs.

In short, make sure that your response to the ABC findings incorporates the collective wisdom and experience that companies have learned about the interaction of quality, cycle time, and cost. When you see very high batch-related costs, use root cause analysis and process value analysis to concentrate your energies on reducing the cause of the cost.

CONCLUSION

Small wonder that activity-based costing has caught the attention so quickly of such a wide group of practitioners—management accountants and operations managers alike. Through activity-based costing (particularly when used in conjuction with business process analysis), companies are finally able to see the dynamics of their overhead costs. Even more important, they are finally able to structure action programs to deal with these costs. Those action programs are able to support—rather than undermine—a company's goals in improving quality, customer satisfaction, and operational speed and flexibility.

The benefits to be gained from ABC are just beginning. Most of the early work in ABC has been conducted in the form of pilot projects. The value of the information from those projects has been so great that companies are now expanding their plans to make ABC a routine part of their costing structure. The message is clear: ABC is here to stay.

CHAPTER 11

Activity-Based Costing—A Tool Kit

Most of what we've discussed throughout this section applies to virtually all businesses whose managers decide to undertake activity-based costing analyses. After all, one of ABC's most notable characteristics is its adaptability. However, certain implementation issues may be more of a concern to some businesses than to others. Rather than discuss each of these issues within our earlier discussions, we've collected them here to avoid disrupting the sequential nature of ABC techniques.

What follows is a kind of ABC "tool kit"—a collection of tips that some readers may find useful, even crucial, and that others may find tangential or obvious, depending on the nature of their companies and the extent of their experience with activity-based costing. Use what you need; ignore the rest.

CONDUCT A THOROUGH REVIEW OF YOUR CURRENT COST SYSTEMS

Before you begin designing a new cost accounting architecture, make sure the ABC team thoroughly understands the architecture of your current system. There are two major objectives for this review.

First, you want to assess how accurate or inaccurate the current costs are likely to be. You will use this assessment to predict the relative value of conducting a full ABC project and to recommend the scope of that project.

Second, it establishes a baseline. In many companies, the current cost accounting system evolved over a period of many years. You are likely to find some aspects you want to keep and others you want to eliminate or change. In any event, the review of the current costing methodology is an important starting point to know "what you're working with." The following discussion encompasses the steps you should take during your review.

Perform a Database Review

Your objectives in this step are:

1. learning what data exists in the system;
2. learning how that database is used in the current costing methodology; and
3. beginning to document the data that might be valuable in the ABC costing effort.

In a service environment, you will want to examine the systems that people use to perform the core work (such as the issuing of policies or processing of claims in an insurance company or the processing of loans or clearing of checks in a bank). These may be customer service systems or service tracking systems. In a manufacturing environment, you will want to examine the systems that maintain bills of material, routings, materials planning, customer orders, and shop floor control. In a distribution environment, you will want to examine inventory planning and inventory tracking systems as well as customer order entry systems. Be sure also to examine the performance measurement systems and other reporting systems, whether formal or informal.

Be sure as well that the team's knowledge is current about major strategic initiatives such as total quality, time-based management, or continuous flow programs. Many companies are in a constant state of change, and these major strategic initiatives are likely to be a source of much of that change. Understanding the dynamics of the business and strategies will provide beneficial insights into the future costing needs of the company.

Identify the Current Cost Flow (If One Exists)

If your company is already costing the objects that are of interest to you, then you will want to examine the current techniques and procedures. If your company currently deals with inventory—either as a manufacturer, distributor, or retailer—then you already have systems in place to cost that inventory. On the other hand, if you are in a service industry, then the costing systems may not exist; or at least they may not exist within your formal accounting system.

The first step in identifying the current cost flow is to develop a schematic of how the costs flow from the general ledger to the objects that are of interest you. This investigation serves two major purposes. The first is to simply understand the current architecture. The second is to establish a control point to make sure you have not overlooked any element of cost that should be included in your analysis.

As you trace cost from the general ledger to the object, you will want to document several flows separately:

- How do material and labor get charged?
- How is overhead charged?
- How many different overhead cost-centers are there?

- How many levels of allocation are there?
- Is overhead assigned directly from the overhead cost-centers to objects, or do intermediate allocations take place?
- If a standard cost system is in place, to what extent has non-value-added cost been buried in the standards?
- Have scrap, shrinkage, rework, and efficiency factors been built into the standards?
- Are there already profitability analyses for the objects? If so, do they include non-inventoriable costs? For instance, do they include marketing, distribution, and/or selling costs? If so, how are those costs determined?

An example of a typical current cost flow model is shown in Exhibit 11-1. Some items of note in the exhibit include:

- The direct material and direct labor flow directly to products from the cost rollup and by-pass any allocation.
- The indirect costs (indirect labor, depreciation, utilities, and the like) flow to one or more manufacturing cost centers. Where there is more than one cost center, this cost assignment is based on headcount or management estimates about the relative consumption of resources by the different cost centers.
- The manufacturing overhead cost pools are then assigned to the product.

Identify the Current Overhead Cost Pools

The next step in the current cost system review is to become familiar with the development of the overhead techniques. In this step you will document the following:

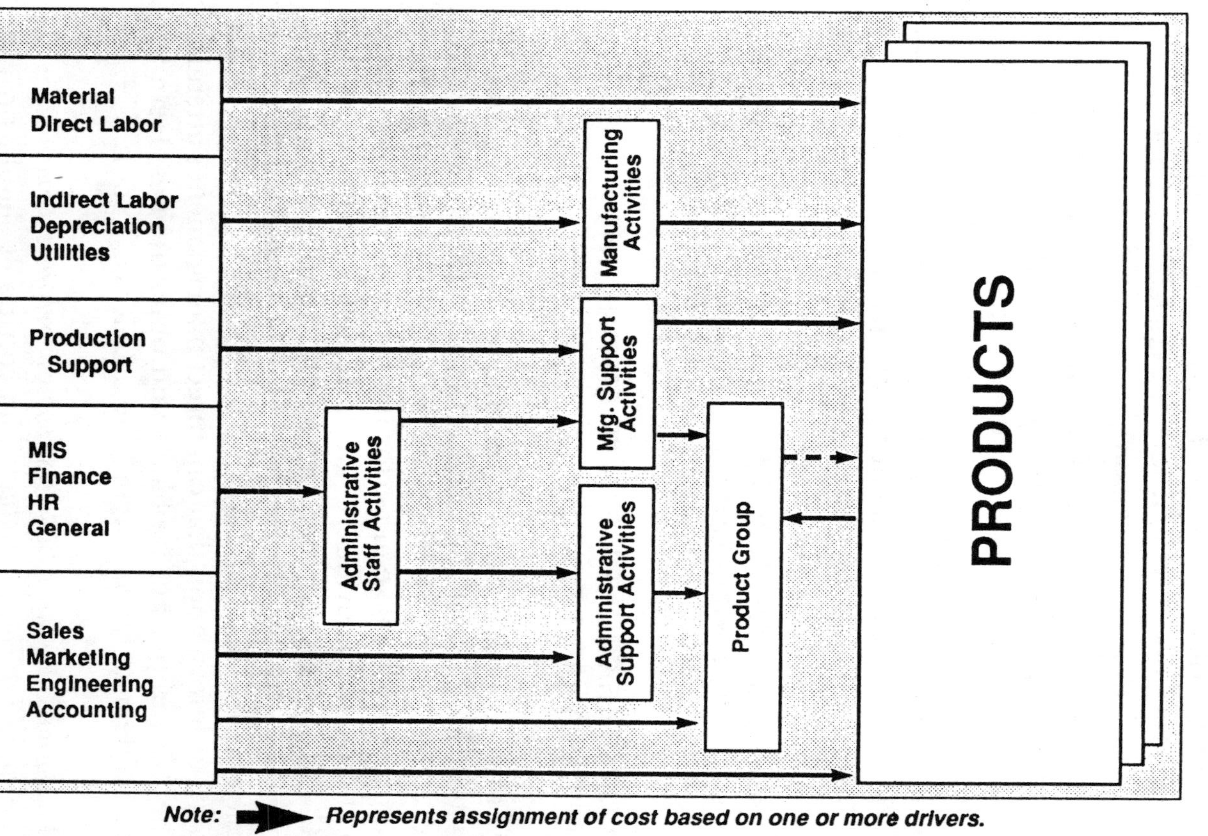

Note: ***Represents assignment of cost based on one or more drivers.***

EXHIBIT 11-1. Example of Cost Flow Model

- *Determine the type of overhead pools.* Are separate pools kept for different types of costs? For example, are separate pools created for indirect labor, indirect materials, or depreciation?
- *Determine the level at which the pools are maintained.* Are costs separated by major workcenter or individual machines? Or are they lumped together for the whole organization?
- *Identify the allocation base used for each pool.* Is it assigned to objects based on labor hours, machine hours, material value, or some other basis?
- *Summarize the extent to which current costs are likely to be inaccurate.* Identify specific dynamics that are likely to cause the current costs to be distorted.

CONSIDERATIONS WHEN SPECIFYING THE ACTIVITY COST POOLS

Now that you have seen the technique for assigning costs to activities, let's revisit the issue of specifying the activity cost pools. This set of specifications is the single most important decision you will make in performing activity-based costing. If you define the activities at an extremely detailed level, the ABC calculations can become overly complex—particularly when taken to the object level. On the other hand, if you define the activities too broadly, the results will fail to reveal important information that can direct management's attention to the most important problems and opportunities. Here are some guidelines for specifying the activity cost pools.

1. *Do not view the activity cost pools merely as intermediate vehicles for attaching cost to product.* The cost pools should provide operational information of a relevant nature. The cost that is collected in a cost pool should answer specific operational questions, such as: What does it cost to generate purchase orders? What does it cost to produce engineering changes?

2. *The types of activities within a pool should be as homogeneous as possible* without creating "cost pool proliferation."

3. *Consider the relationship between the activity cost pools and important dimensions of performance you want to measure.* For example, if your company has high utility costs, and if you want visibility into the utility cost by process, then isolating utilities as a cost pool within each department can provide that information. If, however, the cost of utilities is grouped into one pool with all the other machine-related costs, then the visibility you want will be lost.

4. *Use the findings from the business process analysis to help you distinguish the "significant few" from the "trivial many" possible activity groups.* Select the combination that best captures the essence of your business operations.

5. *Distinguish between the level of detail needed for better management of the process and that needed for more accurate costing of objects.* If the difference in detail is significant, do both. If there is a difference, the extra detail almost certainly will be needed at the process level. After you have calculated the activity costs at the process level, combine similar activities into summary activity cost pools before taking them to objects.

6. *You must be able to specify an "activity driver" for every activity cost pool you want to take to the object level.* You must also have available or be able to collect statistics for each activity driver you specify. If, for instance, you specify "number of calls received" as an activity driver to be used for costing customers, then you must be able to gather the data that shows the number of calls received from each customer.

7. *You should sketch out the definitions for all the activity cost pools before you perform consolidations of the general ledger data.*

An Illustration

During one of our field work projects, the business process analysis revealed that high variability in the workforce was a root cause of many costly problems—among them absenteeism, employee turnover, quality problems, low yield, excessive rework, and excessive setups. The company was very labor-intensive, and the project's steering committee decided to raise management's level of awareness of the workforce instability issue by showing its cost effect. The team created separate activity cost pools within each operations process for direct labor, setup labor, rework labor, absenteeism, and turnover. The work force turnover pool included such activities as recruiting and training. Its cost was estimated at $2,500 per turnover incident. The cost of absenteeism was calculated as a percentage of the fringe benefits. This formula was based on the fact that the company had to carry extra permanent employees in order to compensate for the steady rate of absent workers.

Here, again, the breakdown of costs that was most helpful for managerial purposes was more detailed than was needed for object costing purposes. While these different labor-related costs were kept separate and visible at the process level, they were aggregated into a single pool before they were assigned to objects. This accomplished the goal of providing relevant information for process improvement purposes while keeping the object costing structure simple.

DECIDE WHAT "VERSION" OF COST TO USE FOR YOUR PROJECT

Throughout this chapter, we have referred to the costs in the general ledger as the starting point for your ABC work. We have shown how to restate those costs from their general ledger account/cost-center orientation to an activity orientation, and then how to assign the activity costs to cost objects. But we haven't yet mentioned which general ledger costs to use. In many situations you will find more than one "version" of cost in the general ledger. You may find, for instance, actual costs, one or more sets of budgeted costs, and perhaps projected costs (which combine actual costs to date and forecasts of remaining costs).

There is, in fact, no pat answer about which version of cost to use. The following is a list of issues to consider in making this choice.

1. *Actual costs may not exist at the level you need them.* Particularly if product costing is your objective, you are unlikely to find actual material and labor costs at a product level. You are probably going to have to rely on your standard cost data for costing the material and labor content of your products.

2. *If you want to add a reconciliation step in your project in order to make sure your total ABC costs equal your total traditional costs, working with the budget cost data version may be easiest.* Departmental budgets and the standard costs are likely to have been developed interactively. If this is the case, the reconciliation step will be greatly simplified.

3. *Using the budget data is preferable if there have been any significant changes in the products or processes.* The ABC costs need to reflect the current operating environment.

4. *You also need to consider the relationship between the time period you use for gathering your costs and the one you use for gathering resource and activity driver statistics.* This is most likely to be an issue for activity drivers that reflect transaction counts. If, for instance, you have specified such activity drivers as "the number of material moves," "the number of purchase orders," or "the number of schedule changes," you will probably be getting your counts of those drivers from scans of the history files of the systems that process those transactions. Collecting transaction counts is usually easier when analyzing a previous time period than it is when forecasting a future time period.

DON'T TOUCH THE OPERATING VERSION OF YOUR GENERAL LEDGER

An initial ABC project is analytical in nature. Most companies conduct financial analyses of various sorts on a routine basis. They already have the controls in place to make sure the analyses do not interfere with the official set of books for the company. Make sure your ABC team knows and complies with all such controls. We have two caveats regarding this subject.

The first caveat is one we assume is obvious to anyone reading this book, but we'll mention it anyway. Within an initial ABC project, you are not going to be updating your company's general ledger in any way. You are only using the data that is stored in the general ledger as a basis for your analysis. To conduct your project, you may need to make a copy of the general ledger database, or you may need to secure authorization to use the general ledger report writer to format the data the way you want to see it.

Second, make sure you know the processing schedule for your general accounting department. You may discover that you cannot get access to data you need during certain periods of time—specifically during period-end closing activities. This same issue also applies to systems you may want to access for gathering driver statistics. If you know the processing schedules in advance, you can develop your ABC project plan around those schedules.

CONSIDER USING NON-GAAP CONVENTIONS

Keep in mind that the purpose of activity-based costing is to improve your company's decision-making power by improving the information that supports the decisions. This information is purely managerial in its intent. Even though your financial records are maintained in accordance with *generally accepted accounting principles* (GAAP), you may choose to deviate from GAAP constraints in developing your activity-based costing information. It is very likely that you would want to include *selling, general, and administrative* (SG&A) costs in assessing product/service profitability. There are two additional areas in which you may want to considering using techniques that are not allowed in GAAP reporting.

Imputed Interest Cost

You may want to include an imputed interest cost in your analysis. While GAAP does not allow you to capitalize or inventory your costs of financing assets, you may want to estimate such costs in your ABC analysis—at both the process level and the object level.

If a large investment in fixed assets is required to conduct a particular activity, then the cost of that activity should reflect the cost of capital for the asset. This is particularly true when your business process analysis is able to reflect the time dimension of the activity. For instance, an activity model may show the average time that inventory stays in storage. When you estimate the costs of that activity, your estimate would be more complete if it reflected the cost of financing:

1. the warehouse;
2. any automated retrieval equipment; and
3. the investment in the inventory being stored.

Likewise, at a product level, if two products are otherwise similar but one product has a very fast throughput and turnover rate, while another similar product has slow rates (with many cycles of storage time), then that second product actually costs you much more to make, own, and sell than does the first. The purpose of ABC is to expose exactly such differences. But it is only by explicitly recognizing the different cash flow implications of the two situations that your ABC analysis will fully reveal these differences. Including an imputed interest cost for the money you have tied up in the slow assets and the resources that support them is the way to make the cash flow implication explicit.

Depreciation Issues

You may also want to consider calculating depreciation costs for the ABC analysis using:

1. replacement cost rather than historical cost; and
2. expected life rather than depreciable life.

For many of the purposes for which the ABC costs will be used, these GAAP adjustments make the ABC calculations better reflect the physical dynamics of the business.

Appendix to Chapter 11
Sample Interview Questions

In Chapter 8, we referred to functional interviews as one technique to use within preliminary stages of ABC. What follows is a sample set of questions for conducting these functional interviews.

1. Customer and Customer Requirement Definition.
   - Who are your customers? Who receives your output or your services?
   - What product or service do you provide?
   - What level of support do you provide for them?
   - What do your "customers" expect from you?
   - What attributes of your service are most important to them?
   - What techniques do you use to confirm your customers' requirements?
2. Organization Structure.
   - Describe a high-level functional chart of departments.
   - Identify titles and number of personnel.

- Are any personnel dedicated to particular processes or products?

3. Activity Definition.

- Describe the flow of work in your area.
- What major activities does your organization perform?
- How do these activities relate to the business processes?
- What are the major responsibilities of your personnel?
- What is your estimate of the percent of effort required by your organization to support each of the activities? Describe the logic you use to make those estimates.
- Are there any significant resources, other than personnel (e.g., equipment), that is dedicated to particular activities, processes, or products?

4. Cycle Time Relationship.

- How long does it take to provide the various services?
- Does any information exist that relates the time requirement to a measurement (e.g., time per document)?
- What determines the time required to perform the activities?
- What are the factors or events that most get in the way of your people as they perform their work?
- What other factors affect the workload?
- How long do you think it *should* take to perform these services?

5. Cost Assignment.

- What information is available to develop a cost per unit for your activities?
- What causes complexity or excess variety in your area of responsibility?
- What are the major factors that make your activities or services necessary?
- What would you have to change in order for your service levels to change for each area you support?

6. Process Improvements.

- If you could do one thing to reduce "problem" activities, what would it be?
- Do you foresee any changes in technology used that will change the way you do business?

SECTION 3

Continuous Improvement

CHAPTER 12

Improving Performance Measures

A common objective in organizations today is to continuously improve performance. In keeping with this objective, we will now describe how Total Cost Management can support your company's efforts toward *continuous improvement* by supporting your performance measures and by providing the analytical framework for key decisions.

All the techniques described here use business process analysis and activity-based costing as a foundation for understanding the cost dynamics in an organization. In this chapter, we address ways to improve the information used to measure and monitor performance. In Chapter 13, we describe ways to use the process/activity view of costs to support specific decisions concerning:

1. investments in quality initiatives;
2. new product/service development; and
3. justification of capital investments.

In business, many trends are profoundly affecting how managers view their performance. The quality movement has helped managers gain a new understanding of the relationships among customers, business processes, and financial success. The changing competitive arena has helped people understand that the most important basis for evaluating their own performance lies outside their own organization, and that all people within an organization must work together toward clear, common goals. New techniques like business process analysis and activity-based costing have provided a foundation for understanding the cost dynamics in an organization, and they form the basis for modeling the economics of the business. A natural outgrowth of all this new understanding is that many managers are now convinced that the methods currently used to keep them informed about their companies' performance are missing the mark.

You can hear the complaints at all levels of management, from CEOs to first-line supervisors or "from the top floor to the shop floor."* And though the scope may differ between levels, the nature of these complaints are surprisingly similar.

> "I get fragments of information, but never a balanced picture. And because there's no balance, I'm sure I sometimes respond with suboptimal actions that impede long-term success or undermine other areas of the business."
>
> "The information I receive that's most dependable in terms of timing, accuracy, and objectivity is the monthly Profit & Loss Statement. But because the rest of the performance picture is missing, I've come to view the P&L as part of the problem because it dominates decisions inappropriately."

---

*M. E. Beischel and K. R. Smith, "Linking the Shop Floor to the Top Floor," *Management Accounting*, October 1991, pp. 25–29.

"I launch new programs—whether they're new strategic directions or department-level initiatives—but I seldom receive information about the results of these efforts."

"I receive (or send) mixed messages about the performance priorities. Top management says one thing, but lower-level performance seems to be evaluated on different and seemingly unrelated criteria."

"I get reams of reports, but they are usually too much too late."

"I want to be eager to receive performance information. I want it to be so timely that I can act on it, so balanced that I can act effectively, and so clear that the things that truly need my attention jump out at me."

STRATEGIC CONTROL VERSUS PERFORMANCE MEASUREMENT

Many of the issues in measuring performance are conceptually the same from the top floor to the shop floor; even so, their scope and emphases really do differ. At the very top level of the organization, the objective is to achieve strategic control. Boardroom executives are responsible for determining which elements of performance are most important to the business. They are responsible as well for determining the balance among those elements. By contrast, the objective at lower levels of the organization is to improve tactical and operational control. The boardroom executives need the information to develop and monitor strategy. Middle- and lower-level managers need the information to support the strategy.

Projects with an objective of improving the boardroom information are becoming known as *strategic control projects.* Projects that have the objective of improving the information for lower organizational levels are most commonly known as *performance measurement projects.*

Obviously, the ideal sequence for improving an organization's overall information structure is to develop the strategic control metrics first and then link them to lower-level performance measures.

What follows in this chapter is a generalized view of the techniques for improving your performance measurement practices. The various elements we describe may be easier or more difficult to accomplish, depending on whether you are doing a comprehensive overhaul of your performance measures (starting with strategic control) or whether you have a more narrow or focused scope for your improvement process.

THE NATURE OF PERFORMANCE MEASUREMENT

A performance measurement system has many roles. Three of the most important are:

1. *It allows managers to monitor how the business is doing and to know what aspects of the business may need attention.* Under ideal circumstances, the performance measurement system serves as an early warning system that directs attention to a problem area in time to take corrective action, or else it directs attention to an opportunity in time to take advantage of it. Performance measurement supports proactive management and provides positive reinforcement. It also supports self-management by giving individuals and teams the feedback information they need to do their jobs.

2. *The second role for performance measurement systems is as an important communication tool.* The old adages in business are that "you get what you measure" and that "what gets measured gets done." Whether you like it to or not, your company's performance measurement system communicates the message that the elements of performance you formally measure are the important ones, and that those you do not formally measure are unimportant—or at least less important. The performance measurement system is a constant reminder to people of what is most important for them to achieve.

3. *The third role is that the performance measurement system serves as the basis for companies' reward systems.* Compensation, promotion, recognition, and appraisals frequently are based in large measure on performance results, as reflected by the performance measurement practices.

Unfortunately, many companies' performance measurement systems often reflect what the company *can* measure or or what it is in the habit of measuring, rather than what the company considers to be truly important aspects of performance. In these situations, the performance measurement systems fail to fulfill any of their roles. They fail to keep managers informed about the true performance of the business; they communicate the wrong message about the performance priorities; and they may reward behavior that is contrary to the strategic goals of the business.

Three important improvements needed in most performance measurements systems are:

1. Refining the set of measures so that they collectively present a balanced picture of the different aspects of performance. Once the measures have been refined, the need for two additional changes becomes obvious in many companies. The first is to make sure that the aspects of performance that are important at high levels in the organization are adequately reflected in the performance measures throughout the organization. The second is to make sure that the reward systems supports the broadened understanding of these important dimensions of performance.

2. Providing meaningful context for the performance measures.
3. Presenting the information in such a way that it can be quickly and easily interpreted.

We will address each of these improvements separately, though the first will involve the greatest level of detail.

REFINING THE SET OF MEASURES

The most fundamental analysis needed when reviewing a company's set of performance measures is to confirm which aspects management considers most important. We recommend that you name and prioritize the various aspects of performance before you systematically examine your current performance measurement system. Now let's see how to examine the different elements of performance.

Naming Aspects of Performance

There are three basic techniques for documenting the important aspects of performance. These techniques aren't mutually exclusive. On the contrary, they are most effectively used in combination with each other.

Identifying Critical Success Factors *Critical success factors* (CSFs) are those key areas of the business in which high performance is essential if objectives are to be met.* CSFs reflect both the competitive issues in the business's industry and its own unique objectives.

---

*John F. Rockhart, "Chief Executives Define Their Own Data Needs," *Harvard Business Review,* March–April, 1979.

Identifying critical success factors is based on in-depth experience and knowledge of your business and industry. A key technique for identifying critical success factors is to ask the question, "When our overall performance has been very successful, what specifically were we doing extremely well?" Then you should ask the companion question, "When our overall performance has been poor, what specifically were we doing poorly?" This pair of questions can be asked on many levels. You need to ask them about your own company. You need to ask them about your competitors—both domestic and foreign ones. You need to ask them about other companies in related industries.

Typical enterprise-wide CSFs include:

- Producing products that customers perceive to be of high quality.
- Designing new products quickly.
- Developing unique and innovative new products.
- Keeping the cost of the product or service low.
- Maintaining a reliable source of supply.
- Responding quickly and fully to customer requests.

Some CSFs are specific to particular industries.

- For automobile manufacturers: Maintaining a quality dealer system.
- For business equipment dealers: Providing responsive and timely customer services.
- For software developers: Predicting which hardware platforms will be most popular.
- For consulting firms: Hiring and retaining top-quality associates.

- For insurance companies: Providing responsive, timely, and accurate claims processing and payment.

Some companies also identify *critical failure factors* (or aspects of performance that must be avoided if the company is to achieve long-term success). Typical failure factors include:

- taking customers for granted;
- relying on customers who are unprofitable;
- fixating on traditional competitors and not recognizing emerging competitors; and
- running out of cash.

The emphasis in the reporting system at the company's highest levels needs to reflect the relative importance of the different aspects of performance as indicated by the critical factors.

If you are performing this analysis below the strategic control level, you should also identify success factors tied to the division's or department's specific charter.

Analyzing a Process-Based Business Model Although brainstorming and researching critical success factors is the most important starting point for identifying the key elements of performance, that analysis sometimes leaves gaps in the performance picture. For instance, a company that considers itself to be in an engineering-driven industry may tend to concentrate its identification of critical success factors on the engineering aspects of its business—perhaps even to the point of failing to identify important aspects in sales or operations. (Pharmaceutical companies, for instance, sometimes focus almost exclusively on the development of new products.) These additional aspects of performance are important for two reasons. First, they allow you to test your performance profile for completeness. Second, they will be needed to develop the appropriate performance information for the executives who head these other areas of your business.

A model like that in Exhibit 12-1 can help the project team identify and prioritize the elements of performance. For each box in the model, the team needs to ask, "How do we do that in this company, and what are the important aspects of performance?" They also need to ask such questions as:

- What are the capital requirements of the business and how do we raise new capital?
- What skills do our people need and how are we meeting their development needs? At what level do we pay our people and how does that pay scale compare with their other opportunities?
- How versatile are our people, processes, and technology?
- What are our sources of material? Are the sources reliable and responsive? What is the quality of the incoming materials? What is the cost of the incoming materials?
- What is the technology base of the company? In what processes is technology most important and what is our long-term plan for establishing the ideal technology base?
- How do we win new business? What proportion of new business comes from existing customers and what proportion from new customers? Have these proportions changed over time; and if so, what do those changes imply? What are we doing to keep the pipeline for new business full and how do we assess the quantity and quality of the pipeline?
- What are our products and services? What proportion of our business is coming from new products and

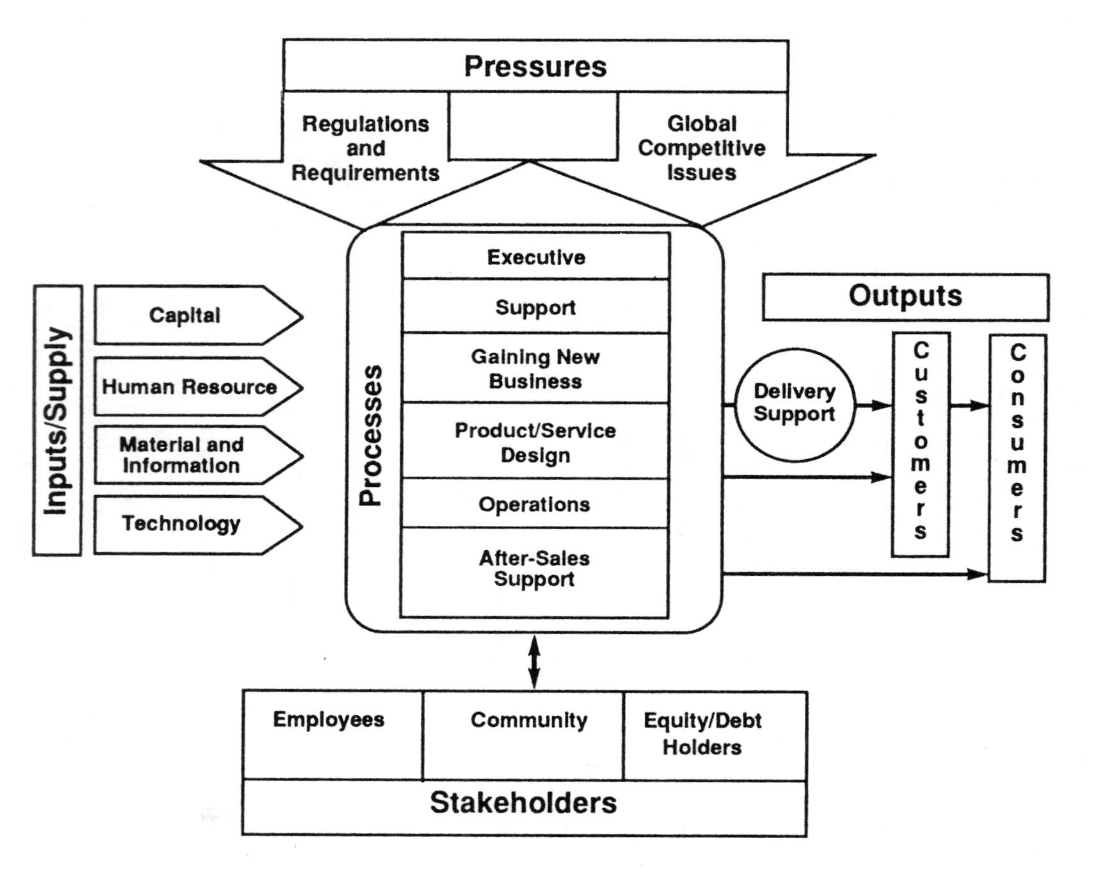

EXHIBIT 12-1. Process-based business model.

services and what proportion is from old ones? What stage of the life cycle are we in?

- • How do we design products and services? How long does it take to produce a new product or deliver a new service? Once a new product is completed, how prepared is the company overall to make, sell, and service it?
- What are the most important elements of our operations? What is the proportion of value-added to non-value-added costs? How long does it take to execute each operation's sub-process? How quickly can our operations respond to customer requests?
- Why do we need to provide after-sales support? How much of the after-sales support reflects poor quality of the product or service? How satisfied are our customers with the after-sales support?
- How effective is our delivery support? What is it about the way we do business that helps make our customers profitable? In what ways do we help our customers serve their own customers?
- What do the different stakeholders expect of the business?

The answers to these questions will undoubtedly add to your model of performance elements. You should develop metrics to measure and monitor all of these aspects.

If you are performing this analysis below the strategic control level, you should rely on the business process analysis results to guide this examination. You may also want to develop function-based success factors. A *function-based success factor* is one common to a business process across all industries, rather than one stemming directly from enterprise-wide success factors. For example, a Payroll Department has to produce a payroll on time regardless of the industry. A

Production Department has to meet a production schedule. A treasurer has to plan the cash needs of the organization. These function-based success factors are also best developed by people who have a wide variety of experience in the process as well as a keen understanding of the organization's higher-level strategy.*

Incorporating Your Root Cause Analysis A third technique for identifying the important elements of performance is to incorporate the results of your business process analysis. Within BPA, you identified major problem areas within your processes and identified root causes of those problems. You may have also used ABC techniques to calculate the costs of the processes. This analysis provided the basis for prioritizing the root causes and developing plans for addressing them.

Typical of costly categories of root causes are:

- Processes that require sequential processing by many individuals.
- Incompatible or redundant systems.
- Organizational structures that distance "work" from its customers.
- Unreliable operating capacity—with frequent unplanned downtime.
- Unwieldy physical layout of operations facilities.
- Lack of training or versatility in the workforce.

A comprehensive performance measurement system should include elements reflecting the important areas of your business that you have targeted for improvement.

---

*John F. Rockart and Christine V. Bullen, *The Rise of Managerial Computing*. Homewood, Ill.: Dow Jones Irwin, 1986.

Prioritizing and Balancing

After you have completed identifying the important elements of performance, the elements need to be structured into a general profile. This structuring forces you to come to terms with the balance or proportionality issue. The task is analogous to an editor's decisions about the format of a newspaper's front page. Only so much information can fit on the front page. The challenge is to make the space dedicated to each topic proportional to its importance. The executives at one company, for instance, developed the following profile of the categories and proportionality of information they wanted to have included in their monthly briefing books.

Customer Trends	15%
New Product Development Information	8%
Flexibility Indicators	5%
Key Business Process Information	25%
Specific Improvement Initiatives	15%
Financial Performance	30%
Competitor Trends	2%

Having set this target profile, the project team realized that it had an abundance of financial information, spotty business process information, and virtually no customer information. The company's collection of information about new product development and competitor trends was very fragmented. Developing the profile was one thing; developing the systems and procedures to provide the information was an altogether different challenge. But the profile provided the target and the vision to the team to build a work plan to support the profile. (The team also recognized immediately that the development of a customer information system or database would eventually become a requirement.)

Assessing the Current System

After you finish identifying and prioritizing the aspects of performance in your company, the next step is to assess your current measures against the performance elements you have identified as important.

Exhibit 12-2 illustrates a way to organize this assessment. We have listed the critical success factors for this enterprise along the horizontal axis. Along the side axis are the value-chain components or the mega-processes for the enterprise. The vertical axis represents the management levels. Each individual cube within this framework allows you to identify the measures currently in use which can provide the needed information to decide whether the current performance is helping the organization achieve the success factor.

When you have finished evaluating every cube, you will be able to categorize:

- success factors that are supported by no performance measures;
- success factors that are supported only in isolated processes;
- success factors that never reach lower levels of management;
- processes that are under-measured;
- processes that are over-measured;
- management levels that are well-supported; and
- management levels that are poorly supported.

This assessment provides the basis for refining the performance measures. The specific refinements, of course, will vary from company to company and from situation to situation. In all cases, though, the objective is to make sure that all success factors are supported by measures, that all measures

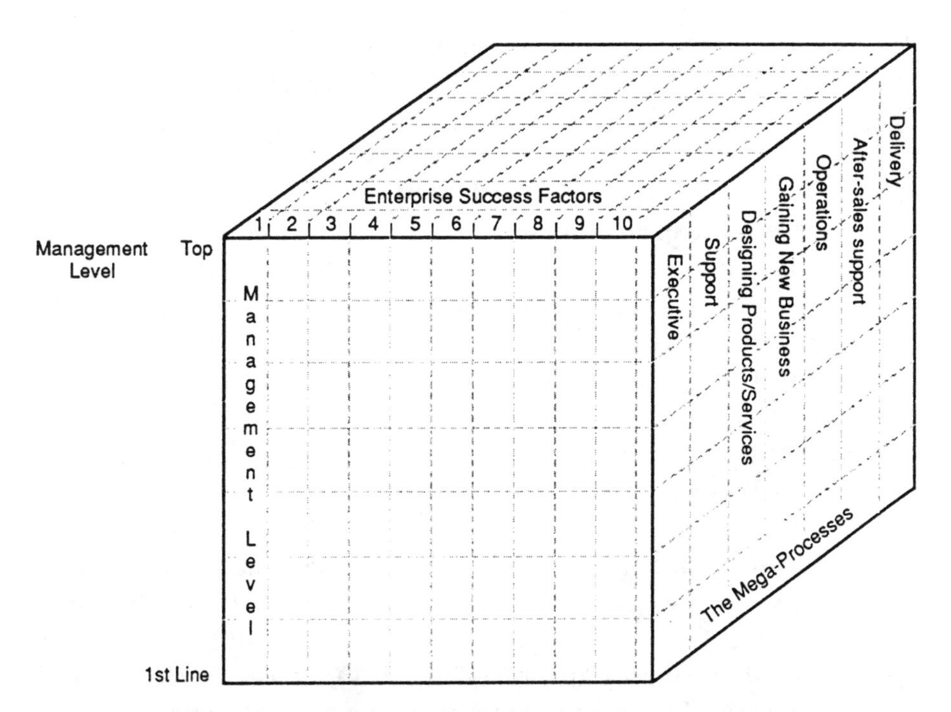

EXHIBIT 12-2. Structure for assessing a performance measurement system

support some aspect of the success profile, and that no measures are used in such a way that they impede performance.

A Conceptual Framework for Developing New Measures

Once you have analyzed your current measures and identified holes and imbalances, the next step is to develop new measures to fill the holes and to make adjustments to make sure that the new set of measures provides a balanced view of the organization's peformance. This section describes the different characteristics of performance measures that you may want to consider as you develop new measures and refine your performance profile.

Process View versus Functional View Throughout this book, we have emphasized that taking a process view rather than a functional view of your organization is the key to analyzing your business. This process view allows you to cost your business appropriately and make important steps in improving it. Once you turn your attention to measuring performance, the process view continues to be the most effective model.

But measuring performance on a process basis forces a company to address the relationship between its business processes and its organizational structures. Most companies use a dual technique for doing so. The first is to name an owner for every business process. The owner is typically the individual on the management team who has the most direct influence (in terms of resources and responsibility) for the performance of the process. The second is to organize all performance data, especially the cost data, in such a way that it can be summarized and reported either by process or by individual manager.

Performance Measures You May Want to Eliminate When companies assess their current measures against desired measures, they generally discover important elements of performance that need to be added to their performance measurement system. It is equally important to identify current measures that should be eliminated. Improvements to the company's performance measurement practices rarely result in additions to the overall number of measures; on the contrary, they often result in a reduction. The improvements result in more comprehensive, more balanced, and more strategically focused views of performance. A necessary step in achieving this improved view is to eliminate unnecessary performance measures.

Common candidates for elimination include:

- Measures that support no success factor.
- Multiple measures that redundantly support a single factor.
- Measures that are unnecessarily detailed.
- Measures that encourage or reward actions that undermine the enterprise's goals and objectives.
- Measures that are beyond the responsibility or influence of the recipient.

Performance Measures You May Want to Change Another area you will want to investigate is whether you have non-value-added activities buried within your costs. It is common, for instance, to find that while calculating costs, average allowances have been built in for setup activities, scrap, rework, "normal" inefficiencies, and other non-value-added costs. For product/service costing purposes, you should cost the non-value-added activities at the product level. But for performance measurement purposes, it is highly desirable not to bury these costs, but rather to capture and report them separately. It is important to report them separately because recognizing those costs and taking actions to reduce them are a major objective of a Total Cost Management effort.

Performance Measures You May Want to Add The kind of measures most companies need to develop and add to their formal performance measurement systems are non-financial measures. In fact, sometimes you will find that forward-looking managers are already collecting some of this information on an informal basis. Some of the more common measures that companies are adding include the following.

1. Quality measures such as:
   - Results of customer satisfaction surveys.
   - Percent of repeat sales to existing customers.
   - Number of complaints received.
   - Scrap and rework costs as a percentage of the cost of goods manufactured.
   - Total cost of quality. (We will describe techniques for reporting the cost of quality in the next chapter.)
2. Flexibility measures such as:
   - Average number of certified skills per employee.
   - Setup time as a percentage of total production time.
   - Inventory turnover and receivables turnover.
3. Time measures such as average and maximum:
   - Time between order submission and order receipt.
   - Production end-to-end lead time.
   - Cycle time for each key business process.

Non-financial measures (such as the examples listed here) are an integral part of a TCM performance measurement system. The non-financial measures serve as leading indicators of cost and profitability. They also provide vital information for interpreting and understanding the underlying dynamics of the financial measures.

PROVIDING CONTEXT

Once you have decided which measures to report, you should consider ways of giving context to those measures. Reporting a single number (such as revenue per employee, percentage of non-value-added cost to total cost, or average cycle time) always begs the question, "Should I be pleased with that number?" The more context you provide for the measures, the more effectively the recipient will be able to assess the performance. For a measure like percentage of non-value-added cost to total cost, the important context may be:

1. to see your own performance over time;
2. to compare your performance against your current target, other divisions within your company, industry averages, or "best in class" performance. (See Exhibit 12-3.)

Seeing your own performance over time is extremely important. Not only does it allow you to see your progress toward your goal, but seeing your performance over time is fundamental to supporting a continuous improvement environment. It is no longer good enough to simply avoid unfavorable variances. The requirement today is to perform better and better each day. The performance measurement system supports that requirement by displaying the trends.

Of course, collecting data about industry averages and best-in-class performance will be a challenging task, but it's not necessarily impossible. As business leaders reflect on the performance of their companies over the past decade, they often describe a previous mistake: "We were guilty of comparing ourselves only against ourselves. We saw how we were doing over time, but we never took our heads out of the sand to compare ourselves to our real competition—or to compare ourselves to what we could be."

More and more companies are expressing an interest and a commitment to comparing important elements of their performance against others in their industry and against the "world's best" performance. The practice is called *benchmarking*. The interest and the demand for benchmarks are great

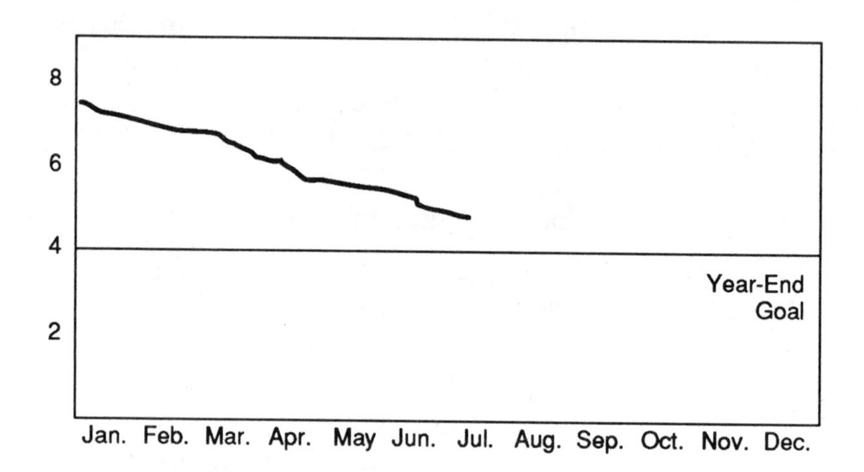

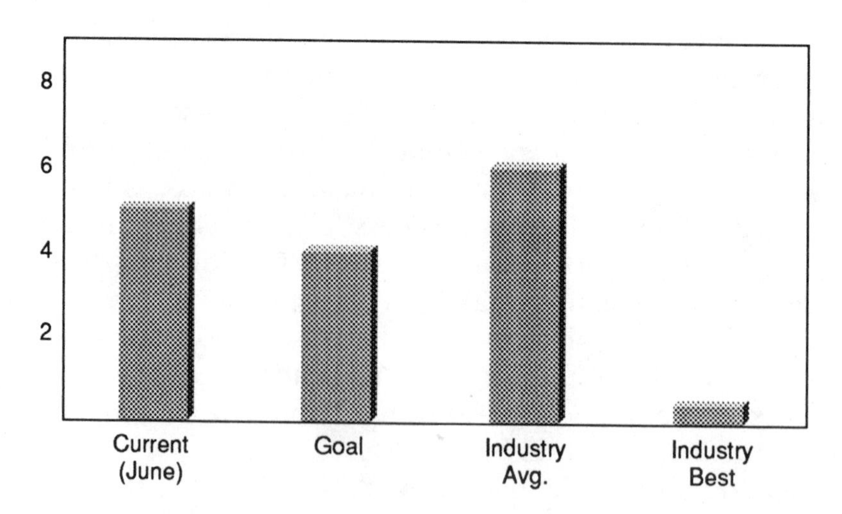

EXHIBIT 12 - 3. NVA as a percentage of revenue: current context and trend NVA.

enough that industry associations and third-party researchers are beginning to collect and provide some of this information.

PRESENTING THE INFORMATION

Keep in mind when you present performance information that you have two objectives: first, to help the recipient understand the overall performance quickly; second, to help the recipient distinguish between elements that are under control and others that need attention. The following are some tips to achieving those objectives.

Be Consistent

One way that a reader will develop speed in absorbing information is in finding the same format and the same design over and over again. If you present information in multiple cycles (for example, weekly flash reports and monthly briefing books), use the same design standards for all the cycles.

Use Graphs

Wherever possible, present the information graphically. The old saying that "a picture is worth a thousand words" is most true for performance information.

We worked once with a company's Chief Information Officer to develop the prototype for an executive information system, which would later be expanded to other offices in the organization. One team worked to develop the data that would be presented; another worked to develop the graphical formats. While development was still in progress, the CIO saw numerous versions of the graphs that reflected only hypothetical data. Once the project was completed and he saw the final results, he commented, "It looks great—but when do I see my real data?" We told him, "You're looking at it." At first he didn't believe us. He said, "No way. I read the old performance report earlier today. The numbers can't be the same." He pulled the report from his desk and compared the numbers with the graph. He then literally dismissed the meeting to take care of the problem that had "jumped out at him" from the graph. It was a problem he had completely missed when he simply read the numbers in a report format.

Help the Reader Decide What to Read

When you design the presentation of the performance information, assume that your reader is a *very* busy person. Present the information at a high level so that the reader can read it and, based on what he sees, choose which areas to examine at a further level of detail.

You can even present the Table of Contents graphically. If you are reporting performance on the different divisions of your organization, the Table of Contents can display the Performance Against Plan for each of the divisions. That way a reader with limited time can use the graphics in the Table of Contents to decide where to spend his time.

CONCLUSION

By building on the process view of the organization, companies have made great progress in improving their performance measurement practices. They have done this by taking a fresh look at the elements of performance that are truly important to achieving both short- and long-term goals. They have then added, changed, and/or deleted practices for measuring and monitoring these elements. They have reviewed the performance metrics from one level of the organization to the next to make sure that the company was sending consistent messages about performance priorities. They have then provided relevant bases for evaluating the performance—within and outside the organization.

CHAPTER 13

Continuous Improvement—Decision Support

Once an organization has begun to view and calculate its costs on a process/activity basis, that new understanding can be applied to improve many of the specific decisions made by management. This chapter explores three categories of decisions that can greatly benefit from a process/activity view of costs.

First, we will describe the technique for calculating the *cost of quality* (COQ) and then show how that technique can be enhanced. Second, we will explore some of the financial models used during the process of developing new products. Specifically, we will look at the techniques of *life-cycle costing* and *target costing*. Finally, we will examine new techniques for *justifying capital investments* and how those models can incorporate the activity information.

USING THE PROCESS/ACTIVITY VIEW OF COSTS TO SUPPORT TOTAL QUALITY MANAGEMENT PROGRAMS

A generation ago, the conventional wisdom in western industry was that a tradeoff existed between quality and cost. The assumptions went something like this: "Higher quality products cost more to make than do lower quality products. Increasing quality means higher costs. You can save costs by reducing quality."

Many people have worked during the last twenty years—especially during the 1980s—to disprove these assumptions. In one company after another, managers have become convinced of a different reality: that poor quality, not high quality, is what costs a fortune.

In the discussions that follow, we present an overview of the cost of quality concepts. We then describe the role of Total Cost Management in improving cost of quality practices.

What has made cost of quality such a powerful communication and analytical technique is the categories it uses to describe and explain the cost relationships. COQ is a way of classifying costs into three broad categories:

1. cost to control;
2. cost of failure to control; and
3. lost opportunity.

Cost to Control

Cost to control represents the effort it takes to make products and services conform to quality specifications, and to reduce the causes of variation. Within cost to control are two subclasses: *prevention* and *appraisal*.

Prevention This sub-class contains costs of actions taken to plan each product and process to ensure that defects do not occur. It includes such activities as documenting procedures, certifying vendors, training employees, assessing capital capabilities, and certifying specialized skills. It also includes organizational changes such as the inclusion of customer service personnel on design teams.

Appraisal This sub-class includes costs of inspecting a service to ensure that it meets customer requirements. It includes any activity where one person is inspecting another person's work—for example, inspecting raw materials upon receipt, testing software before its released to users, and reviewing the data entry of transactions.

Cost of Failure to Control

What the organization incurs when output (products and services) fails to conform to quality specifications is called *cost of failure to control.* Within this class of costs are two sub-classes: internal failure and external failure.

Internal Failure These are costs generated by defects that are identified before the product or service reaches the customer. Examples include the cost of items that are scrapped, and the cost of reworking or correcting defective items. New services may be tested in the form of a "trial run" before they are offered to external customers. The costs of correcting errors in the procedures or in the supporting technologies that are detected in these tests would also be classified as internal failure costs.

External Failure Costs generated by defects that customers themselves discover are external failure costs. Examples include all warranty costs, costs of operating a customer hot-line, and the cost of field repairs.

Lost Opportunity

When customers consider your goods and services to be inferior, and they buy from other sources, the profits lost are known as *lost opportunity.* Lost opportunity costs are usually not included when you estimate COQ because they are difficult to measure; nevertheless, lost opportunity is a significant element of COQ on an intuitive level.*

Uses for Cost of Quality

Managers typically use the cost of quality concept in two ways as a part of their effort to gain support for new quality initiatives. First, project managers estimate the current level of spending in each of the four cost-of-quality sub-classes. The total COQ is usually presented as a ratio: COQ as a percentage of total operating costs or as a percentage of sales revenue. A pie chart or bar graph is used to show the proportion of cost in each of the four COQ sub-classes. (See Exhibit 13-1.)

Then the team presents a profile to project the relationship of these costs over time. (See Exhibit 13-2.) The profile is often developed by using the company's current performance as the base and then making the projections based on the experience of companies in similar industries that have initiated strong TQM programs.

The message is primarily financial: huge returns are possible if you prevent poor quality from occurring. The testimoni-

*Michael R. Ostrenga, "Return on Investment through the Cost of Quality," *Journal of Cost Management for the Manufacturing Industry*, pp. 37–44, Summer, 1991.

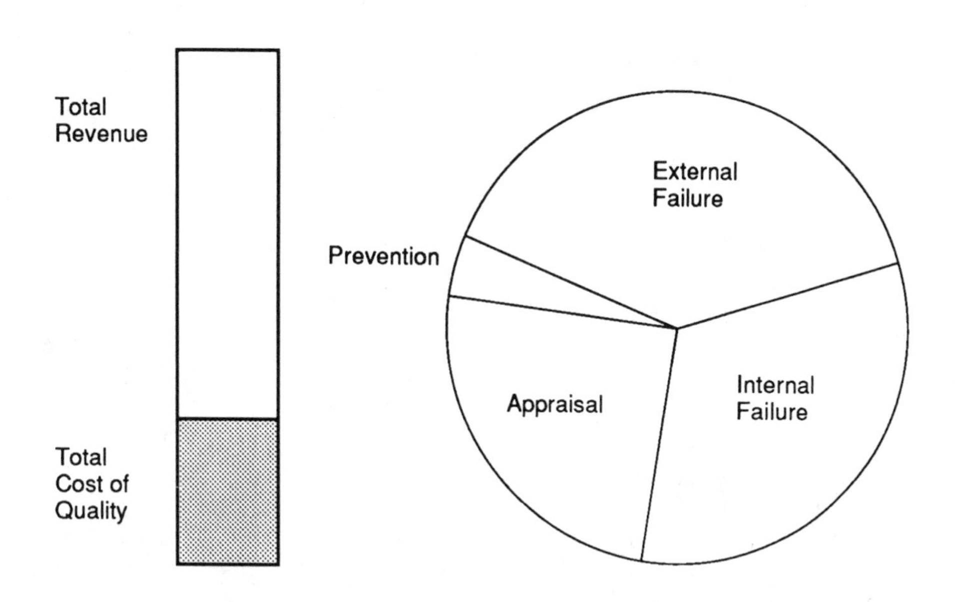

EXHIBIT 13-1. Cost of quality: profile of current state.

als from other companies are striking: "We are experiencing a $14 reduction in appraisal and failure costs for every dollar we spend in prevention. We've been at it for five years now and still haven't reached the point of diminishing returns." The financial objective in TQM programs is usually described as "managing the total COQ number down."

The cost of quality concept has been an extremely powerful model in helping gain boardroom-level sponsorship for adopting TQM as a driving force within companies. There are, however, two improvements needed in many companies' practices in reporting costs of quality.

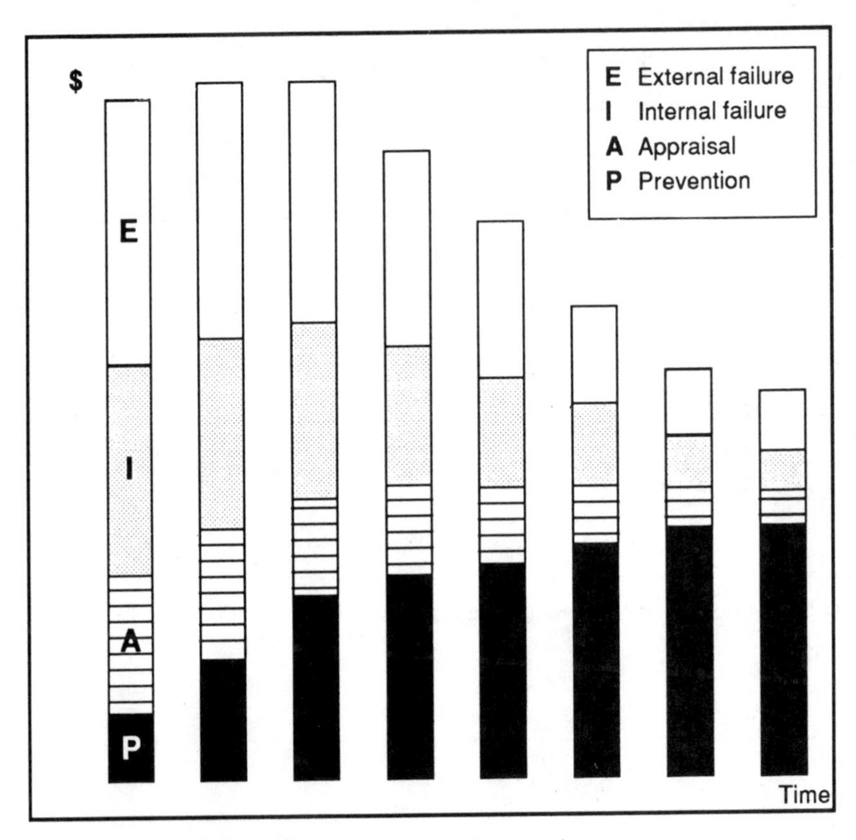

EXHIBIT 13-2. Projected total cost of quality over time.

Improvement #1 Many companies' COQ models ignore overhead areas of the business. The logic for omitting overhead was the same as for omitting lost opportunity: It's difficult to measure. Even without assessing overhead, quality champions teams could make a dramatic case for the financial value of quality improvement initiatives. There is no surprise, then, that the overhead areas have been slower in adopting the new mindset of quality than have their counterparts in the production functions. Yet in many organizations, overhead areas often have extremely high appraisal and failure costs.

Business process analysis and activity-based costing are the techniques used most successfully to understand and document the costs and the causes of overhead. We believe that the time has come for updating the COQ models to fully include the costs from sales and marketing, administrative services, operations support, distribution and logistics, and financial functions. That inclusion is needed in order for companies to make more progress in addressing the quality and cost problems in overhead areas of the business.

Improvement #2 The second improvement needed in many COQ models is that they be made an integral part of performance reporting. In developing the initial COQ models, the quality champions often got by using crude estimates and "back of the envelope" techniques to make the original point to management that poor quality is costly and that preventing poor quality is a wise investment. Once the point is made, however, and once the improvement initiatives are under way, it is important to periodically report the progress by using the same COQ models.

This is important for sustaining and increasing the participation and sponsorship of senior management in the ongoing quality improvement programs. In the past, this follow-up step was often not performed because the data were either not available, or else the estimating techniques were perceived as "self-serving" for the quality function, and lacked an appropriate level of objectivity. Business process analysis and activity-based costing techniques organize cost information in a way that makes it natural to fold into the COQ reporting. Many activities identified in BPA and ABC can be associated with a COQ category.

USING THE PROCESS/ACTIVITY VIEW OF COSTS TO SUPPORT THE DEVELOPMENT OF NEW PRODUCTS AND SERVICES

In many industries, being able to offer high-quality products and services at competitive prices is no longer enough to give a company a competitive edge. High quality is a precondition for staying in business at all; in such industries, companies are placing more and more emphasis on their ability to develop new products and services quickly and to get them to market without delay. But speed in design isn't the only objective. The life expectancy of products and services in those same industries is getting shorter and shorter. A new service has less time to recoup its development costs than was true in the past. Moreover, quality programs have reinforced the lesson that the most important place to "get the quality right" is in its design. Design flaws are very costly if they flow downstream into operations or, worse yet, to the customer. The pressure to develop new products and services better and faster is a huge challenge facing much of American industry.

Total Cost Management offers two different but related techniques for helping to monitor new product/service development: life-cycle costing and target costing.

Life-Cycle Costing

Life-cycle costing is the practice of organizing costs according to the stages in a product's or service's life and then using that profile to make decisions about the product.

Early in the 1960s, the U.S. Department of Defense (DOD) developed the concept of organizing product costs according to the product's life cycle stages. The intent was to provide a method of increasing the effectiveness of government procurement. The two related uses of life-cycle costing were:

1. to encourage longer planning horizons to increase the perspective on total costs by including the operating and support costs; and
2. to increase cost savings potential by increasing spending on design and development efforts that would reduce operating costs.*

Subsequent research has confirmed the DOD's original hypothesis. The constant theme throughout all of this work is that the pre-operating phases of a new product or service (that is, the planning, design, and prototyping phases) determine somewhere between 80 to 90 percent of the total costs that it will ever incur. Despite the fact that design decisions are the leverage point for determining costs, most of the cost control pressure in many companies has focused on sqeezing new efficiencies from operations—where only 10 to 20 percent of influence on total cost is even possible. The time-lapse may be so great between the design of the product or service, and the point where the costs are ultimately incurred, that this relationship between determining and incurring costs may be obscure.

The message of life-cycle costing is similar to that of cost of quality. Both are messages of leverage. The COQ message is that the most cost-effective quality strategy is to prevent defects. The life-cycle costing message is that the pre-operations phases of a product or service are the most highly leveraged place to affect costs.

Three Views of "Life Cycle" At first glance, the discussion of life-cycle costing may seem at odds with the more common interpretation of the "life cycle" that has been used for years to

---

*Michael D. Shields and S. Mark Young, "Managing Product Life Cycle Costs: An Organizational Model," *Journal of Cost Management for the Manufacturing Industry*, Fall 1991, pp. 39–52.

describe a product's marketing stages. Life-cycle costing grew from a producer's view of product life stages. But the idea that there are stages in a product's life have been around for a long time. What is new in Total Cost Management is using those stage models for costing and analytical purposes. For costing purposes, there are actually three important views of the life stages for a product or service:

1. the provider's view;
2. the marketing view; and
3. the customer's view.

Life-cycle costing deals with different issues and helps solve different problems in each of the three views.

The provider's view. From the provider's viewpoint, the names of stages may vary from one company to another, but the major steps include:

- feasibility investigation and concept design;
- detailed design;
- prototyping;
- ramp-up;
- full production and/or delivery;
- after-sale services; and
- phase-out or abandonment.

Typically, a company has a process in place to evaluate ideas for new products and services and to convert selected ideas into development projects. The actual development may be segmented into different stages.

In the recent past, the hand-off from one stage to another was notoriously abrupt in most organizations. The phrase most frequently used to describe this hand-off was "throwing it over the wall." Design engineering would "throw the designs over the wall" to engineers who had to figure out how to make the item. These process engineers would then "throw the process plans over the wall" to the people in production. Somewhere along the way, someone would "throw specifications over the wall" to the Purchasing Department to find suppliers for the purchased components. In many service industries, the hand-off from one stage to another reflected a different set of dynamics. Services would sometimes go from a "bright idea" to "delivery to the customer" without intermediate design steps. Educational offerings (like course offerings) would be created without the expertise of instructional designers. Software would be coded from sketchy or non-existent designs. Professional services would be delivered without methodologies.

Today, most companies are working hard to tear down the barriers to effective interaction and to assemble development teams that bring the downstream expertise to the design phases so that better decisions can be made earlier in the process. The techniques for improving both the quality of designs and the speed of the overall development process go by many names—each with its own special emphasis. *Design for manufacturability* and *concurrent engineering* are common in manufacturing industries. *Quality function deployment* is common across all industries.

In such environments, life-cycle costing is especially helpful in addressing the following two problems:

1. faulty projections of product or service costs; and
2. inaccurate profitability assessments.

Let's look first at faulty projections of product costs (and sub-optimal design decisions based on those estimates). Just as we described how COQ models often omitted overhead costs, the techniques that designers use to estimate costs likewise frequently omit many of the overhead costs or use the same costing rates that ABC has demonstrated to be so inaccurate. The models also largely omit important timing considerations. When engineering models exist, they are usually derived using one of two basic techniques—either from building mathematical models or by using a profile of actual costs for a product similar to the one being worked on.*

Particularly valuable under the second technique would be a profile of actual costs that used ABC techniques to trace costs both to the product or service and to the life-cycle stage; showed the timing of costs; and also provided the activity drivers for calculating overhead costs. Exhibit 13-3 illustrates such a profile.

The second point concerns inaccurate profitability assessments. For financial reporting purposes, GAAP requires that research and development costs (which represent much of the pre-operations phases) be expensed as incurred. For managerial purposes, however, when you assess the profitability of a product or service, you may want to isolate the R&D costs and amortize them over the expected life. A product or service cannot truly be considered profitable until it has covered its own development costs.

The marketing view. The traditional marketing view of product life stages is quite different from the provider's view. In the marketing view, sales volume is the determining factor in classifying the stages. A product goes through the stages of:

- introduction;
- growth;
- maturity;
- decline; and
- abandonment.

---

*[Shields and Young.]

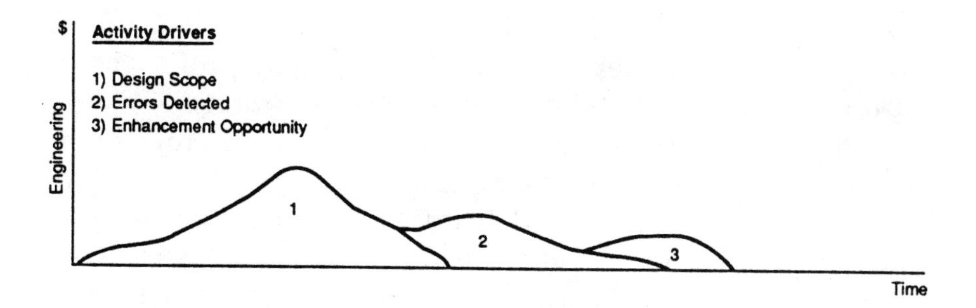

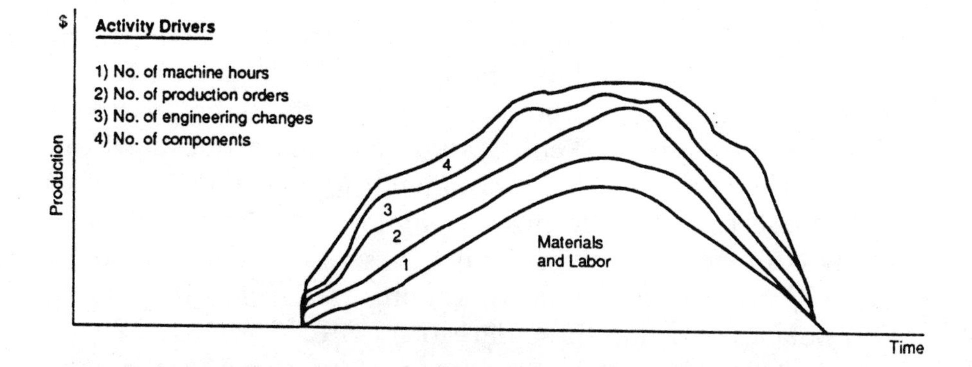

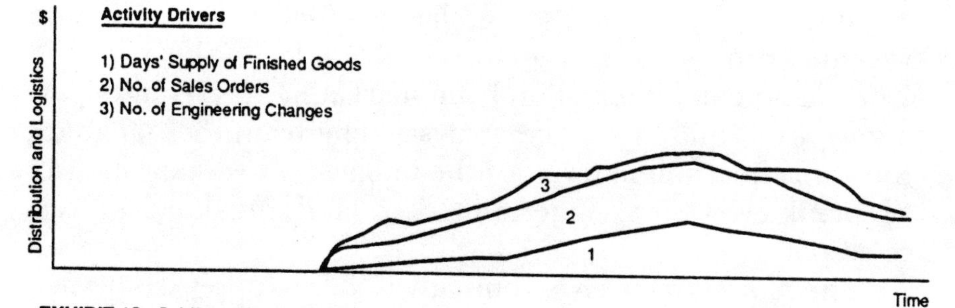

EXHIBIT 13 - 3. Life-cycle cost profiles.

The marketing life cycle concept is used to forecast revenue and to make promotion decisions. By combining information from the provider view and the marketing view of life cycles, you can develop a cost and profitability profile that is extremely useful in guiding development decisions.

The ongoing challenge in development is making scope decisions. During the feasibility phase of new idea development, you identify required features and you estimate cost and time for the development process. As development continues, however, you may have to revisit the orginal scope decisions. Project development teams see new possibilities for additional features. New technologies emerge and the project team asks: "If we take the product or service to market under the old technology, will anyone want to buy it? If we move to the new technology, will we delay the project to the point that we miss the vital marketing window?" These questions are asked daily in almost all development organizations—particularly those that provide high-technology goods and services. Many companies currently make these scope decisions on a purely intuitive basis and are striving to develop techniques and policies to guide these decisions better.

The best approach we have seen in structuring these decisions is the *return map technique* developed at Hewlett-Packard.* Using this technique forces the project team to analyze the impact of proposed scope changes for both the cost and revenue profiles over the foreseeable life of the product. Information and interaction from marketing, R&D, and operations are required for the analysis. The team then analyzes the scope question in terms of the impact on such new metrics as break-even-time, time-to-market, and break-even-after-release.

The more effectively a company is able to apply Total Cost Management approaches to the understanding of the cost

---

*Charles H. House and Raymond L. Price, "The Return Map: Tracking Product Teams," *Harvard Business Review*, Jan.–Feb. 1991, pp. 92–100.

dynamics of the enterprise, the more accurately they will be able to model the cost dimension of these scope decisions.

The customer's view. So far, the discussion of life-cycle costing has been entirely from the perspective of the enterprise that develops, makes, and/or sells a product or service. But the buyer of a product or services will have a very different perspective of the relevant stages in the product's or service's life. There are three stages of cost to the buyer:

- initial purchase cost;
- costs of operating and maintaining the product or service; and
- the cost of disposing of the item or discontinuing the service.

(For industrial products, both hardware and software, there may also be an implementation stage.)

An extension of life-cycle costing (known as *whole-life costing*) comes from combining the provider's view and customer's view of cost. In whole-life costing, the provider asks the question, "What does it cost me to develop, make, and sell the item; then what does it cost my customer to buy, maintain, and replace my product or service?"

Considering cost issues related to a customer's maintenance and service concerns is certainly not an invention of the 1990s. To make such a claim would insult generations of engineers. But in the past, these considerations were often less formal, and they resulted more from individual engineers' experience and intuition than they must today.

To understand what it costs a customer to own your product or receive your service, cannot just guess at the numbers. Gathering this information requires the collaboration of personnel from the vendor all the way to the customer. It involves gathering not only the cost data but also enough information from the people who use the product or service to understand the root causes of cost to the customer.

Formally considering the customer's cost to dispose of a product is a more recent phenomenon—one based on society's growing awareness of the cost and environmental impacts of disposal problems.

Target Costing

A second approach closely related to life-cycle costing is *target costing*. Both techniques are concerned with the development of new products and services. Life-cycle costing evolved in Western industry; target costing evolved in Japanese industry.

From a technical standpoint, the difference between the two might may appear to be nothing more than differences in emphasis and sequence. Both techniques require estimating the cost of the new products or services. Both include estimates of volume. The difference is not so much in the accounting technique, but in the approach to managing the development process. Under both approaches, the company makes a feasibility or market analysis, and a development team defines features of the product or service. In the Western approach, the development team typically designs the product or service and estimates its cost. Then executives make a marketing/management decision about whether to proceed into production. In effect, the marketing/management question is this: "Given what it will cost us to design, produce, market, service, and deliver this item, do we believe that we can sell it at a high-enough price, and at sufficient volume, for it to be a profitable addition to our line?"

The target costing approach asks many of the same questions, but at different times and in a different sequence. There are essentially four pairs of related questions here:

- What is the product or service, and what market share do we want to capture?
- What features must be present, and at what selling price, for us to achieve the target market share?
- What is our desired profit, and therefore what is the maximum amount that we can allow the product or service to cost (over the entire value chain)?
- How can we achieve that cost, and how long will it take to achieve it?

Once you've answered these four pairs of questions, the directive to the product development team is to develop a specific product with specific features that will cost no more than a specific amount. The concepts of business process analysis can be particularly helpful to a development team as they create or refine processes that will allow them to achieve the target cost.

USING THE PROCESS/ACTIVITY VIEW OF COSTS TO SUPPORT IMPROVED TECHNIQUES FOR CAPITAL BUDGETING

Among the most important decisions that executives make—especially in terms of competitive positioning—is the investment in equipment, buildings, and technology. The company's future financial health is largely dependent on these investment decisions.

Traditionally, new technology and other investments have been justified on the basis of return on investment calculated mostly by estimating the reduction of labor costs. Unfortunately, this approach doesn't consider the strategic impact of quality, reliability, lead time, and customer responsiveness. The strategic dimensions of new investments need to be understood and incorporated into the analysis. The use of advanced technology has changed the way we design and produce products. Deployed effectively, improved technology can improve quality, cycle time, and the cost of doing business.

However, caution is appropriate here. As illustrated in the BPA section of this book, investments to automate non-value-added activity tend to hide the real problems. A word or two here to repeat the BPA message may be helpful.

The basic tenet of BPA is to eliminate non-value-added waste by removing the impediments and constraints to improved work flow. In practice, we see many instances where companies have accurately perceived a need for improvement, but the improvement approach was then misguided. In case after case, we have seen companies invest in equipment or systems in an attempt to reduce costs. As shown in the BPA discussion, it is far better to eliminate (to the degree possible) the causes of non-value-added waste; to simplify the process; to stabilize the inputs; and then, and *only* then, to automate. This is an important focus with long-range implications, for it clearly demonstrates the desire to rid the organization of non-value-added activities rather than just doing them faster or cheaper.

The Traditional Approaches

Companies have always performed special kinds of cost/benefit analysis to assess the wisdom of their potential investments. For the most part, firms have used three approaches:

- *The payback method*, which calculates the amount of time required to recover the initial investment in a project.
- *The accounting rate of return method*, which divides income for a fixed period of time by the investment required to generate the income.

- *The discounted cash flow analysis method*, which takes the time-value-of-money into account to calculate the returns.

Company decision makers are, in fact, becoming more and more critical of the traditional investment analysis techniques' ability to provide the right direction for adopting new technology. In a study that Ernst & Young conducted of U.S. manufacturing firms in 1990, only 11 percent of those participating were completely satisfied with their ability to identify the benefits of investments.*

No one is arguing that the current investment concepts and models are in error. The problem is that the information used in these models is either inaccurate, incomplete, or both. Here are some of the problems surrounding the use of these traditional justification techniques.

Financial Information Alone is Not Adequate There is nothing wrong with the use of a "return" or cost savings calculation. The problem exists in the information that we feed the model. The models can only accept information that has been expressed in monetary terms. Therefore, only the "hard" financial data is used in the calculations.

The use of financial hurdle rates as a ranking device implies that the proposed investment with the highest return will be selected regardless of the strategic consequences of non-financial characteristics like quality or time. The problem with this approach is that it will potentially eliminate critical investment opportunities that are best positioned to improve the company's future competitiveness.

Total Benefits Have Not Been Well Understood The benefits of quality and automation have not been well understood, which

---

*American Competitiveness Study: Characteristics of Success, 1990. Ernst & Young.

made it difficult to forecast the projected financial effects in any investment analysis. The result in many evaluations was that intangibles or "non-cost" quantitative benefits were often ignored. Examples include:

- Reduced lead time.
- Number of worksteps combined or eliminated.
- Higher quality and reliability.
- Improved competitive positioning.
- Ability to meet and improve on delivery schedules.
- Improved customer satisfaction.
- Overhead cost reduction resulting from reductions in floor space requirements.

Most companies' practices focus on material or direct labor. They do a poor job of identifying the changes to the costs of overhead. As we've discussed elsewhere in this book, most cost accounting systems in use today provide detailed data about material and labor, but they shed very little light on the dynamics of overhead and administrative support costs. As a result, good information is often available regarding labor and materials, thus providing plenty of hard data to justify a project geared toward reducing labor, inventory, scrap, material usage, and so on. Even when this information about labor and materials does not exist, the process for estimating it is likely to be fairly straightforward.

However, detailed information on the investment effect of changes to customer service, design lead time, automation, and the like, is normally not available under the traditional cost systems. Time and time again we hear of companies attempting to justify investments on a financial basis using the direct labor savings and a variable overhead rate tied to the labor!

Traditional Analysis Assumes Costs Are Controlled at the Point of Incurrence Remember that the source of a cost is its *root cause,* yet the cost may be incurred almost anywhere along the value chain. This difference is important but often misunderstood or overlooked.

For example, a company that is concerned about its high data-entry costs may decide to automate the data-entry process by investing in scanning equipment and the companion application systems. This may appear to be a logical approach, since the cost is incurred in the data-entry activity. But business process analysis can help protect against prematurely proposing such investments. In many cases, the root cause of high data entry costs may be redundant or incompatible systems, poorly designed input formats, or collection of data that is not truly needed. Addressing the root cause is required in order for the most effective cost reduction to take place.

Recommended Improvements for Evaluating New Investments

The purpose of this section is to provide a high-level framework of our recommended approach to improved investment management. We have based these recommendations on advanced work performed by the CAM-I Investment Management Committee, as well as on the integration of activity-based information.

Recommendation #1: Incorporate Activity-Based Information As we've discussed earlier, one of the major deficiencies in traditional investment analysis is in the treatment of overhead costs. The BPA chapters of this book demonstrated that most overhead costs are caused by facts, events, circumstances, or conditions in the process other than direct labor. Yes, some costs are labor-driven, such as direct labor fringe benefits, supervisory costs, and some labor-related supplies. On the whole, however, most overhead costs are caused by factors other than direct labor volume.

We have previously shown how you can identify the root causes of costs in the BPA section, and we've shown as well how to calculate the costs of activities in the ABC section. Once the BPA and ABC work is completed, you have a solid foundation for improving the estimate of cost savings to be used in an investment analysis.

For instance, the results of the ABC analysis may show the following costs for a retail distribution center:

Activity	*Activity Driver*	*Activity Cost Rate*
Handling	per move	$25
Handling	per yard traveled	$ 1
Downtime	per hour	$75
Labor	per hour	$15
Repairs	per hour	$18
Order processing	per document	$10
Error detection	per document	$15
Data entry	per time handled	$ 5

An investment under consideration could streamline and synchronize the order-filling process so that the following improvements would be made:

- the number of material handling moves would be reduced by 15 to 30 percent or 500 moves totaling 20,000 yards;
- increased reliability contributing to improved up-time by 200 hours;
- the cost savings from these improvements would be:

Material handling	500 moves	@ $25 =	$12,500
Material handling	20,000 yards	@ $15 =	20,000

Downtime	200 hours	@ $75 =	$15,000
Labor	200 hours	@ $15 =	$ 3,000
			$50,500

The cost savings would appear to be $50,500. But wait! From the BPA discussion, we've learned that changes in the quality or timing of an upstream process will affect downstream parts of the organization. In this example, the increased quality and smoother work flow to the delivery department was estimated to save that department at least 100 hours of effort. Adjusting for this downstream effect would show:

Original cost savings		$50,500
Downstream effects	100 hours @ $18 =	$ 1,800
	Total Cost Savings:	$52,300

The availability of identifying activity drivers and activity costing rates fill a big gap in a company's ability to estimate the impact on overhead costs of a proposed investment.

Recommendation #2: Use a Decision Model that Considers Non-Financial Impacts There are several different approaches for incorporating the non-financial information into the decision model.

The CAM-I Multi-Attribute Decision Model, for instance, is an effective tool for incorporating non-financial information into an investment decision. It is designed to provide a weighted ranking for a project by using management's policy input about the relative importance of different impacts. It is based on user assessement of three types of factors:

- *financial factors*, such as the net present value;
- *non-financial factors*, such as lead time and quality; and

- *strictly qualitative factors*, such as employee morale.

Once you have identified all the decision factors, you assign weights to each to reflect its relative importance, with the sum of all weights equal to 100. In reviewing independent projects, you assign a value to each critical factor based on the project's expected performance within a predetermined range of possible outcomes. A risk assessment is then made (ranging from 0 to 1) for each factor to reflect management's judgment of whether the value will be reached. Finally, the product of the relative weight, value, and risk assessment is calculated for each factor, then summed across all the factors to arrive at a total project value. Management makes its investment decision by reviewing each project independently, then comparing the results of all options to make a selection among them.

Separate calculations for "hard" and "soft" benefits. Another approach is to estimate a financial value for all the benefits expected to be realized from the investment by means of a three-step process.

The analysis starts by identifying the usual cost savings. BPA and ABC techniques then serve to estimate a financial value for as many of the "non-financial" benefits (e.g., reduced cycle time) as possible. Finally, brainstorming/consensus techniques allow the team to estimate a financial value for the remaining qualitative benefits, such as employee morale. These estimates are then formatted to present the amount and percentage of benefits for each of the three types of factors.

Recommendation #3: Establish Tracking Mechanisms In Ernst & Young's "The American Competitiveness Study: Characteristics of Success," one of the key conclusions was that an ability to track capital investment performance characterized successful companies.

The importance of tracking or post audits should be intuitive. Yet, as shown in a study that Sullivan and Smith conducted, only 12 percent of the respondents regularly performed a post audit of their investment analyses, while 30 percent never conducted such an analysis.*

The technique employed in the post audit should include all criteria originally used to justify the investment, including both quantitative and qualitative information. Linking the TCM techniques of BPA and ABC will provide much of the support for tracking investment results. BPA provides the understanding of the underlying causes of cost; ABC quantifies this understanding. New measures can then be developed for reporting performance. Examples of these post-audit measures are:

- Non-value-added costs by activity and process.
- Cycle time of the process.
- Cycle efficiency (VA time/Total process time).
- Number of worksteps.
- Throughput volume.
- Amount of rework/reconciliation.
- Reduction in floor space.
- Performance in meeting delivery schedules.

Finally, the tracking mechanism should provide information about the issues that may have been categorized as "intangibles" in the original justification. Some of these intangibles may have included:

- Improved market/competitive position.
- Image in the marketplace.

---

*Charlene A. Sullivan and Keith V. Smith, "Capital Budgeting Practices for U.S. Factory Automation Projects." Paper submitted to *Financial Management*.

- Improved customer satisfaction.
- Positive impact on morale or safety.

CONCLUSION

A fundamental theme of Total Cost Management is that routine decision-making can be improved when decision-support information is organized around business processes and activities. The process/activity orientation provides a framework for viewing products and services over their full life cycles. It provides a basis for estimating the effects of capital investments and for tracking the financial impacts of quality improvement efforts. When coupled with critical success factors, it provides a structure for improving the metrics used to assess performance within the organization. It is the analytical foundation for achieving the goal of continuous improvement.

CHAPTER 14

Implementation

The concepts of Total Cost Management are appealing for *many* reasons. Just four of the most obvious include:

1. They address real rather than hypothetical problems.
2. They are conceptually logical.
3. They support the strategic directions of today's businesses.
4. They have been supported by enough successful implementations to indicate that implementation is indeed possible and profitable.

Yet, as executives begin to consider implementing TCM in their own organizations, a whole series of questions come to mind:

- Where do I start?
- How massive a project does this need to be?
- How do I organize an implementation team?

- What level of sponsorship is needed for this kind of project?
- What are the software issues involved in implementing TCM?
- What sorts of challenges or barriers are typical for this kind of project? And what are the best ways to address them?
- How do I make sure the organization actually attains benefits from the work?
- How do I develop TCM from a project to TCM as a routine way of doing business?

What follows is a discussion intended to provide you with some suggestions for answering these kinds of questions.

ONE-TIME ANALYSIS OR MAINLINE CHANGES?

It is possible to use TCM techniques on a one-time basis to solve a specific business problem. For instance, you may use the business process analysis technique as the basis for reducing the cost and cycle time of a particular process. (Examples: reducing the time and cost of processing orders for a distributor or reducing the time and cost of processing claims in an insurance company.) Similarly, you could use the ABC technique to provide information for a specific strategic planning event. Or you could use a combination of ABC and investment justification techniques to analyze a particular investment decision. There are times and places in which one-shot, stand-alone application of the TCM techniques may be appropriate.

Even so, the real power of TCM comes as it evolves from an individual project to a routine way of gathering and organizing information in the business. In this context, TCM is more than a collection of techniques. It is a mindset change and an ongoing process. A TCM implementation strategy is the means to this end: a plan for selecting the initial individual project(s) and then taking TCM from the initial projects to routine, mainstream information.

THE ROLE OF PILOT PROJECTS IN DEVELOPING A TCM STRATEGY

Even if a company's ultimate objective is to change its mainline business systems to a TCM basis, most executives start with pilot projects. Those pilot projects become the foundation for evolving to enterprise-wide implementation and into a way of doing business.

Pilot projects play two important roles in the overall TCM strategy. First, they are a basis for confirming a conceptual design; second, they can be a key source of funding.

Pilots as a Basis for Confirming a Conceptual Design

Even though the TCM principles are well-developed and thoroughly field-tested, there is no cookie-cutter, one-size-fits-all set of specific requirements for TCM. The business issues differ from one company to another and from one industry to another. The root causes differ. The levels of meaningful detail differ as well. From an information systems perspective, TCM is largely a "taker" system—especially in activity-based costing. It "takes" the majority of the data it needs for the cost calculations from other systems (i.e., from general ledger, operations planning and control systems, and the like). The structure of these feeder systems differ from company to company.

By first completing at least one pilot project for each major TCM technique, you can develop, test, and refine specific requirements for how that technique can best be employed on a wider scale within the company.

A pilot project usually has the following characteristics:

1. *It is limited in scope.* Business process analysis and activity-based process costing may initially be limited to certain targeted processes. Activity-based process costing is virtually always limited to a single location. It may even be limited to a sub-set of products. New performance measures may initially be limited to certain areas of the business. Investment justification may be limited to a single investment choice.

2. *It addresses a current business choice.* The usefulness of the results of the pilot project is an important determinant for evolving beyond pilots. The business issue addressed in the pilot needs to be clearly identified so that the pilot is more than an academic exercise. It is important that the results of the pilot be used in an actual business decision.

3. *It is conducted as an "off-line" project.* Permanent changes are typically not made to the company's base information systems in order to complete the pilot project. Much of the data for the pilot may come from the base systems, and software may be developed during the pilot to access or download that data. But the architecture of the base systems is not altered in order to complete the pilot.

Pilots as a Source of Funding

Besides the critical role that a pilot project plays in developing the company-specific TCM requirements, it can also be an important source of funding for the longer-range implementation of TCM. You should plan and sequence TCM in such a way that its benefits are evident throughout the process. An effective way to employ this strategy is to make sure the pilot project includes a business process analysis—including the development of an action plan based on the BPA findings.

DEVELOPING AN ENTERPRISE-WIDE IMPLEMENTATION STRATEGY

There are several dimensions in a TCM strategy. We will describe each of the elements separately, then illustrate how to combine them into an overall strategy.

- *TCM Technique* identifies which TCM techniques are included (i.e., business process analysis, activity-based process costing, activity-based object costing, performance measurement, and so on).
- *Source of Information* identifies whether the data are gathered and organized for presentation within a special project or whether they are performed as part of the day-to-day, transaction-based information processing.
- *Level of Integration with Financial Reporting* identifies whether the activity-based costs calculated for managerial analysis are integrated with or separate from the costs used for financial reporting.
- *Business Processes* identifies which business processes are included within the scope of TCM.
- *Other Scope Limitations* identifies any other factor limiting the TCM scope—for example, location or percent of the value chain to be included.
- *Timing* identifies the time frame for implementation.
- *People* identifies who is going to do the work (i.e., composition of cross-functional teams).

Here is a typical example of a TCM roll-out plan:

1. Begin with a business process analysis project for the process of "procuring materials" in the Wisconsin facility.
2. Extend the BPA to the rest of the operations support processes in the Wisconsin facility (project-based).
3. Concurrently, begin evaluation of performance measurement practices.
4. Add activity-based process and product costing for the Wisconsin facility (project-based—separate from financial reporting).
5. Add business process analysis for sales support and distribution processes in the Wisconsin facility (project-based).
6. Add activity-based profitability assessment for customers in the Wisconsin facility (project-based).
7. Update the databases to reflect attributes for life-cycle costing and cost of quality categories.
8. Repeat sequence 1-7 for the Kentucky facility.
9. Change the budgeting process to be activity-based.
10. Change source of activity-based process costing information from special project to transaction-based collection (refine the general ledger chart-of-accounts and procedures to capture activity information during routine processing).
11. Design new performance measurement system and develop new data collection techniques to support the new metrics.

We patterned this example of TCM roll-out plan after one used by a durable goods manufacturer with operations throughout North American and Europe. The client's full implementation plan included a worldwide roll-out.

TCM strategies differ significantly from one company to another. One company may start with business process analysis and then address an urgent need to improve its product costing before proceeding further. Another company may start its TCM effort by focusing on its performance measurement practices. The strategy that is most appropriate for an individual company is one that satisfies the immediate needs of the company while also progressing in a sequence that takes advantage of the TCM building blocks.

SOFTWARE ISSUES

For many of the TCM techniques addressed in this book, some form of computer software will obviously be required to implement the technique. This section identifies some of the software issues you may need to address. A word of caution is in order, though, before we begin that discussion. Software is, at most, a minor issue in implementing TCM approaches. Be sure that you do not make the mistake of interpreting TCM as a significant systems issue.

There are two different sets of software issues we will deal with:

1. software required to conduct the pilot projects; and
2. software required to migrate beyond the pilots.

Addressing the software issues for pilot projects creates something of a chicken-and-egg situation. On the one hand, a major objective of the pilot is to determine and refine your conceptual design, including the definition of the necessary software features and capabilities. On the other hand, software is likely to be needed to accomplish the work in the pilot.

The approach our clients have found most effective is to conduct the pilot projects using a combination of software options that require only a minimum investment (if any) in new software tools, and then at the end of the pilot projects to define the system architecture for migrating to wider-scale implementation.

Pilot Scenario

For conducting the pilots, commercially packaged software is available that runs on most personal computers. Software of this sort can help you:

- model business processes;
- develop activity-based process costs; and
- develop activity-based object costs.

You can develop the prototypes for new performance measurement formats through a combination of spreadsheets, databases, and graphics packages. (If you already have decision support software or executive information system software in-house, those systems would, of course, be utilized in the pilots.)

Developing the prototypes for cost of quality reporting, life-cycle costing, and target costing primarily requires the capability to associate categories of descriptors for each of the activities you identify. You might define a particular activity, for instance, as value-added or non-value-added. You could define it as prevention, appraisal, internal failure, external failure, or unrelated to the cost of quality. You could define it according to its life-cycle stage. This capability to define attributes for activities is present in many of the packages mentioned, including all of the database systems and many of the application packages specifically designed for TCM analyses.

Software packages are also available to model the investment justification techniques used for evaluating new investment opportunities.

In short, don't consider software an impediment to conducting your TCM pilots. In fact, selecting software for conducting the pilots should be a relatively minor task in developing your pilot project implementation plan.

Beyond Pilots

Once you have completed the pilot projects, you will have the information needed to finalize your system requirements and to develop a software plan within your overall TCM strategy.

There are three basic approaches for planning the software for evolving TCM beyond the pilots: one that relies on off-line packages, one that entails custom-development, and one that involves a combination of the two. The fundamental difference among the approaches is the extent to which you want to change your day-to-day data collection and processing systems to incorporate the TCM principles as opposed to employing TCM primarily through off-line analyses. (Incidentally, when we use the term "off-line," we are not implying any particular hardware platform. We use the term to mean that the work is done in a way that does not alter your current systems.)

The three different approaches use different combinations of the following elements:

- Using off-line packages.
- Developing integration software.
- Changing the existing data-collection practices and procedures to capture TCM information.
- Modifying the use of existing systems (without modifying the systems' code).
- Modifying the code of existing systems.
- Custom-developing information systems for TCM.

Approach #1 The first approach views TCM primarily as an off-line analytical tool. Under this approach, the same kind of off-line packages that were used in the pilot are evaluated for their robustness in handling your finalized system requirements. Most of the PC-based ABC packages have been used successfully for facilities-wide implementation, however, you need to evaluate any specific package for its ability to handle the volume of data you anticipate.

Under this approach, you will also need to evaluate the techniques you used in the pilot for accessing and downloading financial information from your general ledger and resource driver and activity driver information from other systems. You will also need a procedure for updating the resource driver and activity driver data that is not resident in any of these systems (for example, estimates of headcount consumed by the different activities that need to be solicited directly from department managers).

Keep in mind that even though this system approach relies on off-line calculation of costs, its update still needs to be formalized. Procedures and data collection devices need to be developed for confirming and verifying the activities and the driver data. A schedule needs to be formalized for the periodic updating of the TCM information. A procedure needs to be formalized for calculating the cost of any new products and services that are introduced into the company between the updates.

The major benefits of this approach are speed, control, and cost. Because fewer people need to be involved in software selection and ongoing operation, this approach is usually the fastest to implement.

Approach #2 A second approach that companies use relies on their existing systems as much as possible, trying to minimize both the proliferation of functionality and the redundancy of data. They utilize the TCM-specific software only to fill the gaps. Under this approach, a company may:

- Use existing modules within its general ledger for calculating activity-based process costs.
- Exit to one of the special-purpose TCM packages to calculate the overhead costs for individual products.
- Then upload those activity-based overhead costs to its existing product costing systems for performing the cost rollup.

This is a particularly viable approach if the mainline systems have simulation capabilities or the capability to maintain multiple views of data. Its major benefit is consistency. It prevents the problems that eventually surface when a number of people using a number of systems are essentially processing and trying to maintain the same data.

Existing systems vary widely, of course, in the extent to which their current functionality and underlying architecture can support the TCM requirements. In some system environments, the "gap" will be very narrow. In other cases, it may be so wide that this approach is impractical. (In the manufacturing sector, the existing environments in which the gap is likely to be narrowest are those consisting of integrated financial and manufacturing systems specifically designed to support manufacturers in process industries.)

Under the second approach, you may also decide to change your use of your existing software, without replacing the packages themselves. After completing their pilot projects, companies virtually always gain a new appreciation for the factors within their businesses that cause cost. In response to this newfound understanding, they may decide to change the structure through which they routinely collect, calculate, and budget cost information. These changes may be conceptually profound, but they may or may not require new or modified software. For instance, a company may refine its chart-of-accounts to be able to accumulate information about activities and processes in addition to the information it already collects about financial accounts and cost centers. Or a company may change the options in its product costing system to accumulate scrap and rework costs separately rather than embed them in its standard costs. In both of these examples, the change would be a significant one. Developing and implementing the procedures to accomplish the changes would require a commitment of time and resources. But from the standpoint of software functionality, your existing systems may be perfectly capable of supporting these changes.

Approach #3 The third approach consists largely of designing new software. A company may want to make TCM the basis of its routine day-to-day systems and yet find that the gap in functionality is so wide between what it needs and what its current systems can support that a large-scale design effort is its only viable option.

In this third case, the work done in the pilot projects becomes the starting point for the identification of data and functional requirements for new system development.

ORGANIZING THE TCM EFFORT

There are four major stages in a TCM effort:

1. Securing sponsorship.
2. Chartering the project.
3. Executing the project.
4. Acting on the results of the project.

Part II of this book has described the work necessary for stages 3 and 4—executing the project and acting on the results. We will now address stages 1 and 2 in the context of pilot projects. (Note that all four stages are necessary for the full TCM effort.)

Securing Sponsorship

TCM concepts may enter an organization through virtually any function and at any organizational level. The president of the company may read about them in the *Harvard Business Review*. The cost manager may learn of them through professional journals. The operations manager may learn of them through outside seminars. The CFO may learn of them through the company's auditors. The TCM topics are very popular—in the business press, as seminar topics, and as topics of converation among business professionals.

The president may find that the TCM descriptions seem to address important problems within the business, but may not have a sufficiently clear vision of how the techniques could best be used in his particular organization. The cost manager may have found the new cost accounting techniques intellectually interesting, but had no picture of how they might fit within the architecture of the company's existing systems environment. The operations manager may have exciting ideas about improving the performance measurement practices, but have no authorization to modify current practices. In short, many people may introduce the concepts to the organization and become champions for change.

To get TCM off the ground, however, the advocates need to "sell" the idea to an executive who can sponsor the project, and the sponsoring executive needs a clear enough vision of the specific benefits that the company can achieve through TCM to commit resources and energy to the effort.

The first step of the TCM effort, then, is one that emphasizes education and assessment. Often the education component is needed at multiple levels of the organization. Senior managers need to know the general nature of the new techniques and specific benefits likely to be achieved. Middle managers and analysts need to know specific details about how the techniques work and different approaches to employing the techniques. Current systems and practices need to be assessed so that the scope of the needed changes can be estimated and a plan for detailed analysis developed.

The first phase ends when an executive sponsor for the TCM work has:

1. a clear-enough vision of the potential benefits of TCM; and
2. a clear-enough understanding of the resources required to charter a project team to take the work to the detailed level of analysis.

Chartering the Project Team

Chartering a project team involves:

- Defining the objective and scope of the project.
- Naming a project leader.
- Staffing a project team by assigning people to work on the project (including specification for each assignment of whether it is full-time or part-time).
- Authorizing any other resources for the project.

Of course, the specific composition of a project team will vary from company to company, depending on the particular objectives for the project. But we offer these general comments:

First, it is important that the composition of the team reflect the cross-functional nature of TCM work. Activity-based costing projects need team members with specialized knowledge in operations, accounting, and information systems. If the results of the project are expected to affect marketing decisions, then marketing needs to be represented on the project team.

Second, it is vital that the project not end up an accounting-only project or a systems-only project. Companies may try this single-function approach, sometimes with interesting results. But these projects' findings are rarely acted upon, and the results are generally viewed as self-serving to the organization that developed them. The only situation that justifies such a project is when it is conducted on a test basis—with the objective restricted to estimating the potential magnitude of benefit to be derived from adopting certain TCM principles. The company might then use these findings to secure sponsorship for a "real" project more likely to result in tangible benefits.

The project requirements are the same for a TCM project as for any other project:

- It needs a skilled project leader.
- It needs work plans with clear assignments of responsibility.
- It needs an ongoing mechanism for anticipating problems and addressing those problems in a proactive way.
- It needs a clear statement of objectives and scope.
- It needs a formal procedure for addressing any proposed changes in scope.

PREDICTING THE CHALLENGES

In securing sponsorship and support for implementing TCM, you should anticipate what some of the initial challenges will be, and you should also develop ways and means for dealing with those challenges. Here are some of the more common initial issues.

Competing Ideologies

Some people may disparage TCM as "this year's new fad." They say, "One day it's Total Quality Management, the next day it's Getting Closer to the Customer, then it's Time-Based Competition. Now you're talking about Total Cost Management."

It's important always to position TCM as a means of supporting organizational strategy rather than as a competing ideology. It's important as well to be able to describe how TCM supports the specific elements of strategy. Information needs to be organized around activities and processes to identify the best opportunities for improvement. (This is true regardless of whether you seek the improvement in cost, time, or quality.) Information needs to be organized around activities and processes in order to know if performance has improved. You may want to reread Chapter 3 of this book for the language and logic for articulating the relationship between TCM and major strategy emphases in today's businesses.

The Fickle Press

Elements of Total Cost Management have received very wide coverage in business publications. We certainly expect that coverage to continue. Activity-based costing has been particularly popular and performance measurement is gaining ground fast. The popularity of these subjects, however, is a mixed blessing.

On the one hand, this extensive press coverage helps with the overall education process. When publications like *Fortune* and *Business Week* feature articles that explain emerging practices in cost management, the task of promoting and explaining the concepts certainly becomes easier within your own company. On the other hand, detractors will always be able to locate stories offering a contradictory viewpoint: "We tried such-and-such technique and were disappointed with the results."

These detractors can complicate your improvement effort. The way to minimize the controversy is to position all TCM projects within the context of specific improvement objectives. The objective is never simply to implement a new accounting technique, and it should be expressed in business language rather than technique language. For example, you might state your goals as follows:

- improving cost, quality, and time by analyzing business processes;
- improving the price-setting process by improving the accuracy of product costs;
- making the performance measures more reflective of the business goals; or
- improving the process of evaluating investment decisions.

The Organization's Capacity for Change

One of the things you'll need to do when you develop your TCM Strategy is to assess your organization's capacity to learn and change. Effective implementation of TCM requires that managers think about the business in terms of its business processes and their underlying activities. This requires people to develop new understandings about what causes cost in an organization. It also requires that people change how they assess their own performance and how they assess the performance of the people who work for them. It may call into question long-standing policies about which products and services to offer and which customers and markets to serve.

In short, the decisions that TCM supports are not trivial. Moreover, they are often decisions that involve more than one functional area. TCM can change the very process by which these decisions are made. It may even affect the power balance in an organization. When companies believe, for instance, that their product costs are unreliable, then the process of establishing prices may be highly political. After ABC techniques are used to calculate accurate product costs, it is important that the decision-making process be changed to take this new information into account. Without this change, the TCM work will have been futile.

The broad subject of managing organizational change has become a refined discipline with its own set of tools and techniques. Describing all the tools and techniques of that discipline is beyond the scope of this book. But it is important to acknowledge that the discipline exists and that there are effective approaches to help make sure that the required changes can take place.

Some of the key elements concerning capacity for change that need to be assessed in a TCM project include the following.

1. The ability of the person sponsoring the project to:
   - have a clear vision of what needs to change;
   - have an in-depth understanding of the resources needed to accomplish the change and have the power to commit those resources; and
   - fully appreciate the extent to which people will be asked to change.
2. The ability of the project team to:
   - plan and execute the project in manageable segments of work;
   - develop a truly collaborative work environment for the project;

- use the multi-functional organization of the project to generate understanding and enthusiasm for the project outside the project team; and
- recognize when the TCM project (either the work or its results) affects other areas of the business.

3. The ability of the people being asked to change to:
   - incorporate this change with all the rest of the changes they are being asked to make (again, positioning TCM as a means to support the strategic emphasis is key to helping make this happen); and
   - have a clear enough understanding for the need for change to believe that it is real and in their best interest.

The implementation strategy needs to consider these aspects of the organization's readiness for change and work to make sure that it will be able to make the changes anticipated from the TCM series of projects.

Conclusion

Total Cost Management is a sophisticated set of approaches and techniques capable of producing significant changes and cost-savings in today's business world. Should your company use TCM to control its costs? Only you and your fellow executives can make that decision.

To conclude, however, we offer the following points to recapitulate and underscore the discussions throughout this book.

First, your cost information must support your strategy. Whether your company's strategic focus is quality, close-to-the-customer, time-based competition, or something else, you need good information to back your decisions. Lacking good information, you can't reach your strategic goals. Acquiring good cost information is the fundamental power that Total Cost Management provides.

Second, you should try to see your organization as a collection of processes, not as a set of organization charts. In fact, your view of the processes needs to capture all of the interactions among the organizational units. What this means is essentially that your analytical framework should be more open to concepts of how the work really gets done and less focused on the reporting relationships used to manage the work.

Third, once you've made the fundamental shift in how you perceive your company, you should manage cost by managing activities. Only when you focus on activities can you make sustainable changes in your cost structure. Total Cost Management makes it possible to organize information in ways that point out opportunities for reducing cost—a process that depends most significantly on identifying activities and their root causes. This focus on activities is the power behind all the TCM principles: business process analysis, activity-based costing, and continuous improvement.

Fourth, you should organize information by identifying the value of activities to your customers. This holds true whether the customers are internal or external. Here, too, you can identify improvement opportunities by determining which activities are value-added or non-value-added to your customers or which are disproportionately costly to you.

Fifth, the findings of your TCM analyses must make their way into action plans. Don't fall into the trap of simply reorganizing the numbers.

Finally, you must monitor your business by aligning performance measures with the critical success factors you have identified. Again, the process view allows you to establish metrics for measuring and monitoring the important elements of performance.

If we could combine these points into one single statement, it would be something like this: Total Cost Management isn't an objective in and of itself; rather, it's a way to support your business objectives, whatever they may be. To elaborate slightly, we'd say that reaching a new understanding of your company's numbers isn't the goal you should seek. Instead, you should focus on understanding the numbers to develop an information support structure that allows you to accomplish your strategic goals.

TCM, in short, is a means to an end. Cost management is the means. The end is greater competitiveness and corporate excellence in the global marketplace.

Bibliography

BUSINESS PROCESS ANALYSIS

Harrington, J. *Business Process Improvement,* [New York: McGraw-Hill, Inc., 1991].

Mehra, P., Kammalade, J., and Ozan, T. "A Process Approach to Overhead Management," *Journal of Cost Management for the Manufacturing Industry*, Fall, 1989.

Sullivan, E. "OPTIM: Linking Cost, Time, and Quality," *Progress*, April 1986.

ACTIVITY-BASED COSTING

Berliner, C. and J. Brimson (eds), *Cost Management for Today's Advanced Manufacturing: The CAM-I Conceptual Design*, [Boston: Harvard Business School Press, 1988].

Cooper, R. "The Rise of Activity-Based Costing, Part Three: How Many Cost Drivers Do You Need, and How Do You Select Them?" *Journal of Cost Management for the Manufacturing Industry*, Winter 1989.

Drucker, P. "The Emerging Theory of Manufacturing," *Harvard Business Review*, May–June, 1990.

Ernst & Young, *American Competitiveness Study: Characteristics of Success*, 1990.

Ernst & Young, *Integrated Cost Management, Phase II: Implementation,* [Montvale, NJ: National Association of Accountants, 1990].

Ostrenga, M. "Activities—The Focal Point of Total Cost Management," *Management Accounting*, February, 1990.

Peters, T. *The New Masters of Excellence*, [City: Publisher, date].

Raffish, N. and P. Turney (eds), *The CAM-I Glossary of Activity-Based Management [Arlington: CAM-I, 1991].*

Simpson, J. and D. Muthler, *Journal of Cost Management for the Manufacturing Industry,* Spring 1987.

DECISION SUPPORT

Performance Measurement

Blackburn, J., *Time-Based Competition: The Next Battle Ground in American Manufacturing,* [Homewood, IL: The Business One—Irwin/APICS Series in Production Management, 1991].

Kaplan, R. (ed), *Measuring for Manufacturing Excellence,* [Boston: Harvard Business School Press, 1990].

McNair, C., W. Mosconi, T. Norris, *Meeting the Technological Challenge: Cost Accounting in a JIT Environment,* [Montvale: National Association of Accountants, 1988].

Turney P. (ed), *Performance Excellence in Manufacturing and Service Organizations*—Proceedings of the Third Annual Management Accounting Symposium, San Diego: March 1989.

Cost of Quality

Morse, W., Roth, H., and Poston, K. "Measuring, Planning, and Controlling Quality Costs," *National Association of Accountants*, 1987.

Ostrenga, M. "Return on Investment through the Cost of Quality," *Journal of Cost Management for the Manufacturing Industry*, Summer 1991.

Life-Cycle Costing

Ernst & Young, "Cost Management System Research: Activity Accounting Project Guide," CAM-I CMS Project R-90 CMS-02.

House, C. and R. Price. "The Return Map: Tracking Product Teams," *Harvard Business Review*, January–February 1991.

Shields, C. M. and S. Young, "Managing Product Life Cycle Costs: An Organizational Model," *Journal of Cost Management for the Manufacturing Industry*, Fall 1991, pp. 39–52.

Susman, G., "Product Life Cycle Management," *Emerging Trends in Cost Management*, B. Brinker, Ed., [Boston: Warren, Gorham, Lamont, 1991].

Target Costing

Ernst & Young, *Cost Management System Research: Activity Accounting Project Guide*, CAM-I CMS Project: R-89 CMS-02, 1990.

Sakuri, M. "Target Costing and How to Use It," *Emerging Practices in Cost Management*, B. Brinker, Ed., [Boston: Warren, Gorham, Lamont, 1991].

Worthy, F. "Japan's Smart Secret Weapon," *Fortune*, August 12, 1991, pp. 72–75.

Capital Investment Justification

Brimson, James A. *Activity-Based Investment Management,* [New York: Membership Publications Division of *American Management Association,* 1989].

Ernst & Young, *American Competitiveness Study: Characteristics of Success*. New York: Ernst & Young, 1990.

Ernst & Young, *Total Quality—An Executive's Guide for the 1990s*. Homewood, Ill.: Dow Jones Irwin, 1990.

Howell, Robert A., James D. Brown, Stephen R. Soucy, and Allen H. Seed. *Management Accounting in the New Manufacturing Environment*. Montvale, N.J.: National Association of Accountants, 1987.

Santori, Peter and Clarence Rixter. "National Machine Tool Builders Association: Capital Justification."

Sullivan, A. Charlene and Keith V. Smith, "Capital Budgeting Practices for U.S. Factory Automation Projects," paper submitted to *Financial Management*.

Sullivan, William G., James M. Reeve, and S. Rapinder S. Sawhney, "Strategy-Based Investment Justification for Advanced Manufacturing Technology," *Cost Management Systems Research, Phase III*.

Terborgh, G. *Business Investment Management*. Washington, D.C.: Machinery and Allied Products Institute and Council for Technological Development, 1967.

INDEX